THE BIGGEST BOOK OF
GAMES FOR ONE
EVER!

First edition for the United States, its territories and dependencies, and
Canada published in 2005 by Barron's Educational Series, Inc.

All inquiries should be addressed to:
Barron's Educational Series, Inc.
250 Wireless Boulevard
Hauppauge, NY 11788
www.barronseduc.com

ISBN-13: 978-0-7641-3273-5
ISBN-10: 0-7641-3273-3

Library of Congress Card Catalog Number 2005921552

Project Editor: Martin Corteel
Project Art Direction: Zoë Dissell
Designer: Barbara Zuñiga
Production: Lisa French

Printed in Great Britain
9 8 7 6 5 4 3 2 1

THE BIGGEST BOOK OF

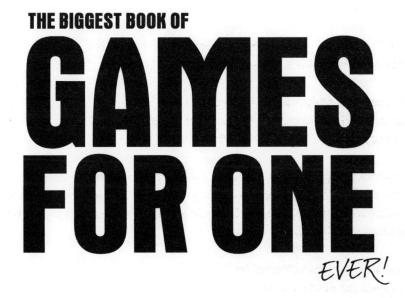

GAMES FOR ONE

EVER!

Over 500 games of luck, skill, and patience
for players of a solitary disposition

CONTRIBUTORS

Robert Allen, David Ballheimer,

Jacqueline Harrod, and John Paines

Contents

Introduction

Here is a great collection of games that you can play on your own. That's right—there's no need to drag unwilling family members along to help you, so you can play at any time you like. A quiet evening at home can become an interlude full of fascination. Alternatively, you can spend your coffee break engaged in one of the many shorter games included.

The games include over 100 versions of solitaire, as well as chess problems, matchstick and coin games, word, number, and logic puzzles, crossword puzzles, and a host of trivia quiz questions. There are some games that will take you only a few minutes and others that can last for a satisfyingly long time.

This book contains everything you need to experience many hours of gaming pleasure. Your pencil will be chewed to a stub by the time you finish this book!

solitaire
card games

ALHAMBRA SOLITAIRE

You will need two decks of cards for this game, somewhat strangely named after the citadel and palace in Granada, built at the behest of the Moorish Kings of the thirteenth century.

Remove the Ace and the King of each suit from one deck, putting these eight cards at the top of the table as Foundation cards.

The aim of the game is to build the Aces up in sequence and in suit to the King (Ace, Two, Three, Four, Five, Six, Seven, Eight, Nine, Ten, Jack, Queen, and King). The Kings build down in sequence and suit to the Ace.

Shuffle the remaining cards together very thoroughly and deal out a reserve of four rows of eight cards each, face up, from left to right. Overlap the rows so that the layout resembles eight upright columns, with the value of each card clearly seen.

Use any suitable exposed card (those at the base of a column with nothing upon them) to build on the Foundation cards. By doing this you release the cards above for use.

When you can do no more, play out the cards in your hand one by one, building up or down wherever possible.

There is no building on the reserve. Discard useless cards to a single heap, the use of which is somewhat different from the norm. Exposed cards in the reserve can be played to the top of the heap, if their numbering is consecutive, either up or down. Suit is of no importance. For example, if the card on the top of the heap is a Seven, an exposed card valued at Six or Eight can be moved onto it. This is very useful in unblocking trapped cards, as you will find out!

The heap can be turned over and played through again twice at the end of the first deal, but careful planning is needed for a successful conclusion.

A horrible variation of this Solitaire begins with the reserve dealt out in eight piles of four cards, with only the top card facing up. This may be impossible to resolve successfully. (Well, I can't do it ...)

Notes:

All Solitaire card games are played with one or two standard decks of fifty-two playing cards; the jokers are not included. In some games, a "piquet" deck is required: this is a standard deck with all the Twos, Threes, Fours, Fives, and Sixes removed, leaving just 32 cards.

Always shuffle the cards thoroughly between games.

On the opposite pages is a glossary explaining some of the common terms in Solitaire.

ALTERNATE SOLITAIRE

One deck of cards – and a great deal of space – is needed for this game. (All cards face up.)

Remove the Ace of Diamonds, the King of Clubs, the Ace of Hearts, and the King of Spades and put them in a row at the top of the table. Each of these is to head a vertical column of thirteen cards, none of which should overlap.

The aim of the game is to build up in sequence and alternating color on each Ace to the King (black Two on red Ace, red Three on black Two and so on) and down in sequence and alternating color on each King to the Ace (red Queen on black King, black Jack on red Queen, etc.).

Deal out the cards in your hand one by one, building whenever the opportunity arises. Discard unplayable cards to one of four heaps which can be placed any way you like. As always, top cards remain available for you to use—but you can only move them to a Foundation pile, not from one heap to another.

When all the deck has been dealt, the heaps can be gathered up and played through once again. (Resist the urge to shuffle them!)

The end of a successful game will show four vertical columns, thirteen cards in each, filling the table. The Ace columns will end with a red King; the columns headed by a King will end with a black Ace.

Glossary:
Foundation – the all-important base cards of the piles, on which are to be built the entire deck (or decks) in the required order. The Aces often take this role, but not always.
Tableau – cards arranged on the table at the beginning of the game in the way the game requires.
Reserve – cards on which no building takes place, ever!
Heap – the cards which cannot be played at that moment, but will be brought back into play as soon as possible. All cards in the heap face up, but only the top card is available for use.

AULD LANG SYNE SOLITAIRE

You will need one deck of cards for this game. Take the four Aces from the deck and place them in a row, face up.

The object of the game is to build on these Aces, or Foundations, in sequence and in suit up to the King.

Shuffle the deck thoroughly and deal out four cards, face up, in a row below the Foundation cards. Stop to see whether any card can be used (Two of Diamonds onto Ace of Diamonds, for example), then place a further four cards upon those dealt previously, or onto the gaps if you have been lucky enough to be able to use them.

Continue to lay down four cards at a time, building on the Foundations after each deal whenever possible. A card having been removed enables the exposed card beneath to be used, too.

No redeal is permitted. The four Foundation piles must be crowned with their Kings, or the game is lost.

A variant to this game, called Tam O'Shanter, will not permit the Aces to be removed first. You have to wait until they emerge in the course of play! "Had we but world enough, and time ..."

BAKER'S DOZEN SOLITAIRE

One deck of cards is needed for this, and a lot of thought. (When being sentenced to the stocks—or worse—was the punishment for short weight in loaves of bread, bakers protected themselves by selling thirteen for the cost of twelve. The thirteenth loaf was called the "vantage." I do not suggest that this version of Solitaire is either that ancient or was invented by a baker!)

Shuffle the deck thoroughly and deal out four rows of thirteen cards, face up. Overlap them so that the Tableau resembles thirteen vertical columns and the value of all cards can be seen.

The merciful originator of this Solitaire dictates that the Kings must be transferred to the tops of their respective columns—which eases life a great deal. If you have more than one King in a column, put one King above the other. With them safely penned, the game can begin.

Your object is to place the four Aces, as they emerge in play, in a row above the Tableau. Build up on these Foundations, in sequence and in suit, until the piles are crowned with a King.

Take any Aces available in the exposed cards (an exposed card being one at the base of a column with nothing on it) and any cards that can be built on them, moving one card at a time. The removal of a card frees the one above it.

When nothing more can be played, build down on the Tableau columns in sequence, but ignoring suit, until these cards can take their positions on the Foundation piles (any Five on any Six, any Four on any Five). But you must only move one card at a time and not a sequence of cards. A gap in the Tableau is not to be refilled.

If the game comes out well, you may wish to attempt a variant, called Good Measure. (Does this title refer also to bread, or something more exotic?)

Good Measure is played in almost the same way, differing only a little in the original layout. Two Aces are removed before the game begins, awaiting the other two, and placed above the Tableau. This consists of five overlapping rows, ten cards in each.

BARONESS SOLITAIRE

One deck of cards, with the four Kings removed, is needed for this.

This time-honored version of Solitaire may be simple, but it is addictive. Try it.

Deal out a row of five cards from left to right, face up.

Remove any two cards which total thirteen when added together, such as Ace and Queen, Seven and Six, Five and Eight, and so on. (Now you understand why the Kings, valued at thirteen, are removed before the start of play.) Look closely at the cards which remain: there may be more pairs adding up to the number required.

Deal another row of five cards across spaces or cards not taken away and play as before.

Continue this until all the cards in your hand have been dealt. (The final row will contain eight cards.)

A successful game will have all the cards paired and removed from the board.

BELEAGUERED CASTLE SOLITAIRE

One deck of cards is needed for this game. The layout is as depicted in Figure 1, with all the cards facing up.

The four Aces are removed from the deck and placed in a column down the center of the table.

To the left and right of each Ace, deal a line or "wing" of six overlapping cards, so that only the card at the end is totally exposed, though the value of each card can be seen.

The object of the game is to build up in suit on the Aces to the King (Ace, Two, Three, Four, Five, Six, Seven, Eight, Nine, Ten, Jack, Queen, and King).

Only the exposed card on the end of each wing can be played, either immediately onto the correct Ace or onto the end of another wing.

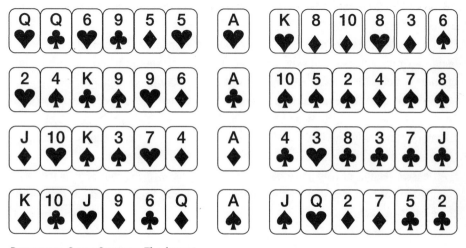

BELEAGUERED CASTLE SOLITAIRE: **The layout.**

If built onto a wing, the sequence is built down with no regard to suit – any Five on a Six, any Jack on a Queen – until cards necessary to the Ace piles can be released. Only one card can be moved at a time.

When a space has been created by the removal of all the cards in one wing, any exposed card can be put there. In this way a card which is blocking play can be transferred, freeing those beneath for use.

It is very important to plan ahead if you wish to bring this Solitaire to a successful conclusion.

In the example above, the Two of Clubs can be put onto the Ace of Clubs immediately, the Jack of Clubs onto the Queen of Diamonds, the Seven of Clubs onto the Eight of Spades, enabling the Three of Clubs to join the Two on the Ace of Clubs, and so on ...

A shamefaced but truthful footnote: I have never been able to bring this Solitaire to a successful ending. After I confessed this to a friend, he played and finished it in ten minutes! I retain my belief, however, that it is a difficult game.

LA BELLE LUCIE SOLITAIRE

One deck is needed for this unusual and visually pleasing Victorian Solitaire. As it also requires thought and planning to bring it to a happy ending, one cannot ask for more!

(Do allow yourself plenty of room in which to play this charming survivor from more spacious days.)

Play out the cards, face up, in groups of three, each trio overlapping one another in the form of a fan. (There will be eighteen of these groups in the Tableau, but the last "fan" will have one card only.)

The object of the game is to take the four Aces as they emerge in play, building up on them in sequence and in suit to the King.

In this game, the "exposed" card is that card uncovered at the end of a fan. Should any Aces be seated there, desperate to catch your eye, put them in a line at the bottom of the table. These are the Foundations. (The removal of a card releases the one beneath for play.)

Build any suitable exposed card onto a Foundation pile. If this cannot be done, build down in sequence and suit, which adds greatly to the difficulty, upon the end of another fan until needed. (A fan removed during play is not replaced.)

Should the game become stuck, pick up all the cards not yet correctly placed on a Foundation pile and shuffle them thoroughly. Redeal this "new" deck into fans of three, as before. (Obviously, the last fan of this redeal may consist of only one or two cards.)

You may replay the cards twice, but no further chances are given.

An easier version of this game named Trefoil begins with the four Aces placed as Foundation cards at the start of the game. The Tableau comprises sixteen fans, with three cards in each.

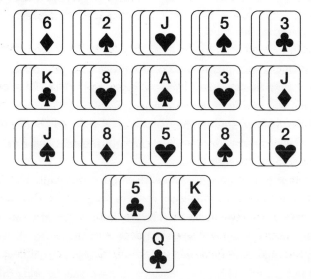

La Belle Lucie Solitaire: The Ace of Spades is immediately available, together with the Two of Spades to be built upon it. (All cards face up.)

BRITISH BLOCKADE SOLITAIRE

Two decks are needed for this game, a more modern and less interesting title of which is Parallels. All cards must face up.

Shuffle the two decks together very thoroughly. Remove one Ace and one King from each suit, putting the four Kings in a vertical column to your left and the four Aces, in the same way, to your right. Allow plenty of space between the two. These are the Foundation cards.

The object of the game is to build up, in sequence and suit, on the Aces to the appropriate King and down, in sequence and suit, upon the Kings to the appropriate Ace.

Deal ten cards in a row between the parallel Kings and Aces as a reserve. Pause to consider whether any of these can be used for building. Fill any spaces made with the next cards to be dealt from the deck.

When nothing further can be done, deal a second row of ten cards below the first, but do not overlap them.

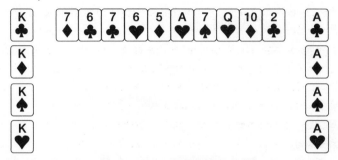

BRITISH BLOCKADE SOLITAIRE: The Two of Clubs and the Queen of Hearts can be removed to their Foundation piles. Gaps are to be filled immediately from the deck.

The cards in both rows are now available for play to the Foundation piles. Continue to fill the gaps with the next cards taken from those you hold.

Deal a third row of ten cards below the second when play comes to a standstill.

Now only the top and bottom row are available. The second row finds itself blockaded, the title of this Solitaire is validated, and a card here is only freed for use when the card immediately above or below it is taken away. Build everything possible, refilling gaps as before.

Blocked again? Deal a fourth row of ten below the previous three. Now there are two inner rows awaiting the order of release. Play on, remembering that cards in the inner rows must have a free edge above or below (or both) before you can use them.

No redeal of the reserve is allowed when the deck is exhausted.

Running a blockade has its difficulties; so too does this game – although it's not as frightening!

A truly horrible variation does not allow the top row to possess any available cards until all the deck has been dealt. The less said about that the better.

CAPTIVE QUEENS SOLITAIRE

One deck of cards is required for this game. Remove the four Queens from the pack and place them face up, one upon another, in the center of the table. These are the "captive Queens."

All the Fives and all the Sixes are arranged in a circle around the Queens, also facing up. Once the opening Tableau has been arranged, the Solitaire is ready to begin.

The Fives and the Sixes are the Foundation cards. The object of the game is to build up on the Sixes, in suit, to the Jacks and to build down, in suit, on the Fives to the Kings. (This last runs Five, Four, Three, Two, Ace, King.)

Using the cards in your hand, build on the Foundation cards if possible. Place those not immediately needed face up on a single heap. The top card is always available for use.

You are permitted to replay the heap once, but there must be no reshuffling of the cards, however useful this might be to a happy ending!

Captive Queens Solitaire: **Ready to begin.**

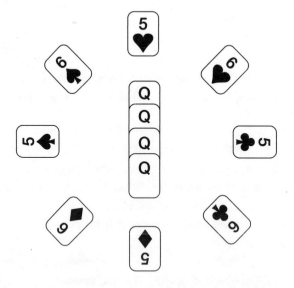

CARPET SOLITAIRE

This simple Solitaire requires one deck of cards. Place four rows of five cards each on the table, all facing up. This forms the "carpet" of the title.

As the Aces emerge, put two to the right and two to the left of the carpet.

Build up on the Aces, in suit, to their respective King. Any of the cards in the carpet are available for use. Use the cards in your hand to build on the Aces or to form a single heap of those not immediately playable. As always, the top card of the heap is available.

As "holes" are made in the carpet, fill the gaps with cards from the heap or from those in your hand.

It is not permitted to gather up and replay the heap; neither is this often necessary.

CLOCK SOLITAIRE

Only one deck of cards is needed for this. Shuffle the cards thoroughly, then deal out, face down, twelve cards in the shape of a clock face. Place a thirteenth card in the center, also face down.

Repeat this until you have thirteen piles of four cards, then turn the top card on the thirteenth pile face up. If, for example, this is the Five of Diamonds, place it face up underneath the five o'clock pile on your clock face. Leave it protruding somewhat so that its number can be seen. Take the top card from the five o'clock pile and put it under its appropriate number pile.

An Ace is placed at one o'clock, a Jack at eleven o'clock and a Queen at twelve o'clock. A King is placed under the pile in the middle.

The object of the game is to have all the cards face up in the right piles, but this happens only rarely because once all the Kings have turned up it is impossible to continue.

CLOCK SOLITAIRE

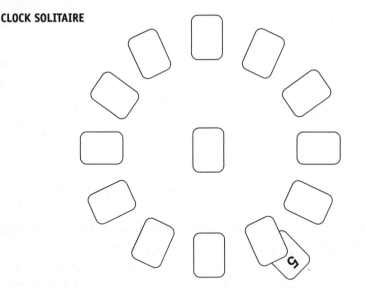

COLORS SOLITAIRE

One deck of cards is needed for this simple—but aggravating—game.

Begin by dealing out the deck, face up, into up to six heaps. Pile these as you please; the top cards are always available for use.

You are looking for a Two, Three, Four and Five to become the Foundation cards. The Two and Four must be one color (suit is not important) and the Three and Five the other. Obviously, the first Foundation card to emerge dictates the color of the others.

When they are found, put these cards in numerical order, side by side, at the top of the table.

Colors Solitaire: **Begun**

Colors Solitaire: **Ended**

The object of the game is to build up on these, in color and in thirteen-card sequence, to a card of a value one below the Foundation card.

Build from the cards you hold and watch the tops of the heaps with an eagle eye. (Discard cards with some care, or you will find yourself becoming hopelessly blocked.) You must not move a card from heap to heap, only to a Foundation pile.

Redealing the heaps is not allowed. A successful game shows the four Foundation piles topped by an Ace, Two, Three, and Four, respectively.

CZARINA SOLITAIRE

One deck of cards (well-shuffled) is needed for this game.

Deal five cards onto the table, face up and in the shape of a cross; this is the Tableau. The next card from those you hold is put, face up, into the left-hand corner. This is the first Foundation card. Three other cards of the same value must be placed in the remaining corners as soon as they emerge in play.

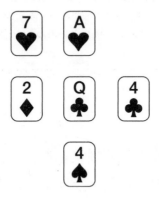

CZARINA SOLITAIRE: **The first Foundation card has been placed.**

The object of the game is to build a thirteen-card sequence, up and in suit, on each Foundation. (The Tableau has the Seven of Hearts as an example. Thus, the sequence will run Seven, Eight, Nine, Ten, Jack, Queen, King, Ace, Two, Three, Four, Five, and end with a Six.) To achieve this, you will be building down, regardless of suit, onto the cross cards until these cards can be removed to a Foundation pile.

Build any cards that can be used from the Tableau onto the Foundations, filling gaps from those you hold. (Later in the game, a gap may be filled with any card available; that is, the top card of the heap, of a Tableau pile, or those in your hand.)

If, in the initial Tableau, you are fortunate enough to deal consecutively numbered cards, for example, a Jack and a Queen, you can build down immediately by placing the Jack on top of the Queen. Then another card can be dealt into the space that is left. This rarely happens if the cards are well shuffled.

Now begin to deal your cards, one by one. Play them up onto the Foundations, or down onto the cross cards until needed. Unplayable cards are put face up onto a single heap and, yes, the top of this is always available for you to use!

When all the cards have been used, no redeal of the heap is permitted.

The game has succeeded if each Foundation pile contains thirteen cards, built up in suit, causing the central cross to vanish silently away.

DEAUVILLE SOLITAIRE

Why this game is named after a French coastal town I do not know; but I am positive that two decks of cards are required to play this excellent Solitaire. A great deal of thought is also needed to bring it to a successful conclusion.

After the two decks have been well shuffled together, deal three overlapping rows with ten cards in each, all cards face down. Deal a fourth row of ten cards to overlap the third, this row face up. These are the "exposed" cards.

Remove any Aces that are immediately available in the exposed cards, placing them in a row below the Tableau. The others will emerge in the course of play to join them. These are the Foundation cards.

The object of the game is to build up, in suit and sequence, on each Ace to the King.

The Tableau

Six Aces are needed to complete the Foundation row

The Foundation

DEAUVILLE SOLITAIRE

When an exposed card has been removed, turn the card beneath it over, so that it becomes available for use.

You can build down on exposed cards in the Tableau in sequence but in alternating colors (red Five on black Six, black Four on red Five, and so on). When you do so, place the cards in such a way that the tops of any other cards there can be seen. This helps to plan the best move possible.

Play the cards in your hand one at a time. These, and all the exposed cards in the Tableau, can be played in the following way:

(a)   Immediately onto the Foundation cards, hopefully ...

(b)   If this is not possible, build down in sequence in alternating colors on the Tableau until these can be moved to the Foundations.

(c)   Any exposed card can be used to fill a gap caused by the removal of all the cards in one column. This is very useful when a card is blocking play.

Cards played from those held in your hand can be discarded onto a single heap if they cannot be used. The top card of the heap is always available.

Resist the temptation to move sequences into a space or onto other exposed cards in the Tableau. Each card must be moved singly.

There is no redeal of the heap. The game is won if each Foundation stacks up, in suit and sequence, to the King.

DEMON SOLITAIRE

One deck is needed for this; a rarity among Solitaire games in that it is known to many.

Deal out a neat pile of thirteen cards, face down, to the left of the table. Turn the top card face up. This reserve is the "Demon" of the title.

Take the next card from those you hold, putting it face up at the top of the table as the first Foundation card.

The "Demon" Reserve

DEMON SOLITAIRE:
The layout.

The Foundation Row
– three more Foundation cards to find

The Tableau

Beneath this deal a row of four cards as the Tableau. Again, these must be face up.

The object of the game is to take the other three cards, of equal value to the first, to the Foundation row as they emerge in play: building up on each, in sequence and suit, until each pile contains thirteen cards, thus absorbing every card in the deck. The top card will be one lower in value to the base. (In the example given using the Seven of Hearts, a successful sequence will run as follows: Seven, Eight, Nine, Ten, Jack, Queen, King, Ace, Two, Three, Four, Five, and Six of Hearts.)

You can build in a downward direction on the Tableau, in sequence but alternating colors (e.g. red Ace on black Two, black King on red Ace, and so on). Spread each column towards you; it helps!

A space in the Tableau is filled with the top card of the reserve. The face-down card below it is then turned up for use.

Deal the cards from your hand in groups of three to a single heap, face up. When you have dealt the trio, look at the top card. Remove it, if possible, to a Foundation pile (either founding it or building on it). Otherwise, build it down on the Tableau until required.

If you are able to play the heap's top card, the one below is free and the game continues in the same way.

Pause to consider what is to be done between each deal of three. (The last group will, of course, only consist of one card.)

The top of the Demon reserve is always available. (Remember to turn the face-down card up when the one above is removed.) So, too, is each exposed card of the Tableau. These can transfer singly between the columns, or in any length of sequence, provided the "join" complies with the rules of downward sequence and alternating color.

Should the Demon vanish, fill the gap with the top card from the heap only.

When the deck is dealt, turn the heap over and play it through again, redealing in batches of three as before.

This is done until the game is successful, or until it becomes hopelessly blocked.

If the latter, there is nothing to be done but to gather up the entire deck and accept defeat gracefully. (Sweeping the cards before you onto the floor with muttered vulgarities is frowned on by most players!)

I wonder why this infuriating and aptly named game is so popular.

DOUBLE OR NOTHING SOLITAIRE

You will need one deck of cards for this Solitaire. It bears a vague resemblance (distant cousin?) to several other Solitaire versions, but its oddities single it out.

After shuffling the deck, deal out seven cards as a Tableau as shown. (All the cards must face up.) Put three cards in a column to the left and three cards in a column to the right. They do not overlap. Between them, at the top, place the seventh card.

If you have dealt any Kings, remove them to the bottom of the deck and replace them with the next card.

Now deal another card, the Foundation card, putting it between the columns at the bottom. (Again, this must not be a King. If it is, replace it as before.)

The aim of the game is to build on the single Foundation, doubling the value of each card, until all the deck has been gathered to it.

DOUBLE OR NOTHING SOLITAIRE: **The Two of Hearts is the Foundation card. The Four of Spades can be built upon immediately and replaced by the next card from the deck. (There is, as yet, no heap.)**

When the value of a doubled card exceeds twelve, subtract thirteen and play on. (The Jack is worth eleven and the Queen, twelve. Fortunately, suit is ignored.)

The sequence runs continuously: Two, Four, Eight, Three, Six, Queen, Jack, Nine, Five, Ten, Seven, Ace, Two, Four, Eight, and so on.

In the example shown above, the Foundation card is a Two, but you will join the numbering wherever you came in. For example, if you dealt a Queen, you would top this with a Jack, followed by a Nine, etc.

Play out the cards in your hand one by one, to the Foundation pile if possible, or to a single heap, the top of which is always available.

Use the seven cards in the Tableau whenever suitable, filling gaps made in it with the top card from the heap or your hand.

Kings play no part in this game. They can be used to fill a space in the Tableau (after the original layout has been dealt) but move nowhere else.

The heap can be turned over and dealt out again twice when you have exhausted all the cards in your hand.

A successful game will have forty-eight cards built correctly on the Foundation, with the four Kings sitting disconsolately upon the table.

(The example, which began with a Two, ended as it should, with an Ace.)

DOUBLE PYRAMID SOLITAIRE

Two decks of cards are necessary for this game; all cards are dealt facing up.

Begin by building a pyramid the easy way. Put one card at the summit and deal ten cards on either side of it. (The cards can overlap if space is a consideration.) You now have a pyramid as the Tableau.

The next card of those in your hand will be the first Foundation card and is placed inside the Tableau. In the example below, this is a Five, but it could be anything!

The other seven cards of the same value are placed as they emerge in play. Put them inside the pyramid, beneath the first Foundation pile, in a row of three and a row of four. The "double pyramid" of the title is thus explained.

The aim of the game is to build up in suit and sequence upon the Foundations, ending with a card one less in value to the card at the bottom of the pile (for example, Five, Six, Seven, Eight, Nine, Ten, Jack, Queen, King, Ace, Two, Three, and Four).

Use any suitable card in the Tableau for building, at any time. A card removed from here is never replaced.

DOUBLE PYRAMID SOLITAIRE: A demonstration of the layout. (The Six of Diamonds and the Six of Clubs can be played onto the Foundations from the Tableau.)

The Tableau

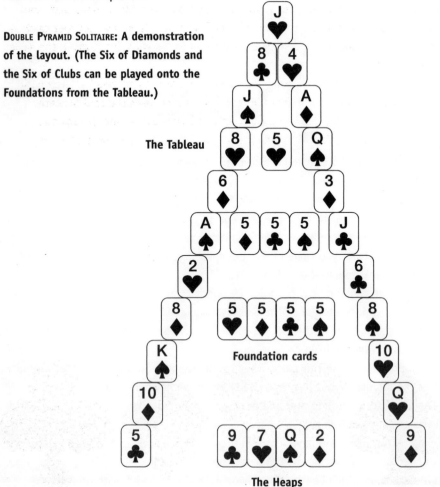

Foundation cards

The Heaps

Play out the cards in your hands one by one. If they are of no immediate use, pile them as you choose onto one of the four heaps that form the base of the pyramid. The top cards of these remain always available for moving to a Foundation pile; they may not, however, be moved from one heap to another.

No redeal is allowed. A successful game will find each of the eight Foundation piles containing thirteen cards and the large, outer pyramid gone.

DRIVEL SOLITAIRE

You will need one deck of cards for this game. It is a simple Solitaire, but I think the alternative title, Idiot's Delight, is going too far.

Shuffle the deck very thoroughly and deal four cards in a row, face up.

If any of the cards are of the same suit, remove those of a lower value and put them to one side. The highest card in that suit remains in its place. (Aces are of a higher value than Kings in this game.)

Fill the gap, or gaps, with the next card from those held in your hand. Should that card be lower than another in the same suit on the table, remove that, too.

Continue until you have four cards of a different suit, then deal out four cards at a time on top of the previous four, discarding all the lower value cards in the same suit as before.

Gaps made by the removal of all the cards in a pile must be filled at once with the top card from one of the three other piles. This releases the card beneath, hopefully for removal. It is wise to play an Ace into a gap whenever possible.

A successful conclusion to the game sees the four Aces in a row, all the other cards of lower value having been removed.

DUCHESS DE LUYNES SOLITAIRE

You will need two decks of cards for this game.

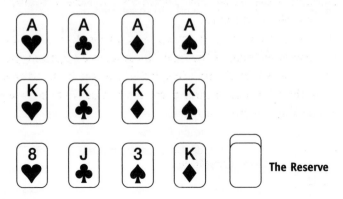

DUCHESS DE LUYNES SOLITAIRE: The layout.

Deal out four cards in a row side by side, facing up, with two more cards (called the reserve pile), one upon the other beside them, facing down.

The object of the game is to take one King and one Ace from each suit as they appear, building up on the Aces, in suit to the King (Ace, Two, Three, Four, Five, Six, Seven, Eight, Nine, Ten, Jack, Queen, King). The Kings are built down, in suit, to the Aces (King, Queen, Jack, Ten, Nine, Eight, Seven, Six, Five, Four, Three, Two, Ace).

Remove any Aces or Kings there might be in the row of four and place them as shown above; a row of four Aces at the top and a row of four Kings in the middle are required.

Continue dealing four cards onto the previous four and two cards onto the reserve pile. Pause between each deal to see whether there are any Kings and Aces to be removed or any building (up or down) that can be done.

When all the cards in your hand have been used, spread out the reserve pile and remove any cards that can be used immediately. Then check to see whether any exposed cards on the row of four can be built onto the King/Ace piles. If so, build them accordingly.

After this, gather up the four piles from right to left and put the unused remnants of the reserve pile on top. Continue the game as before. Three redeals are permitted, but on the last redeal omit the reserve pile and just deal out one row of four cards.

I am told that there is a Solitaire game called Parisienne with precisely the same rules, the only difference being the removal and placing of the four Kings and the four Aces before the game begins. It makes life a little easier, I suppose ...

EAGLE WING SOLITAIRE

One deck of cards is needed for this game. Begin by dealing out a pile of thirteen cards, facing down. For some reason, this is given the odd name of "trunk," and is to be placed in the center of the table.

Now deal out a further eight cards, facing up, as a reserve: four in a row to the left and four in a row to the right of the trunk. These are the eagle's wings.

The next card you deal will be the first Foundation card and is placed above the reserve. (The other three Foundation cards of the same value are to be moved into position beside it as they emerge in play.)

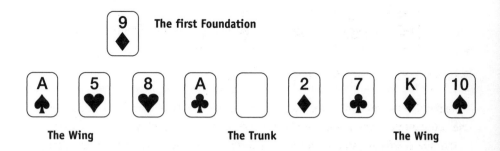

EAGLE WING SOLITAIRE: **The layout.**

Your aim is to build up, in suit, a sequence of thirteen cards ending with the card one lower in value than the card which began it. The example above shows the first Foundation to be the Nine of Diamonds. This will run as follows: Nine, Ten, Jack, Queen, King, Ace, Two, Three, Four, Five, Six, Seven, Eight.

Deal out the cards in your hand one by one, building upon a Foundation pile wherever possible. Discard useless cards to a single heap, the top card of which remains available to you.

Use the eight cards that form the wings for building on the Foundation piles. Fill a vacancy here by removing the top card from the trunk and placing it, face up, in the gap.

When you have dealt all the cards, the heap can be turned over and played through again, twice. I hope you find this leniency of some help—usually, I don't!

EIGHT ACES SOLITAIRE

You will need two decks of cards for this Solitaire. Remove the eight Aces and place them in two rows of four. These are the Foundation cards and are to be built up in suit until each pile is topped by the King.

Play the cards (which should have been well-shuffled, naturally) from your hand onto one of the Foundation cards or onto one of six heaps, only the top card of which is available for use. You must not move a card from heap to heap, only to a Foundation pile.

A vacancy caused by the removal of an entire heap is either filled by any exposed card or by the next card in the deck. But it is not necessary to fill gaps immediately if this moves the game along.

When all the cards have been dealt out and the game has ground to a halt, remove the top card from each of the heaps and place it face down beneath its pile. This may restart the game. Play on until you are stuck again, then repeat the placing of the top card face down under its pile. When you arrive at the cards which have been turned over, they can be played normally, if possible.

If you only have one card in a heap and the game has ground to a halt, you may turn the card over and place another exposed card on top of it. But, if you wish the game to be more difficult, you should leave the card face up. You can choose either of these methods, but must not swap between the two.

The top cards can be removed only twice. No further chances are allowed.

EIGHT OFF SOLITAIRE

One deck of cards is necessary for this game. All cards face up.

Shuffle the deck thoroughly, then deal six rows of eight cards each. Overlap the rows so that the Tableau resembles eight vertical columns.

Place the four remaining cards in a line beneath the layout. These are your reserve.

The object of the game is to remove the four Aces to the top of the table as they emerge in play, building up on each, in sequence and suit, to the King.

The exposed card at the base of each column, together with all cards in the reserve, are there for you to use. (As usual, the removal of a card frees the one beneath.)

Take anything possible to the Foundation row, or build down in sequence and suit upon the Tableau until needed. Move cards singly—never a lengthy sequence, however tempting.

A column removed in play must be replaced by a King; no other value will do. (And this does not mean that you can extricate the royal personage from the obscurity of cards awaiting release; the space remains until he becomes available.)

This is followed by a helpful rule. Any exposed card can be transferred to the reserve row as you choose, provided the quantity of cards here does not exceed eight (as in the title). Good luck!

FLOWER GARDEN SOLITAIRE

One deck is needed for this Solitaire. All cards are dealt face up.

Begin by playing out thirty-six cards, making six rows of six cards, with the rows overlapping. This is the Tableau or "garden" of the title.

The sixteen cards that remain, called the "bouquet," are placed above the six columns of the garden in the shape of a crescent.

The object of the game is to remove the four Aces as they emerge in play, building up in sequence and in suit upon them until they are crowned by the appropriate King.

When released, these Foundation cards are put in a row below the garden.

The Bouquet

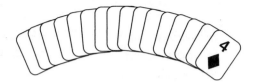

The Garden or Tableau

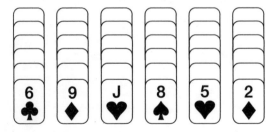

FLOWER GARDEN SOLITAIRE: **The beginning, Aces as yet unfound.**
(All cards face up.)

The base of each column in the Tableau is the "exposed" card and, yes, is available for play. The removal of a card frees the card beneath for use.

Any card in the bouquet is instantly available for building and is not replaced.

Moving cards one by one (including cards in the bouquet), either build up on a Foundation pile or, if that's impossible, build down in sequence on the columns of the Tableau, ignoring the suit, until they can be played off (any Eight on any Nine, any Seven on any Eight, and so on).

If all cards in a column have been removed, the space can be filled with any available card. (Obviously, it is sensible to move a King into a space whenever possible. The cards blocked by him are then set free.)

The game is won if the garden and bouquet have gone and the four Foundation piles are topped by their Kings.

FLY SOLITAIRE

Two decks of cards are needed for this game. Shuffle the two decks together, first removing the eight Aces. These are placed in a row upon the table and become the Foundation cards.

Now deal a pile of thirteen cards face down and put them to your left. Having done this, turn the top card of this pile face up. For some inexplicable reason, this is the "fly" of the title.

The aim of the game is to build up on the Foundation cards (in sequence, but paying no regard to suit) to the King.

As one would expect, the top card or "fly" is always available for use. Once removed, the card beneath is turned face up. Should the entire pile be played off, it is not replaced.

Begin to play the cards in your hand one by one. Any that are of no immediate use are discarded on up to five heaps, piled as you like. Use the top cards of these heaps as soon as it is feasible—but do not move a card from heap to heap.

(Try to avoid placing cards of a higher value on those of lower rank as the heaps form; you can become stuck very easily.)

No redeal is permitted. Unless the "fly" and all the other cards have been correctly absorbed onto the Foundation piles, the game is not a success, unfortunately.

FOLLOWING SOLITAIRE

One deck of cards is required for this game, together with a good memory and the ability to remain unflustered.

All cards are face up; additional difficulties are not needed.

Begin by dealing a Tableau of six cards, placed in a row from left to right.

The object of the game is to remove the four Aces to the top of the table as they surface in play, building up in sequence upon them to the King.

That is simplicity itself. Here is the hard part: only a Club is to be placed on a Heart, a Diamond on a Club, a Spade on a Diamond, and a Heart upon a Spade. (Thus, Ace of Spades, Two of Hearts, Three of Clubs, Four of Diamonds, Five of Spades, Six of Hearts, Seven of Clubs, Eight of Diamonds, Nine of Spades, Ten of Hearts, Jack of Clubs, Queen of Diamonds, and King of Spades.)

Remove from the Tableau all Aces, and cards to be built upon them, to the Foundation row. Fill spaces with the next card taken from those you hold.

Build down on the Tableau if possible, following the same required arrangement of suits as above, i.e., Club on Heart, Diamond on Club, Spade on Diamond, and Heart on Spade.

Any length of sequence can be moved between columns, provided the rotation of Diamonds, Spades, Hearts, and Clubs is engraved on your memory.

The obvious difficulty will be that, in removing cards to the Foundation piles, only one card can move at a time, the order being back to front.

Play out the cards in your hand one by one, building wherever possible and discarding useless cards to a single heap, the top of which is there to be used at any time.

Do not forget to fill spaces in the Tableau with any available exposed card taken from the heap, hand, or base of a Tableau column.

When the deck is exhausted, turn the heap over and play it through once again in the same way as before.

A successful game will show the four Foundation piles crowned with a King of the same suit as the Ace at the base!

This is a difficult Solitaire and I have played it out only rarely; I wish you greater success.

GATE SOLITAIRE

One deck is needed for this and all cards face up.

Deal out ten cards, putting five in an upright column to the left and five in an upright column to the right. These are the "gateposts," or reserve.

Now deal another two rows one above the other, four cards in each, between the parallel columns to represent the "bars" of the gate. This is the Tableau.

The object of the game is to remove the four Aces to a line above the two bars of the gate, as they emerge in play, building up upon them to the Kings, in sequence and suit.

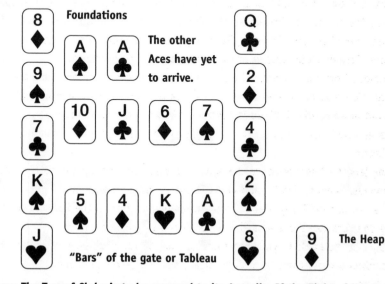

GATE SOLITAIRE: The Two of Clubs is to be removed to its Ace pile. If the Eight of Hearts is taken to fill the gap, the Two of Spades above is freed to be built upon the Ace of Spades.

Remove any Foundation cards, together with anything to be built upon them, from the Tableau or from the exposed cards at the base of the reserves to the side. (As always, this frees the card above for use.)

Build down in alternating colors on the Tableau, moving one card at a time and also using any suitable exposed cards from the base of the reserves.

Spaces made in the Tableau are refilled with the next available card taken from the posts. When the gateposts have vanished – and this can happen very quickly at times, because the reserve is not replenished – use the top card from the (as yet) non-existent heap.

Begin to play out your cards one by one; to a Foundation pile if you can, otherwise building down on the Tableau until they can be removed. (Please remember the rule of alternating color.) Sequences must not be transferred between columns.

Discard unplayable cards to that good old solitary heap, the top of which is available. There is no second chance in the guise of a redeal of the heap.

GEMINI SOLITAIRE

Two decks of cards are needed for this game. As with all games in this book, shuffle the cards well before beginning. Take the first four cards of different values and place them face up on the table. Leave a space between them as twin cards, of any suit, must be placed beside each as they turn up.

Deal out the cards in your hand onto one of five heaps, piling them any way you want. When you deal a card of the same value (of any suit) as one of those first four cards (its twin), place it in the space left for it. Then, when a card one degree higher (of any suit) than this twin pair emerges, place it above the pair. Once you have that card's twin placed beside it, you then build up, again not paying any attention to suit (any Four on any Three, any Five on any Four, etc.). In each case, before further building up is allowed, cards placed above the original twins must also have their twins beside them (in the example shown below you would need a Three on top of both the Two of Hearts and the Two of Diamonds before you could put a Four on either of them).

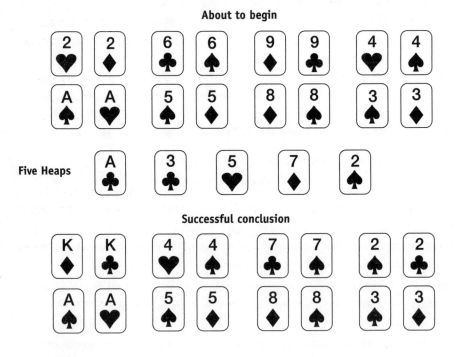

About to begin

Five Heaps

Successful conclusion

GEMINI SOLITAIRE.

Only the top card of each heap is available for use (which must not be transferred between heaps) so great care must be taken in laying out cards on the heaps, otherwise one becomes hopelessly stuck.

A successful end to this Solitaire shows the original twins, each with a pile above it crowned with the card next below it in value. If one is not successful immediately, you get a second chance by gathering up the heaps, unshuffled, and playing these cards through again; only two heaps may be formed this time, and no further attempt is allowed.

This game can be made even more perplexing by playing one of the twin cards up and the other down. The end result is the same, but very difficult to achieve. Do not try it if there is anybody "helping" you!

GRANDFATHER'S SOLITAIRE

Two decks are necessary for this most venerable of games. All cards are to face up.

Shuffle the decks together and deal out two rows of ten cards each, horizontally, parallel to each other, as a reserve. Remove any Kings or Aces as Foundation cards (but only one from each suit; the duplicates are treated in the same cavalier fashion as any other value). Put the Kings in a line above the reserve and the Aces in a line below the reserve. Also take anything that can be built on them. Fill gaps, as throughout this game, with the next card from the deck.

The object of the game is to take the Kings and Aces as they emerge in play; building up in sequence and suit upon the Aces to the King, and building down on the Kings, in sequence and suit, to the Ace.

Deal the cards you hold one by one, building on a Foundation pile if possible. Unplayable cards can be placed in one of two ways: either discarded to a single heap, the top of which is always available; or, if you choose, played to the reserve, not more than one card upon each of the twenty. If you do this, only the uppermost card can be used.

This can be most helpful in bringing the game to a successful conclusion, but great care must be taken in avoiding the inadvertent blocking of vitally needed cards.

The heap can be turned over and played through once more, when all the cards have been dealt.

If, near the end of the game, you have used up all the heap and you have spaces in the reserve, you may fill these spaces with top cards of the reserve.

A successful game will find four piles in the row above, each topped by an Ace, while the four piles below are crowned with a King. And the reserve has vanished away ...

GRANDFATHER'S CLOCK SOLITAIRE

The Foundation

The Tableau

GRANDFATHER'S CLOCK SOLITAIRE:
A good beginning – the
Five of Diamonds, Three of
Hearts and Ace of Clubs can
be removed to their
respective Foundation piles,
immediately freeing the
cards above them for use.
(All cards face up.)

One deck of cards is needed for this Solitaire. The twelve Foundation cards – see
below – are set out in a circle before play begins. (All cards must face up in this game.)

Remove the following to be used as the Foundation cards, putting them in the
position of the corresponding hour on the clock face:

Nine of Clubs – twelve o'clock	Ten of Hearts – one o'clock
Jack of Spades – two o'clock	Queen of Diamonds – three o'clock
King of Clubs – four o'clock	Two of Hearts – five o'clock
Three of Spades – six o'clock	Four of Diamonds – seven o'clock
Five of Clubs – eight o'clock	Six of Hearts – nine o'clock
Seven of Spades – ten o'clock	Eight of Diamonds – eleven o'clock

The object of the game is to build up on each card, in suit and in sequence, until
the appropriate number to its position on the clock face is reached. You will
remember that the Jack is valued at eleven and the Queen at twelve.

After shuffling the remainder of the deck, deal out five rows of eight cards each,
overlapping the rows so that the Tableau resembles eight vertical columns.

The exposed, or available, card at the base of each column can be played to a
Foundation pile, if at all possible, or used to build down in sequence (but ignoring
suit) on another column until needed. Move only one card at a time.

Fill a column emptied in play with any available card. A successful ending to this
game will see all cards gathered to the Foundation piles and the "hours" correct.

HERRINGBONE SOLITAIRE

I have a weakness for the more colorful layouts: this is one such, and the title is appropriate. Two decks are needed.

After shuffling the decks together, deal out two rows of three cards as a Tableau, one above the other. (All cards in this Solitaire face up.)

If a Jack is among the original six, remove it to the center of the table, replacing it with the next card from the deck.

Put all the Jacks, as they emerge in play, into the center of the table to form a non-overlapping, upright column of eight. These are the Foundation cards.

The aim of the game is to build down, in sequence and in suit, upon the Jacks to the Ace (Jack, Ten, Nine, Eight, Seven, Six, Five, Four, Three, Two, and Ace).

The King and the Queen are of no value in this game, other than to add verisimilitude to the title. When a Jack is in place, the King and Queen of matching suit are put at an angle on either side of it; the "herringbone" takes shape in this way.

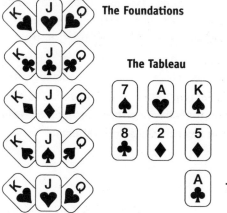

The Foundations

The Tableau

The Heap

HERRINGBONE SOLITAIRE: A demonstration of the layout, with three Jacks still to emerge. Nothing can be built upon the King of Spades in the Tableau; he awaits the arrival of the second Jack of Spades for his removal.

The royal couple must not be placed before their Jack emerges, being discarded to the solitary heap or remaining in waiting upon the Tableau, if they arrive at the wrong time.

You don't need to have both King and Queen before moving them into place.

Deal the cards in your hand one by one. Play anything suitable to a Foundation pile or build up, in suit, upon the cards in the Tableau until they are needed.

The whole, or part, of a Tableau pile can be built upon another if the rules of upward sequence and matching suit are observed. (Fill gaps in the Tableau with the top card from your hand or from the heap.)

Do not build higher than a Ten on these. If the original layout had any Kings, Queens, or Tens in it, they cannot have anything placed upon them. Your only chance is a speedy removal to a Foundation pile.

Discard unplayable cards to the single heap, the top of which is always available.

When all cards have been dealt, turn over the heap and play it through once again.

This game is one of many for which you will find a very large table, or miniature cards, helpful. The more adventurous will scorn these suggestions and sit upon the floor.

HIGGLEDY-PIGGLEDY SOLITAIRE

Two decks of cards, well shuffled together, are needed for this messy and enjoyable game.

Scatter the decks higgledy-piggledy all over the table, ensuring that all the cards are facing down. Clear a space in the middle (you will now wish that you had chosen to play this game on the floor) and choose any card to be a Foundation card. If you have drawn a Queen, for example, you will build on her, ignoring suit and color, as follows: King, Ace, Two, Three, Four, Five, Six, Seven, Eight, Nine, Ten, and Jack on top. The other seven cards of the same rank are built on in the same way as they are found.

Begin to turn the cards over at random. If they can be placed on a Foundation card, well and good. If they cannot, form four heaps, piled as you please, with only the top cards available for use. These top cards can only be placed on the Foundation piles, not moved from one heap to another.

When all the scattered cards have been turned face up and no card can be placed from the heaps, take the heap on the left and play it out, hopefully onto one of the eight Foundations, or onto the three remaining heaps in rotation. Next take the third heap (again the one on the left) and play it out onto either the Foundation cards or the two heaps that are left, then play out one of these heaps onto the Foundation cards or onto the one remaining heap.

If the sequences on the Foundation cards have not been completed after the last heap has been played, you have been unsuccessful in your attempt.

HOUSE ON THE HILL SOLITAIRE

Two decks are required for this space-consuming game. All cards face up.

Shuffle the decks together and deal out thirty-four groups of three cards, overlapping each trio in the shape of a fan. The thirty-fifth and final fan has only two cards in it, but is none the worse for that.

(If, having a literal mind, you have built the Tableau in the shape of a pyramidal hill as the title suggests, the small fan is placed at the apex.)

The object of the game is to remove the eight Aces as they surface in play, and to build up on each of these Foundation cards, in sequence and suit, to their Kings.

The top card of each fan is there for your use; its removal frees the one below.

Transfer anything possible to the Foundation row; otherwise build down on the top cards of the Tableau, in suit, until those cards can be played through. Move one card at a time, never a sequence.

A fan which disappears is not replaced. There is no redeal. A successful game will show eight piles of thirteen cards, topped by a King.

IMAGINARY THIRTEEN SOLITAIRE

I like this Solitaire very much, although it appears rather complicated at first. It is very satisfying when it ends well.

You will need two decks of cards for this game. Place on the table eight cards of any suit, running in sequence from the Ace to the Eight. Below these put a card of any suit which is double the value of the card above. (The Jack is valued at eleven, the Queen at twelve, and the King at thirteen.) So put a Two below the Ace, an Eight below the Four, a Queen below the Six, and so on. A brief difficulty, speedily resolved, is caused by the doubling of the Seven and the Eight. This is where the Imaginary Thirteen of the title is used. Two Sevens are fourteen, for which no card exists. If you deduct the imaginary thirteen from fourteen, you are left with one. Therefore, place an Ace beneath the Seven. The same thing happens with the Eight. Two eights are sixteen; the imaginary thirteen is deducted, and so a three of any suit is placed below the Eight.

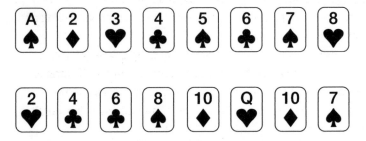

IMAGINARY THIRTEEN SOLITAIRE: **The Two of Hearts is the Foundation card. The Four of Spades can be built upon immediately and replaced by the next card from the deck. (There is, as yet, no heap.)**

Begin to deal out the deck in your hand. If you deal a card with a value equal to the total of the upper and lower cards, place it on the card in the lower row. For example, place a Three (one plus two) below the Ace, a Six (two plus four) below the Two, a Queen (four plus eight) below the Four, and so on. Again, when the value of the upper and lower card exceeds thirteen, deduct the imaginary thirteen and use a card that's the value of the amount left over. A Queen and a Five would total seventeen, so deduct thirteen and place a Four on the lower card.

If a card cannot immediately be placed onto one of the lower cards, place it on one of four heaps, reserving one of these heaps solely for the Kings.

Take the cards for the lower row from the heaps whenever possible before taking from the cards you hold; in that way, you have more chance of bringing the game to a successful conclusion.

Continue adding to the lower row until both upper and lower cards total thirteen, and place the King on the lower card. If you can do this on each of the eight piles, the game has been worked out correctly.

INTELLIGENCE SOLITAIRE

Two decks and a large table are needed for this colorful Solitaire.

INTELLIGENCE SOLITAIRE.

Shuffle the two decks together very thoroughly, then deal out eighteen groups of three cards (face up, overlapping one another) in the shape of a fan. This is the Tableau. If any Aces emerge in this deal, remove them and replace them with the next card from your hand.

The object of the game is to take all Aces to a row at the top of the table, as they emerge in play, and to build up upon them in sequence and in suit to the King.

The exposed card of each fan (the one with nothing covering it) is available for use. These can be transferred to another fan pile if suitable, freeing those beneath. Build up or down in suit as you please on the Tableau piles, even changing direction on the same pile, until it is possible to transfer to a Foundation.

A fan removed in play is replaced by the next three cards taken from the deck.

If you have exhausted the entire deck or, your nerves stretched to breaking point, you can do nothing more, gather up all cards not yet placed on a Foundation pile and shuffle them together. Now deal out as many fans of three as the new deck will allow—obviously, the last fan may have a meager one or two cards in it—and play on. (Do not forget to pull out any Aces from the redeal.) This can be done twice in all.

INTERREGNUM SOLITAIRE

This game requires two decks of cards, along with some thought to finish out! Even
the title is something of a puzzle. The only historical Interregnum I know of is the
gap between the execution of Charles I in 1649 and the accession of Charles II in
1660, so gloomily filled by Cromwell.

Begin by shuffling the two decks together very thoroughly and deal out eight
cards, in a row from left to right, at the top of the table. They are called the
indicator cards and face up, as do all the cards in this game.

Leave sufficient space beneath these for the Foundation cards to be placed as
they emerge during play. Then deal out a bottom row of eight cards.

Your aim is to find the card one step higher in value than each indicator card.

Build up on each one, ignoring suit, in thirteen-card sequence until its respective
indicator card can be used to crown the pile. (These elusive eight Foundation cards
take up their position as the second, or middle, row directly
below their appropriate indicator cards.)

For example, if the first card in the top row is a Two, the Foundation card
beneath will be a Three. The sequence will run as follows: Three, Four, Five, Six,
Seven, Eight, Nine, Ten, Jack, Queen, King, Ace, and, finally, the indicator card Two.

All eight cards in the bottom row are available for use, either as Foundation cards
or for building.

When you can do no more, deal out another eight cards upon the bottom row,
covering remaining cards or spaces, and play as before. (To remove a card frees
the one beneath for use.)

Continue, pausing between each deal of eight cards to build upon the Foundation
piles whenever possible, until all the cards in your hand have been exhausted.

No redeal is permitted. A successful game will find you able to play out all the
cards in the bottom row onto the Foundations, and give yourself a pat on the back.

JUBILEE SOLITAIRE

Two decks of cards are required for this game. It was in 1887 that Queen Victoria celebrated her Golden Jubilee. Today a similar occasion would be marked by the sale of lurid T-shirts, souvenir tea-towels and color supplements galore. Then, a loyal populace devised games of Solitaire (the British call it Patience) in her honor, of a difficulty to make one tear your hair out!

If you are feeling strong enough to make the attempt, begin as follows.

Remove all eight Kings and put them, facing up, in a row at the top of the table.

The aim of the game is to build up on the Kings to the Queen, in suit, in the following way: King, Ace, Jack, Two, Ten, Three, Nine, Four, Eight, Five, Seven, Six, Queen.

Begin to deal the cards in your hand; either onto the King piles if you can, or to one of four heaps. (I think it wiser to reserve one of the heaps for the Queens alone and beware of blocking cards that will soon be needed.) As always in these games, the top card of each heap is available for use. But, you are not allowed to move it from heap to heap—only to a King pile.

When you have played all your cards, turn over and gather up the heaps, without shuffling them, and redeal. This can be done twice.

That doyenne of Victorian writers on the game, Miss Mary Whitmore Jones, has the last word: "... Success is difficult to attain; it is not the lot of every Queen to have a Jubilee."

KNAVES' DIAL SOLITAIRE

This is one of the simpler games, requiring two decks of cards, for days when only a gentle brainteaser is needed. This does not mean that a happy ending is automatic.

Begin by shuffling the two decks together, very thoroughly. Turn the top card—this will decide the suit of the twelve Foundations.

Excluding the Jack (or knave), arrange the cards of this suit in a semicircle, as they emerge in play, running from the Ace to the King. All cards face up.

The eight Jacks play no part in this game. They are placed in two rows of four, inside the half circle or "dial."

The object of the game is to build the other seven cards, of the same value, upon each of the corresponding cards in the semicircle, alternating the colors. (The suit being Diamonds, a black Ace will be placed on the Ace of Diamonds, a red Ace on the black Ace, and so on.) But you need all the Foundation cards in place before you can put any cards of the opposite color on top of them.

Deal out the cards in your hand one by one. If possible, play these upon the Foundation cards or discard them to a single heap, the top of which remains available, as always.

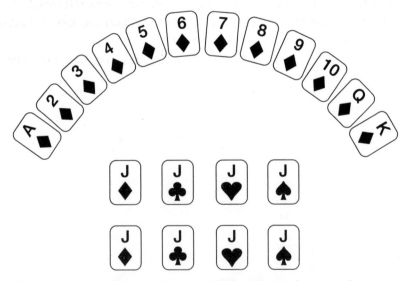

KNAVES' DIAL SOLITAIRE: In this game, the Ten of Diamonds was the top card.

All cards having been used, turn over the heap and play it through again, once. If you have been successful, the dial will have changed color, in this example from red to black.

LABYRINTH SOLITAIRE

One deck of cards is needed for this version of Solitaire. Remove the four Aces from the pack and place them in a row at the top of the table, face up. These are the Foundation cards.

The object of the game is to build in sequence and in suit on these cards, up to the King.

Begin by shuffling the deck thoroughly. Now deal eight cards in a row from left to right, face up, beneath the Foundation row.

Play any suitable card onto the appropriate Ace, then fill any gap (or gaps) thus produced with the next card taken from those you hold in your hand.

When nothing more can be played, deal another row of eight cards immediately below the first and play as before, with one important exception—don't fill in any gaps you may make. This is done in the first row only. This is how the labyrinth effect appears.

Continue playing in the same way until all the cards are used.

Exposed cards, those at the top and at the bottom of each column, are available for play onto the Foundations after every deal.

(Using a card from the top row releases the card immediately below it. In the same way, a card taken from the bottom row frees the card above it for use.)

Should the game grind to a halt, it's OK to take one card from anywhere to build on a Foundation. Hopefully, this will get the game moving again.

There is no redeal. The game is won if all the Foundation cards have been built in sequence and suit up to the King.

LADY OF THE MANOR SOLITAIRE

You will need two decks of cards for this game. Remove the eight Aces, putting them to one side momentarily. Shuffle the remaining cards, then count out four piles of twelve cards each, laying them in a row face up (see below).

Now place the eight Aces in a row beneath these piles. The remaining cards are arranged in a semicircle above the four piles, according to their value, from the Two to the King. Now begin to build on the Aces (Two, Three, Four, Five, and so on) without regard to suit. Take the cards from the semicircle to do this until an appropriate one appears on one of the four piles. This must be taken in preference to those in the semicircle, the object of the game being to use all the cards in the four piles. If you don't succeed in this, the game has failed.

LADY OF THE MANOR SOLITAIRE.

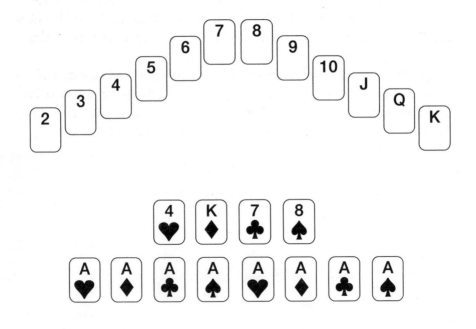

LEGITIMIST SOLITAIRE

I remain in cheerful ignorance as to the identity of the supporter of the French royal house of Bourbon who (presumably) invented this Solitaire. It doesn't stop me from playing it.

Two decks of cards are needed. Shuffle both decks together, first removing one King and placing it upon the table. (All cards are placed face up in this game and the suit is of no importance.)

As they emerge in play, put in a row beside the King (from left to right): a Queen, Jack, Ten, Nine, Eight, Seven, and Six. These are the Foundation cards (or *origines* as the French has it). There is one difficulty: Foundation cards must be moved into position in the order stated (the Queen before the Jack, Eight before Seven, etc.).

The object of the game is to build, in sequence, down on these, paying no attention to suit. Thus, in a successful game, the King finishes the thirteen-card sequence topped with an Ace, the Queen with a King, the Jack with a Queen, Ten with a Jack, Nine with a Ten, Eight with a Nine, Seven with an Eight, and Six with a Seven. But you don't have to wait until you have all the Foundation cards in place before you start building.

Play the cards in your hand one by one upon any available Foundation card. If they cannot be used immediately, put them in a single heap, the top card of which is always available.

The heap can be turned over and redealt twice. If you have not succeeded ... well, *"c'est la vie!"*

LIMITED SOLITAIRE

Two decks are needed for this difficult game. Shuffle the cards together very thoroughly and deal out three rows of twelve, all cards face up. These Tableau cards must not overlap.

Take any Aces in the bottom row and put them in a line at the top of the table. (Hopefully, any other Aces will emerge—or be freed from the top two rows—during play!) The object of the game is to build up, in sequence and in suit, upon these Foundation cards to the King.

The base card of each of the twelve "columns" of the Tableau is exposed and free for use. Removing a card frees the one above it. Do any building possible onto the Foundations, then begin to play out the cards in your hand.

Those unable to be placed can be discarded to a single heap or built down on any exposed card in the layout, but it's here that the difficulty begins. One is very "limited" in the way this is to be done. Only a single card, of the same suit and one lower in value, can be put upon another, taken either from those you hold, the top of the heap or another exposed card in the Tableau (Four of Diamonds upon the Five of Diamonds, Ten of Clubs upon the Jack of Clubs and so on).

And here's the tricky part...this pair is now totally immovable until both cards can be played to their Foundation pile. They must not be built upon further or, even worse, removed to a space. A space made by the emptying of a column is filled by any available card, if that is what you want. But beware, it is sometimes wiser to leave the gap empty.

When all the cards have been dealt, there is a second chance for success. Turn the heap over and take the top four cards from it. Place the four cards in a line facing up and, if possible, play them to a Foundation pile or pair with another on the Tableau, or put them into a space. (Now you see how useful spaces can be.) This will get the game moving once more, if luck is with you.

Anything taken from this reserve of four cards is to be replaced by the next card (or cards) from the heap. When no card of this quartet can be moved, the game has ended. No further helps are permitted.

MARIA SOLITAIRE

This two-deck game is simple to describe, but difficult to play through successfully.

After shuffling the two decks together, deal out four rows of nine cards, all face up.

You are supposed to keep the rows separate, but I always overlap them so that the Tableau resembles nine vertical columns of four, with the value of all these cards clearly visible.

The aim of the game is to take the eight Aces as they emerge in play (putting them in a row at the top of the table), building up upon them, in sequence and in suit, to the King.

Remove any Aces among the exposed cards (those with no other cards upon them, initially at the base of the columns) and anything that can be built on them. In this way the cards above are freed for use. Then build down in sequence upon the columns of the Tableau, in alternating colors, until needed (black Six on red Seven, red Five on black Six, etc.). Any single exposed card in the Tableau can be moved to another column, provided that the rules of sequence and color are observed.

When nothing more can be done, play out the cards in your hand one by one. Place them on the Foundation piles wherever possible, or build them down on the Tableau.

A gap in the layout, caused by the removal of a column, is filled by any exposed card.

Discard unplayable cards to a solitary heap, the top of which is always there for you to use.

As no redeal of the heap is permitted, a lot of forward planning is needed to free vital cards and bring this classic Solitaire to a satisfactory conclusion.

MARTHA SOLITAIRE

One deck is needed for this satisfying game. After shuffling the deck very thoroughly—absolutely vital—remove the four Aces and put them in a line, face up, at the top of the table.

These Aces are the Foundation cards and the object of the game is to build up, in sequence and in suit, until a King crowns each pile.

Deal out four rows of twelve cards: the first and third rows face down, the second and bottom rows face up. Overlap these cards (the Tableau) so that they look like twelve vertical columns.

The card at the base of each column, having nothing upon it, is "exposed" and available for use. Removing a card frees the one above. (If that faces down, turn it over with a nonchalant air and play on!)

Move all possible exposed cards to the Foundation Aces, then build down in sequence and alternating colors onto the Tableau columns until they can be played off (black Five on red Six, red Four on black Five, and so on).

Any one exposed card, or a sequence of whatever length, can be played to another column if you remember the rule of alternating colors.

A gap in the Tableau, caused by the removal of a vertical line, can't be filled so easily. Only one available card is placed there—not a sequence—as a new beginning.

With careful consideration, this game should end well.

MATRIMONY SOLITAIRE

For this game, only one deck is required. Shuffle the cards very thoroughly, then place forty-eight cards, face up, in six rows of eight cards each. If, as you deal out the cards, you find two cards of equal value (such as two Fours, two Jacks, etc.) in the same perpendicular column, don't lay the second card down. Put it at the bottom of the deck in your hand and substitute the next. The four cards remaining are the reserve and should be put to one side face down. The success of the game depends on them.

The object of the game is to pair off all the cards, but you can only use the bottom card in each perpendicular column. In the example below, there are two Fives and two Tens to be happily married and taken away.

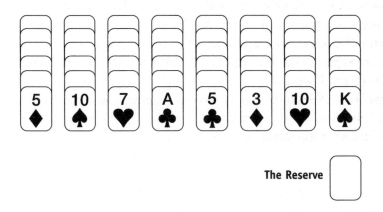

The Reserve

MATRIMONY SOLITAIRE: **The layout. (All cards, except those in the Reserve, are placed face up.)**

Their departure will uncover other cards and may enable other pairs to be made. If this is not the case, and the game is at a standstill, take the top reserve card and try to get the game moving again. When the reserve pile is exhausted, if all the couples are not married, the game has failed.

MISS MILLIGAN SOLITAIRE

Two decks are required for this classic game. No collection is complete without the maddening Miss Milligan, although some might be happy to see her go!

Shuffle the two decks together very thoroughly and deal out a row of eight cards, facing up, from left to right. This is the beginning of the Tableau.

The aim of the game is to move the eight Aces, or Foundation cards, into a line at the top of the table as they emerge in play, building up upon them, in sequence and in suit, to the King.

Remove any Aces, together with any cards that can be built upon them, from the first row of the Tableau. Follow this by dealing a second row of eight cards upon the first, all the cards facing up.

Overlap the cards that remain, or any spaces made, ensuring that the values of all cards can be easily seen. View the Tableau as eight upright columns.

Pause to consider what you need to do. The exposed cards in the Tableau can be built down in sequence and alternating colors upon exposed cards in another column until they can be removed to the Foundation piles (red Seven on black Eight, black Six on red Seven, and so on).

There is no limit to the number of cards in a sequence which can be removed from one column to another, provided that the rules of alternating color and downward numbering are observed.

An empty column can be filled only by a King, or a sequence of which the King is the beginning.

Deal another row of eight cards as before and play on. (Obviously, the columns will be of unequal length.)

No move is to be made until each deal of eight cards is set down.

An unusual help, called "waiving," is allowed when the last eight cards have been placed. Any one exposed card at the base of a column can be put to one side, thus permitting the removal of cards trapped above it. The card taken must eventually be played back into the game, either to the Tableau or a Foundation pile.

"Waiving" can be done as many times as you wish, but the card removed must find a new home; you cannot "waive" a second card if the first is "homeless." If it cannot be replaced, the game is a failure, because the eight Foundation piles will not have gathered all the cards to themselves beneath the King.

MISSING LINK SOLITAIRE

One deck of cards is needed for this. It is important to shuffle the cards very thoroughly before attempting it.

Cut the deck and remove one card from the middle without looking at it. Put it to one side, face down; this is the "missing link" of the title.

The object of the game is to remove the four Aces, as they emerge in play, and to build up on each in sequence and suit to the King.

Deal the cards in your hand one by one, all facing up, to an Ace pile (if you are lucky) or discard unplayable cards to one of up to seven heaps. These heaps are to be formed as you think best. (Obviously it is not wise to put a high card on one of lower value and the same suit, if this can be avoided.) The top of each heap remains available for use throughout the game but cannot be transferred to another heap.

A vacancy caused by the removal of an entire heap is filled by any exposed card or the next card from the deck.

When you can play nothing more, turn the "missing link." Hopefully this will revive the game. There is no redeal.

A successful game will show four piles of thirteen cards, each topped with a King.

MOUNT OLYMPUS SOLITAIRE

In the real world, Mount Olympus is a little under 10,000 feet in height and situated in northeast Greece. To most of us, as to the unknown Victorian composer of this game, it is the home of the ancient Greek gods and goddesses.
The layout of the game shows this very well.

Two decks of cards are needed and the cards face up.

Begin by removing all the Aces and all the Twos from both decks. Put them in a semicircle, alternately, at the top of the table. These sixteen Foundation cards represent the clouds which shroud Mount Olympus.

The object of the game is to build up, in suit, on these in the following way:

Ace, Three, Five, Seven, Nine, Jack and King;
Two, Four, Six, Eight, Ten and Queen.

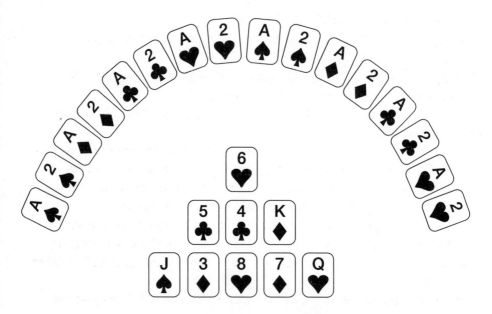

MOUNT OLYMPUS SOLITAIRE: The beginning—the Three of Diamonds can be placed on the Ace of Diamonds immediately, and the Four of Clubs on the Two of Clubs. The gaps will be filled by the next cards from those in your hand.

Shuffle the remainder of the two decks together and deal out a triangular Tableau of nine cards beneath the arc of the Foundation row: one card in the top row, three in the second row, and five in the third row. (This symbolizes Mount Olympus.) Allow plenty of space between the nine cards.

Remove suitable cards in the layout to the Foundations; otherwise, build down on the Tableau cards, in suit and by twos (Seven of Diamonds on the Nine of Diamonds and so on). Make a downward column of each so that you can see the values.

Exposed cards can be moved singly between Tableau piles, or in any length of sequence provided the "join" is correct, until they can be played to the Foundation piles.

Gaps must be filled immediately by the next card from those in your hand. Don't be tempted to do anything else, no matter how much the blocked cards may provoke you!

When the game is stuck, deal another nine cards, one to each Tableau pile, and play on.

There is no second chance in the shape of a redeal when all the cards have been played. But, if when you have dealt out all the cards you are left with gaps in the Tableau, you can move the top card from another pile to fill the spaces.

A successful ending will show the Foundation piles topped by Kings and Queens— gods and goddesses peering benignly from their home.

NAPOLEON AT ST. HELENA SOLITAIRE

The apparent simplicity of this Solitaire masks the difficulty of bringing it off successfully. (Like life, I suppose.)

It possesses several titles, "Forty Thieves" and "Big Forty" among them, but "Napoleon at St. Helena" seems to be the most popular.

Two decks are required and all cards must face up; you don't need to add any unneccessary challenges!

Begin by shuffling the two decks together and deal out four rows of ten cards as the Tableau. Overlap them so that they resemble ten columns, with the value of each card clearly visible. If you deal any Aces in these rows, remove them to use as Foundation cards and replace them with the next card in the deck.

The aim of the game is to take the eight Aces, when they emerge, building up upon them in sequence and in suit to the King (Ace, Two, Three, Four, Five, Six, Seven, Eight, Nine, Ten, Jack, Queen, and King). When found, put these Foundation cards in a row above the Tableau.

The card at the base of each column, having nothing upon it, is exposed and available for play; removing this card frees the one above.

Move any suitable card to the Foundation row. Otherwise build down on other columns of the Tableau in sequence and in suit (this is the stumbling block) until needed (Eight of Hearts upon the Nine of Hearts, Seven of Hearts upon the Eight of Hearts, and so on). Move single cards only, not sequences.

When you have done all you can, deal out the cards you hold one by one, to the Foundation piles or to the Tableau. Discard unplayable cards to a solitary heap, the top of which is always available.

A space in the Tableau caused by the removal of a column is filled with any available card.

No second chance in the way of a redeal is allowed.

NARCOTIC SOLITAIRE

You will need one deck of cards for this Solitaire. I think the title of this game is highly inappropriate. It does not soothe. On the contrary, it goads you until nothing is more important than to bring it to a successful end!

Shuffle the cards very well and deal four cards in a row, face up. If there are two of the same value, place the card on the right onto the card on the left. (The same rule applies if there are three of the same value. The duplicates are always piled upon the card of the same value to the left.)

Continue dealing four cards at a time on top of the previous four, pausing between each deal to move those of equal rank to the leftmost card.

When all the cards in your hand have been used, gather up the piles from right to left without reshuffling or disturbing their order in any way, and deal them out again (and again and again!). There is no limit to the number of times this can be done.

Should the four cards you deal have the same value, remove them from the game. The game is won when all fifty-two cards have been taken away in this way.

I refuse to say how long this took me, but I will admit to more than one hour...

NUMBER ELEVEN SOLITAIRE

Only one deck is needed for this game. Place twelve piles of four cards each in three rows, only the top cards being placed face up. The last four are kept as a reserve as shown.

Remove any two cards that add up to eleven. The face cards have no number value and can only be taken away when any King, Queen, and Jack are displayed at the same time.

When you have found all the available elevens, there will be piles face down; turn the top cards of these face up and look for the number eleven, in two cards, as before. As the piles become exhausted, fill the vacant space with a card taken from the four in reserve.

If you do not succeed in removing all the cards, you have failed.

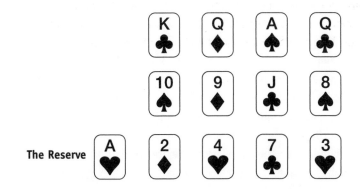

The King of Clubs, the Queen of Diamonds and the Jack of Clubs can be removed since they are there simultaneously. (Suit is of no importance.) The remaining Queen will have to wait for another King and Jack to surface. The Eight of Spades and Three of Hearts, the Seven of Clubs and the Four of Hearts, together with the Nine of Diamonds and Two of Diamonds, can be taken away, since each pair totals eleven.

OCTAVE SOLITAIRE

Two decks are necessary for this most enjoyable and colorful Solitaire.

Remove the eight Aces as Foundation cards, putting them in a row at the top of the table, alternately red and black.

Shuffle the remainder of the two decks together very thoroughly and deal out three rows of eight cards each; the first two rows face down and the third row face up. Overlap the rows so that the Tableau resembles eight upright columns of three.

The objects of the game are (a) to build up in suit and sequence to the Tens and (b) to have beneath each Foundation pile a column containing a King, Queen, and Jack in alternating colors.

Available cards in the Tableau are built down on the columns, in alternating colors, until taken to the Foundations. When an exposed card is removed, turn the one above face up.

Now play out the cards in your hand one by one, either to a Foundation pile or onto the Tableau (remembering the color rule). Discard unplayable cards to a single heap, the top of which is always available.

(Only one card at a time, not a sequence, can be moved around the layout.)

Fill a column that's emptied in play with any available card, but beware: remembering the second objective, it is wiser to put a King at the top of an empty column where possible.

Having played all the cards in your hand, gather up the heap and turn it over. A second chance is given. Deal out eight cards in a line below the Tableau. Use any of these eight cards for building on the Foundation piles or Tableau, filling up spaces with the next card from the heap.

When none of the eight can be placed, the game is practically at an end, but the anonymous inventor permits a last desperate fling. Play the next card from the heap to see if this will reanimate the game. After this, you have no more chances of ending successfully (but I trust you already have).

ODD AND EVEN SOLITAIRE

Two decks of cards are requisite for this Solitaire. Shuffle the decks together thoroughly and begin by dealing out nine cards, in three rows of three, facing up. These are the reserve.

Remove one Ace and one Two of each suit as they emerge in play. These are put in a line above the reserve, totalling eight Foundation cards in all. If at the beginning of the game, you deal any Aces and Twos into the reserve, you can use these as Foundation cards and fill the spaces left behind by them with other cards.

The object of the game is to build up, in suit and sequence, on both the Ace and the Two as follows:

Ace, Three, Five, Seven, Nine, Jack, King, Two, Four, Six, Eight, Ten, and Queen.
Two, Four, Six, Eight, Ten, Queen, Ace, Three, Five, Seven, Nine, Jack, King.

In this way, the title is justified!

Begin to deal the cards in your hand one by one, building on the Foundation piles whenever possible. Cards not playable for the moment are discarded to a single heap, the top card of this being always available.

Use the cards in the reserve whenever you can. A space (or spaces) here must be filled immediately with the top card from the heap. (Should this have vanished or not yet begun, use the next card from those you hold.)

Turn over the heap and play it through once again (and once only) when all cards have been dealt.

ONE FOUNDATION SOLITAIRE

One deck of cards is needed for this game. This Solitaire differs from most in having only one Foundation, and beware...it's not as simple as it first appears!

Shuffle the deck and deal a row of seven cards side by side, face up. Deal a second row in the same way, overlapping the first; continue this until five rows have been dealt. This has the appearance of seven columns, the bases of each being the exposed cards.

Deal the next card, face up, onto the table. This is the Foundation card. The object of the game is to gather all cards to it.

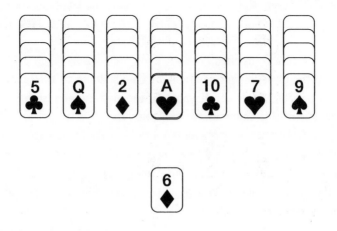

One Foundation Solitaire: **The beginning. (All cards are facing up.)**

The peculiarity of this game is that one may build, in sequence and regardless of suit, up or down, changing direction at any time. Exposed cards at the foot of the seven columns are used to build. Each time a card is used, the card above it becomes available for use. (If you use up all the cards from one column you don't replace them, but leave an empty space.)

For example: the Foundation card in the example above is a Six. Either a Five or a Seven can be built upon it. One must plan ahead to avoid becoming blocked too soon. And here is the difficulty: An Ace must not be placed upon a King, a King cannot be played upon an Ace. (A Queen is the only card permitted to be dealt upon a King and the Two upon an Ace.)

When further play from the columns is impossible, deal the next card from those held in your hand onto the pile. This is a new Foundation.

Play available cards onto this until you become stuck, yet again. Deal another new Foundation from those cards you hold and continue until all have been used.

The game is won if all fifty-two cards sit one upon another on the Foundation.

PAIRS SOLITAIRE

This is a very simple version, but addictive in that you tend to want to play on until successful!

Only one deck is required and it is vital that it is well shuffled. Place nine cards in three rows of three, face up. Remove any pairs that there may be and fill the vacant spaces from the deck. (See below.)

If you come to a stop, you may take one card from the deck in your hand and lay it down. This usually gets the game moving again, and can be done as often as is needed.

Should this card not find a pair, the game has failed.

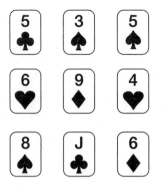

PAIRS SOLITAIRE: **There are two pairs to be removed.**

PAS SEUL ("SOLO DANCE") SOLITAIRE

One deck of cards is needed for this. Pas Seul, peering back through the mists of time to ballet classes, is that golden opportunity yearned for by budding Pavlovas, the solo dance—a most suitable title for a Solitaire.

All cards in this game face up. Begin by dealing out six cards in a row for the Tableau.

Your object is to take the Aces as they emerge in play, building up upon them in suit and sequence to the King. (Put these Foundation cards, when discovered, in a line at the top of the table.)

Start by removing any Aces, and cards that can be built upon them, from the Tableau. Fill the resulting gaps, if any, with cards taken from those you hold.

If your Tableau consists of consecutively numbered cards of alternating colors (e.g., a red Seven and a black Eight), build these cards down on each other (e.g., place the red Seven onto the black Eight). Again, fill any resulting gaps with cards taken from those you hold.

After this, deal out the deck one by one. Build on the Foundation piles wherever possible or build down on the Tableau cards, in sequence but alternating the colors, until they can be removed. Overlap these cards to make six columns of differing lengths.

Discard unplayable cards to a single heap. Cards available for you to use are the top card of the heap (naturally), the top card of those in your hand, the exposed card at the base of a column or any part of a downward sequence, provided that the rule about alternating colors is observed. This is very useful in extricating a vital card.

Gaps in the Tableau, a column having been played through, are filled by any one available card or a sequence.

No second chance is given in this game, as you may not redeal the heap.

PERPETUAL MOTION SOLITAIRE

Never was a game so well named. It is also addictive to a maddening degree.

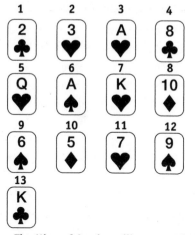

PERPETUAL MOTION SOLITAIRE: **The Nine of Spades will move to beneath the Two of Clubs, missing the correctly placed King of Clubs.**

You will need one deck, well shuffled. Begin by dealing out, face up, thirteen piles of four cards. Imagine that these piles are numbered from one to thirteen and line them up in whatever way helps you to remember. (As usual, the Jack equals eleven, the Queen twelve, and the King has the value of thirteen.)

The object of the game is to eliminate the deck, in batches of thirteen, in the following way.

Take the top card from the pile numbered one, putting it beneath pile number two. Move the top card from pile number two to the bottom of pile number three, continuing in this way until you arrive at pile number thirteen. The top card from this pile returns to the bottom of pile number one. (The Perpetual Motion of the title.)

However, whenever the top card of a pile agrees with your numbering of it, do not remove it. Instead, move the card you have taken from the previous pile to the bottom of the next pile which is not topped with its correct number. (There will be less and less of these as the game progresses.) Going back to the beginning, if there was an Ace on the first pile as the game began, the first card to move would be the top of pile number two.

Hopefully, all top thirteen cards will soon be where they should be, running in sequence from the Ace to the King. Then is the time to remove them, putting them to one side. They take no further part in the game.

The last card removed before the thirteen cards were taken away is now placed beneath the next pile to it (or the next available under the rules should that be already topped by its correct number) and play continues as before.

Should you have succeeded in spiriting away three sequences of thirteen, the game is won. The last layer will be correct, but do not ask me how!

PICTURE SOLITAIRE

You will need two decks of cards for this game, but do not shuffle the decks together.

To begin, take one deck and lay out nine cards in three rows (three cards in each row), face up. Then play out the cards in your hand into a heap; placing the four Aces, as they appear, in a perpendicular line on the left. The four Kings, as they appear, are placed to the right. The Aces are built on up, in suit. (Two of Hearts to be placed on the Ace of Hearts, Three of Hearts to be placed on the Two, and so on.) The final card on these piles will be a King.

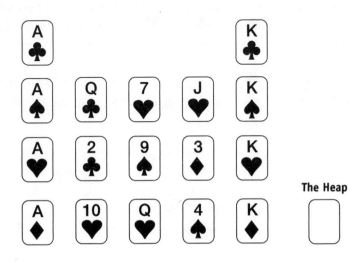

PICTURE SOLITAIRE: **Ready to begin. (All cards face up.)**

The Kings are built on down, in suit. (Queen of Hearts to be placed on the King of Hearts, Jack of Hearts to be placed on the Queen, and so on.) The final card on these piles, if successfully worked out, will be an Ace.

Whenever you can use a card from the center nine, replace it with the top card from the heap. When you have worked your way through the first deck, continue with the second. The Aces and Kings from this deck are put on the waste heap or become one of the nine central cards until they can be correctly placed. The heap can be turned over when all the cards are used, and played through once again to give one a second chance. If all the cards are not placed in their proper sequence after this, the game is unsuccessful.

PUSH-PIN SOLITAIRE

Two decks are needed for this very simple Solitaire. Shuffle the decks together very thoroughly, then deal out the cards from left to right and side by side, face up.

Whenever one or two cards are between two others of the same value or suit, discard them and close ranks. (Seven of Clubs and Three of Diamonds between the Queen of Hearts and the Queen of Spades, discard the Seven and Three. Eight of Hearts and Two of Spades between the Five of Diamonds and the Jack of Diamonds, discard the Eight and Two.)

Should there be three or more cards caught in this way, all can be removed only if they are of the same suit. (Queen, Ten, Six, Three and Two of Diamonds imprisoned between the Four of Clubs and Jack of Clubs, take away all the Diamonds.)

The game is won if two cards remain side by side at the end, all the others having been taken away.

(There is a second chance, however, if a line of whatever length remains when all the cards have been played out. Switch any two cards in the row to revive the game.)

PUSS IN THE CORNER SOLITAIRE

One deck of cards is needed for this game. Remove the four Aces and put them on the table, face up, in the shape of a square. Follow this by shuffling the deck.

The object of the game is to build up in sequence (Ace, Two, Three, Four, and so on) and in color (red card on red card, Hearts or Diamonds, and black on black, Spades or Clubs regardless) to the King.

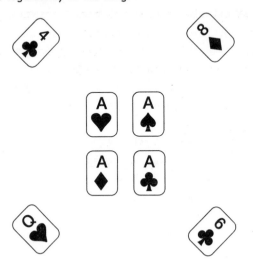

Puss in the Corner Solitaire.

Play out the cards in your hand one by one, face up. Those unable to be placed on a Foundation pile are put into one of four heaps, piled as you choose. (It is very helpful—but not always possible—to avoid putting a higher card upon one of lower value.) The top cards of these are always available for moving to a Foundation pile; they may not, however, be moved from one heap to another.

The heaps are positioned at an angle, one to each corner of the square, mirroring the game for children which lends its name to this Solitaire.

All cards having been dealt, pick up the heaps in a clockwise direction and, without shuffling them, play your "new" deck out once again. No more chances are given. I hope the ending was happy.

PUZZLER SOLITAIRE

One deck of cards is needed for this, with all the Twos, Threes, Fours, Fives, and Sixes removed. (This is known as the piquet pack, referring to a French card game for two people played with a deck from which all cards below the Sevens are omitted.)

After shuffling the deck, deal out four cards side by side, facing up. If these cards include any Kings, put them in a line above the original row. They will be the Foundations and will be joined by the remaining Kings as they emerge in play. Fill any gap left by a King with the next card in your hand.

The object of the game is to build down in suit and sequence on the Kings, to the Sevens (King, Queen, Jack, Ten, Nine, Eight, and Seven).

PUZZLER SOLITAIRE: **A happy ending.**

Begin to play out the cards in your hand, face up, onto the lower row. Stop between each deal of four cards to see if anything can be built on the Foundation row. The removal of a card exposes the card beneath for use.

When the cards in your hand have been exhausted, gather up the lower piles from left to right and redeal them once.

If the game has been successful, each Foundation pile will be topped by a Seven, while the Aces remain in a row below.

PYRAMID SOLITAIRE

One deck of cards is needed for this simple Solitaire. Shuffle the deck thoroughly (absolutely vital in this game) and construct a pyramid in the following fashion.

Deal out, face up, five rows of cards as a reserve in the shape of a pyramid: one card in the top row, two in the second, three in the third, four in the fourth, and five cards in the bottom row.

The object of the game is to remove the four Aces, as they surface in play, to the top of the table, building up upon each in sequence and in suit to the King.

Every card in the reserve is available for use. Take away from there any Aces, and cards to be built on them, filling spaces from the cards you hold.

Now deal your cards one by one, either to a Foundation pile or to a single heap, remembering that the top of this yearns to be of assistance.

No redeal of the heap is permitted when all your cards are played.

A successful ending will find the pyramid vanished and four neat piles remaining, each crowned with a King.

Q.C. SOLITAIRE

Two decks are needed for this difficult Solitaire, named after a Victorian member of the English Bar (perhaps Sir Edward Marshall Hall?), who played this when Whist was not possible. Whether the attorney devised the game is unknown.

After the obligatory thorough shuffling together of the decks, deal out twenty-four cards in four rows of six; this is the Tableau. (All cards in this game face up.) Overlap the rows so that the layout resembles six vertical columns.

The object of the game is to remove the eight Aces to the top of the table as they emerge in play, building up on these Foundation cards in sequence and suit to the King.

Remove any Aces that happen to be skulking among the exposed cards in the bottom row, with anything that can be built on them. This frees cards above them for use.

Single available cards (not sequences) can be transferred to other suitable columns, building down on the Tableau in sequence and suit until they can be played to a Foundation pile.

Begin to deal out the cards from your hand one by one. If a Foundation pile is not yet attainable, try to play them into the Tableau. Discard useless cards to a single heap, which has a greater importance than in other games.

If a column is emptied, the gap must be filled with the top card from the heap. A second annoying rule requires the top card of the heap to be built onto a Foundation pile in preference to a duplicate card at the base of a Tableau column.

This is remarkably effective in blocking the game and raising your blood pressure.

It is allowable to turn the heap over, the deck in your hand having been dealt, to play it through again once. (However, truth compels me to add that this is not permitted by some.)

QUADRILLE SOLITAIRE

This decorative Solitaire is one of several named after a dance. (Seeking always to inform, I have discovered that the quadrille was a square dance of French origin, reputed to have been introduced into England in 1813 by the Duke of Devonshire!) Only one deck of cards is required for this. Shuffle the deck very thoroughly and deal the cards out onto a heap, removing the Aces and Twos as they emerge and placing them to form the figure of a quadrille.

Once all eight Foundation cards are laid out, they must be built on according to suit, but not as in most of the other games in this book. This time you must build in alternate numbers: for example, on the Ace is placed first a Three, next a Five, then Seven, Nine, Jack, and finishing with a King; on the Two is placed a Four, then a Six, followed by Eight, Ten, and finishing with a Queen.

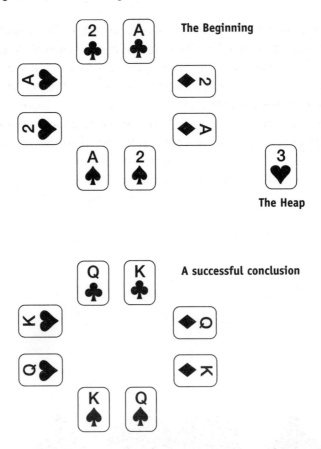

QUADRILLE SOLITAIRE.

There is only one heap, so progress can be very difficult sometimes. The heap can be used twice more after all the Aces and Twos have been found, but no further chances are allowed.

QUADRUPLE ALLIANCE SOLITAIRE

One deck of cards is needed for this game. Ignoring suit, remove any one Ace, Two, Three, and Four and put them in a row, face up.

Below this make a second row, consisting of any Two, Four, Six, and Eight. These last four are the Foundation cards.

You must aim to build up, still disregarding suit, on the lower row until a King tops each base. The sequences run as follows:

(a)   Two, Three, Four, Five, Six, Seven, Eight, Nine, Ten, Jack, Queen, King.

(b)   Four, Six, Eight, Ten, Queen, Ace, Three, Five, Seven, Nine, Jack, King.

(c)   Six, Nine, Queen, Two, Five, Eight, Jack, Ace, Four, Seven, Ten, King.

(d)   Eight, Queen, Three, Seven, Jack, Two, Six, Ten, Ace, Five, Nine, King.

This is not too complicated, if you remember that the cards in the top row are there solely to remind the player by what amount the cards below are to advance.

Play the cards in your hand one by one. Build on a Foundation if possible, otherwise discard them face up onto a single heap, the top card of which is there to be used whenever possible.

All cards dealt? Turn over the heap and play it through again twice. After this, the Kings have no further chance to seal their alliance.

LES QUATORZES SOLITAIRE

Two decks of cards are needed for this game. Shuffle the cards and deal out twenty-five cards, face up, in five rows, each containing five cards. The object of this Solitaire is to make the number fourteen with any two cards, taken only from a perpendicular or from a horizontal row. The cards paired in this way are placed to one side and their places taken by the cards in your hand.

The Jack counts as eleven, the Queen twelve, and the King thirteen.

If, during the game, the number fourteen cannot be made, you have a second chance. Any two cards may be taken from their proper position and may change places with two other cards in order to make one or more fourteens. This exchange of cards can be done only once in each playing.

If you are successful in this game, the entire deck will be paired off.

In the example given, the Queen of Diamonds can be paired with the two of Spades, the King of Hearts with the Ace of Clubs, the Jack of Hearts with the Three of Diamonds, and the Six of Spades with the Eight of Hearts.

LES QUATORZES SOLITAIRE.

QUEEN OF ITALY SOLITAIRE

Two decks are needed for this most interesting Solitaire. (Another name given to this is Terrace, a self-explanatory title, as you will see.) All cards face up.

When you have shuffled the decks together very thoroughly, deal a row of eleven cards at the top of the table as a reserve, overlapping them from left to right. (This is the Terrace.)

Below these deal a second row of four cards. Choose one of these as the first Foundation card. The object of the game is to remove the other seven cards of the same value to the Foundation row as they emerge in play. You must then attempt to build up, in sequence and in alternating colors, until each pile contains thirteen cards with the top card being one lower in value than the base card. The value of the cards is continuous, the Ace being above the King and below the Two.

Before deciding on your Foundation card, look at the reserve to see what it contains. This row can be built only to a Foundation pile, so think carefully. (In the example, I chose the Five of Spades as the first Foundation. As you can see, the Nine of Clubs is the exposed card on the terrace; had I chosen either the Two of Spades, Ace of Spades, or Jack of Diamonds as Foundations, the cards in the terrace would have remained, unmoving, for a long time.)

If you deal two (three, or even all four) cards of the same value among these four cards, you will probably decide to keep both (or all) as Foundation cards.

Take the rejected cards to begin a third row beneath the second and deal some more cards to bring the total number of cards in the bottom row to nine. This is the Tableau.

Play what you can from the Tableau to the Foundations, building up in sequence and in alternating colors. Below, the Foundation card is a black Five. The sequence there will run thus: black Five (Five of Spades), red Six (Six of Hearts), black Seven (Seven of Spades), red Eight (Eight of Hearts), and so on until you reach a black Four.

If you cannot play the cards in the Tableau directly onto a Foundation pile, play them on each other, building down in sequence and alternating colors until needed. When building down on the Tableau, it is better to place the cards in such a way that the value of all of them can be seen. Unfortunately, only single cards can be moved when building down, not sequences of cards.

The exposed card to the right of the reserve, or terrace, is built onto a Foundation pile and nowhere else, as I have already said. Using this card frees the one beside it for use.

Spaces made in the Tableau are to be filled from the heap if this is already in existence, from the top of the cards you hold if not. Now deal out the deck one by one, building up on Foundation piles where you can. Unplayable cards must be abandoned to a single heap, the top of which remains available throughout. There is no redeal.

If you were fortunate in your choice of Foundation, the end of the game will find eight piles of thirteen cards beaming back at you, while the terrace has crumbled away!

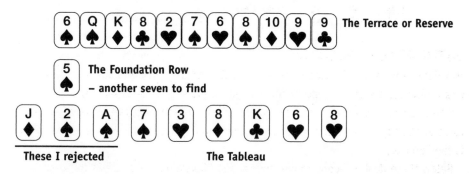

6♠ Q♦ K♣ 8♣ 2♥ 7♠ 6♠ 8♥ 10♠ 9♦ 9♣ **The Terrace or Reserve**

5♠ **The Foundation Row**
– another seven to find

J♦ 2♠ A♠ 7♠ 3♥ 8♦ K♣ 6♥ 8♥

These I rejected   **The Tableau**

QUEEN OF ITALY SOLITAIRE: (a) The Six of Hearts can be built upon the Five of Spades, Seven of Spades upon the Six of Hearts and the Eight of Hearts upon the Seven of Spades. The exposed card from the terrace—the Nine of Clubs—is placed upon the Eight of Hearts. (b) Place the Two of Spades upon the Three of Hearts in the Tableau. As there is, as yet, no heap, fill the gaps with the next cards from the deck in your hand and play on.

QUEEN'S AUDIENCE SOLITAIRE

Only one deck is needed for this game. All cards face up.

After shuffling the deck, deal out sixteen cards in the shape of a square, four to each side. The space enclosed is called the "audience chamber," the sixteen cards the "antechamber."

The aim of the game is to move the Ace and Jack of each suit into the audience chamber as they emerge in play, to build down upon them in sequence and suit to the Twos (Jack, Ten, Nine, Eight, Seven, Six, Five, Four, Three, and Two). The Ace is hidden beneath its Jack and plays no further part in the game. An annoying rule dictates that both Jack and Ace of the same suit must be simultaneously available before taking up their position as a Foundation pile.

Play out the cards in your hand one by one, hopefully onto a Foundation pile, while discarding useless cards to a single heap, the top of which is there to be used at any time.

All the cards of the antechamber can be moved to the Foundation piles for building when possible. Spaces made here must be filled with the top card from the heap; if there is no heap, use the next card from those you hold in your hand.

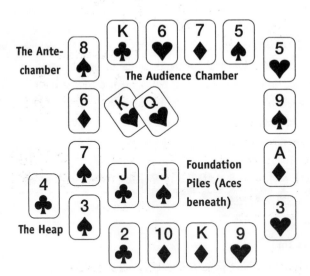

The Ante-chamber
The Audience Chamber
Foundation Piles (Aces beneath)
The Heap

QUEEN'S AUDIENCE SOLITAIRE: Two more Foundation piles are still to be found. The Ace of Diamonds must remain in the Antechamber until the Jack of Diamonds emerges. The Kings of Clubs and Diamonds await their consorts before removal to the Audience Chamber.

The Kings and Queens play a decorative role. The regal couple (same suit, naturally) are put together above a Foundation pile in the audience chamber. Place the Queen on top of the King to illustrate the title of the game. As before, both must be available at the same time before removing.

There is no redeal of the heap. A successful game has caused the antechamber to vanish into the four piles which remain, topped by a Two.

RAGLAN SOLITAIRE

One deck of cards is necessary for this game. The Solitaire differs slightly in that all cards are dealt out, face up, before the game begins. (I find it easier to play this game with miniature cards...or perhaps my tables are smaller than average!)

Begin by removing the four Aces, putting them to your right on the table. These are the Foundation cards.

The object is to build up in sequence and in suit on these Aces to the King.

The deck having been shuffled, deal six cards as a reserve, lining them up below or to the side of the Foundation cards, as you please.

The remainder of the deck is placed in the following way. Deal seven overlapping rows of cards with nine cards in the top row, eight in the second, seven in the third, and so on, decreasing by one in each row until the seventh, which contains three cards only.

The Tableau has the appearance of nine columns, the card at the base of each column being the "exposed" card. These exposed cards—and any of the six cards in the reserve—are available for building onto the Aces, if possible. (The cards in the reserve are not replaced when removed.)

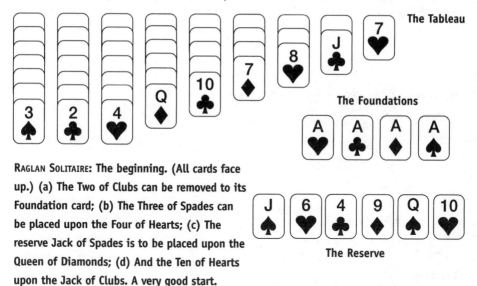

RAGLAN SOLITAIRE: **The beginning. (All cards face up.) (a) The Two of Clubs can be removed to its Foundation card; (b) The Three of Spades can be placed upon the Four of Hearts; (c) The reserve Jack of Spades is to be placed upon the Queen of Diamonds; (d) And the Ten of Hearts upon the Jack of Clubs. A very good start.**

When you have moved all possible cards to the Foundation piles, build in descending sequence and alternate colors on the exposed cards of the Tableau (red Six on black Seven, black Five on red Six, and so on) until they can be played to the Foundation piles. Cards must be moved singly, not in groups, however tempting. Cards from the reserve can also be used for building.

Should a column be removed, any exposed card can be put there, but it is not obligatory to fill the gap.

A successful ending has all cards sitting quietly in sequence and suit on the Foundations, a King on top of each pile.

ROLL-CALL SOLITAIRE

Roll-Call Solitaire is the simplest game of all, with absolutely no skill required. I have included it here because children love it and feel grown-up playing it. It can also help them to count and recognize shapes. One deck is needed.

Remove all cards below Seven, but retain the Aces. (This is sometimes called a piquet deck.) Shuffle, then deal out the cards face up, one upon another, saying as you do so: Seven, Eight, Nine, Ten, Jack, Queen, King, Ace. If a card of the right number turns up, put it to one side.

Once you have dealt out all the cards, deal them out again but don't start each new deal counting from Seven; just follow on from the last number called out. Continue playing until either: (a) all the cards have answered correctly to the roll-call, or (b) you find that you can remove no more and the cards always come around in the same order. If this happens, you have failed in your attempt.

Note: Children tend to continue this until stopped by the removal of the cards by an adult who considers two hours quite sufficient!

ROSAMUND'S BOWER SOLITAIRE

You will need one deck of cards for this Solitaire. This quaintly-named game commemorates "Fair Rosamund" Clifford, the mistress of King Henry II, who lived in the royal palace of Woodstock in Oxfordshire. A legend states that she was hidden away in a secret bower within a maze, to protect her from Henry's wife, Eleanor of Aquitaine.

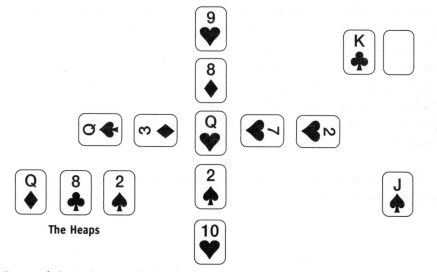

The Heaps

ROSAMUND'S BOWER SOLITAIRE: **The beginning.**

Remove from the deck the Queen of Hearts (or Rosamund), the King of Clubs, and the Jack of Spades. The Queen is placed in the center of the table with eight cards as guards around her: two above, two below and two on either side. All these cards face up.

The King of Clubs is placed above these to the right. Beside him is dealt a pile of Seven cards, facing down, as additional guards.

The Jack of Spades is placed at the bottom of the table. Using the cards in your hand, build on the Jack of Spades in a downward direction, paying no attention to suit (Jack, Ten, Nine, Eight, Seven, Six, Five, Four, Three, Two, Ace, King, Queen, and so on).

Three heaps are formed of cards not used immediately, piling them as you please. The top card of each heap is always available for use but must not be moved to the top of another heap.

If there is a suitable card on the outside of the eight cards protecting the Queen, this must be used in preference to the cards in your hand or on top of the heaps. Fill the gap immediately with the card on top of those lying face down beside the King of Clubs.

It is allowable to gather up and replay the heaps three times. (These must not be shuffled.)

The game has succeeded if the King of Clubs and the Queen of Hearts sit triumphantly atop the Jack pile.

ROUGE ET NOIR ("RED AND BLACK") SOLITAIRE

You will need two decks of cards for this game. Begin by removing the eight Aces from the decks and place them side by side in a row, face up.

Below these Foundation cards deal out a row of eight cards, also face up and side by side. This is the Tableau.

The object of the game is to build up, in sequence, on these Ace Foundation cards to the King. The difference in this game is that the piles are built in alternating colors, the red and black of the title (a red Two on a black Ace, a black Three on a red Two, and so on).

Take any suitable cards from the Tableau and place them on the Foundations. Fill any gaps from the cards you hold in your hand.

If you have consecutively-numbered cards in the Tableau of opposing colors, you can build down on them, e.g., place a black Seven on a red Eight. Again, fill any gaps from the cards you hold in your hand.

Begin to play, dealing one card at a time. Anything that cannot be placed immediately on the Foundation cards can be built down on the Tableau until needed or onto a single heap, the top card of which is always available for use.

Single cards can be moved from the top of each Tableau pile onto the Foundations, or from the top of one Tableau pile to the top of another, if this is helpful; but never to fill a gap.

Gaps in the Tableau line must be filled immediately from the top of the heap. If the heap has been used, fill the spaces with cards dealt from those you hold. If those have been exhausted, the gap must remain a gap!

One redeal is permitted when all the cards have been dealt. Pick up the heap, turn it over and play on as before.

The game is won if all the Foundation piles have been built in alternate colors up to the King.

ROYAL COTILLION SOLITAIRE

Two decks are required for this game. Originally the cotillion was a dance for four couples, in which the ladies lifted their skirts to reveal an inch or so of ornate petticoat (*cotillon* in French). Later the name was given to a fast waltz.

Shuffle the decks together very thoroughly and deal out, face up and not overlapping, twelve cards, in three rows of four, to the left of the board. (The "left wing.")

Next deal sixteen cards in four rows of four to the right of the board—yes, the "right wing." These cards also do not overlap and are all face up.

Between these wings, as they surface in play, are placed the Foundation cards in two upright columns of four, comprising one Ace and one Two from each suit.

The aim of the game is to build up, in suit, on these Foundations by two. Each thirteen-card sequence runs as follows:

Ace, Three, Five, Seven, Nine, Jack, King, Two, Four, Six, Eight, Ten, and Queen.

Two, Four, Six, Eight, Ten, Queen, Ace, Three, Five, Seven, Nine, Jack, and King.

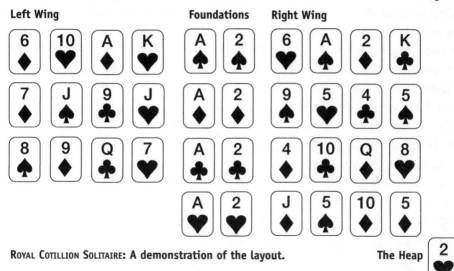

ROYAL COTILLION SOLITAIRE: A demonstration of the layout.   The Heap

All the cards on the right wing are available for building onto the Foundation piles, gaps being filled by the next card from those you hold or from the top of the (as yet unformed) solitary heap. (Obviously, preference must always be given to the heap if the game is to have a happy ending.) Of course, if you deal any Aces or Twos into the right wing at the start of the game, you can use these as Foundation cards and fill the spaces they leave behind with other cards from the deck.

The cards in the left wing are not so easily caught. Only the bottom row is available, a removal from here freeing the card above for use, while spaces remain unfilled.

Play out the cards in your hand one by one, discarding useless cards to the single heap mentioned above, building on the Foundation cards whenever possible.

Redealing the heap is not permitted. A successful conclusion shows the four Kings partnered by their Queens and ready to dance.

ROYAL RENDEZVOUS SOLITAIRE

Two decks are needed for this rather unusual Solitaire. Take the four Twos from one deck, one from each suit, together with all eight Aces from both. Place them as demonstrated: the eight Aces in two rows of four, one beneath the other, at the top of the table. Put two Twos to the right and two Twos to the left of the lower row of Aces. These are the Foundation cards.

Shuffle the remainder of the two decks together very thoroughly, then deal out two rows of eight cards each beneath the Foundation cards, as a reserve. (These do not overlap and all must face up.)

The object of the game is: (a) to build up in sequence and suit to the Queens on the Aces in the top row (Ace, Two, Three, Four, Five, Six, Seven, Eight, Nine, Ten, Jack, and Queen); (b) to build, in suit, by steps of two upon the bottom row of Aces to the King (Ace, Three, Five, Seven, Nine, Jack, and King); and (c) to build, in suit, again by steps of two upon the Twos (Two, Four, Six, Eight, Ten, and Queen).

Each of the sixteen-card reserves is available for immediate use. Build whatever you can from here to the Foundations, filling spaces with the next cards from the deck.

Begin to deal out the cards in your hand one by one, to a Foundation pile, with luck. Discard unplayable cards to a single heap, the top of which remains available for you.

Now the heap is in existence, fill gaps in the reserve with the top card from here. Only when this has dwindled to nothing can you revert to using the next card from your hand, as before.

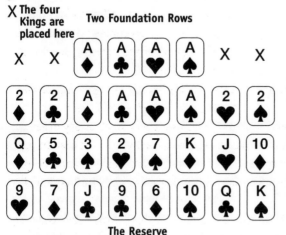

X The four Kings are placed here

Two Foundation Rows

The Reserve

ROYAL RENDEZVOUS SOLITAIRE: (a) The Three of Spades can be built upon the Ace of Spades in the lower Foundation row immediately. (b) The Two of Hearts is placed upon the Ace of Hearts in the top row. The two spaces will be filled by the next two cards from the deck, there being no heap, as yet.

Four Kings, one of each suit, remain unaccounted for. Place these above the appropriate two Foundation piles when their twins have crowned their Ace piles in the lower row.

There is to be no redealing of the heap at the end of the game.

If you are successful, all cards will have been gathered to the correct pile and the rows will read, from left to right, as follows:

Top Row: King, King, Queen, Queen, Queen, Queen, King, King.

Bottom Row: Queen, Queen, King, King, King, King, Queen, Queen.

SALIC LAW SOLITAIRE

Two decks of cards are needed for this game. The Salic Law, not repealed in Spain until 1830, gave preference to a male succession to the throne. This explains why the eight Queens are removed before the game begins and placed in a row, side by side and facing up, at the top of the table. Their splendid isolation ensures that they take no part in the game at all.

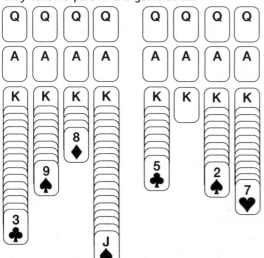

SALIC LAW SOLITAIRE: (All cards face up.)

Shuffle the decks together thoroughly and put one King at the extreme left, leaving a generous amount of space between it and the row of Queens. (All cards face up.)

Play out the cards you hold, one by one, upon the King, overlapping down so that the value of each card can be seen. Remove all Aces as you deal, placing them in a row below the Queens. The Aces are the Foundation cards.

The object of the game is to build up on the Foundations, in sequence but paying no regard to suit, to the Jacks. As you deal out each card, check whether it can immediately be placed onto a Foundation pile. If it can, check whether any other exposed cards (those at the ends of a column) can be moved onto a Foundation pile.

When you come to a second King, put it beside the first and deal out down on the second King until the third pops up. Continue dealing down on the last King found once all eight have been placed.

Build on the Foundation piles from exposed cards at the end of the columns during the deal. Afterwards continue in the same way. (Only exposed cards can be played onto the Foundation piles and must not move from column to column, however necessary.) Whenever possible, play to empty a column. A King that is alone is considered an "empty" column and any exposed card can be put there (but not until you have dealt out all the cards). This enables the game to keep moving, as it removes cards blocking play.

A successful game will show a row of Queens, beneath which will be a row of eight Foundation piles topped by the Jacks. The bottom row will consist of eight Kings.

SCOTCH SOLITAIRE

Perhaps this Solitaire should be more properly named Scottish Solitaire, but the name is so time-honored that it would take somebody braver than me to tamper with it.

Only one deck of cards and a good memory are necessary for this.

Deal out a Tableau of eighteen piles, face up, in three rows of six. Sixteen piles contain three cards each, the seventeenth and eighteenth have two in them.

As you deal, try to remember where the Aces are placed, because the object of the game is to free them in play and build up upon them in sequence, but in alternating colors, to the Kings (red Ace, black Two, red Three, and so on). As the Aces surface, put them in a row below the Tableau.

Begin by removing any Aces that are among the exposed cards, together with all cards that can be built on them, thus freeing those beneath.

Build down on the Tableau, ignoring suit and color (any Queen on any King, any Jack on any Queen, etc.), moving cards singly from pile to pile until they are needed on the Foundations.

Used piles are not replaced and there is no redeal. I confess that I have been unable to progress further than three completed sequences. Try as I may, the fourth continues to elude me. Maybe you can do better.

SIR TOMMY SOLITAIRE

This is supposed to be the first Solitaire ever invented, but who Sir Tommy was I do not know. (Many people who think that Solitaire has only one version know this one.)

The object of the game is the usual one—to build on the Aces up to the King—but it is not necessary to follow suit, i.e. Diamonds on Diamonds, Clubs on Clubs, as with some games of Solitaire. The number on the card is the only thing of importance.

You will need one deck of cards. Shuffle these well and begin to lay out four piles facing up. You can place the cards on whichever pile you like as the piles do not have to contain an equal number of cards. Remove the four Aces as they appear. The Aces are placed in a line below the four piles and if there are any Twos, place these on the Aces, followed by Threes and Fours and so on, as far as possible.

If the cards cannot be placed on an Ace pile, put them on the ordinary piles above as you please. But take care—it is a good idea to put the face cards on one pile so that the low cards, so necessary to be immediately available if the game is to be successful, are not blocked.

You must not transfer a card from one ordinary pile to another. It must stay in the pile chosen until it can be placed on an Ace Foundation pile in the usual way.

If you have not been able to place all the cards on an Ace Foundation by the time all the cards have been dealt, the game has been a failure. (Shuffle again and better luck next time!)

SIX BY SIX SOLITAIRE

One deck of cards is needed for this unusual and difficult Solitaire.

Deal out, facing up, a Tableau of thirty-six cards in six rows of six, overlapping them so that they are in six perpendicular columns.

Remove any Aces from the exposed cards at the base of each column (automatically freeing the card above), placing them above the layout. All other Aces are put in the Foundation row as they emerge or are released from the Tableau during play.

Your aim is to build up on the Aces to the King, in sequence and in suit.

Deal out the cards in your hand one by one, building them up onto the Foundation piles where possible or building down onto the Tableau, in sequence but ignoring suit, until they are needed.

Any exposed card in the Tableau can be moved singly between columns, provided the rule of downward sequence is kept. But a sequence of cards (more than one) can only be moved if all the cards in it are of the same suit and placed on an exposed card of correct number and suit. These are rare!

This game is odd in that unplayable cards do not form a heap; they are placed one by one onto the first Tableau column to the left, regardless of value, spreading down. The card at the end of this column—or any sequence if the rules are followed, as above—is always available for you to use.

A space caused by the removal of a Tableau column is to be filled by any available card or a downward sequence in suit. (You guessed it!)

With no redeal allowed, great care is necessary to prevent the game becoming hopelessly blocked.

If luck is with you, the end of the game will see all the cards gathered to the four Foundation piles, topped by their King.

SNAIL SOLITAIRE

You will need two decks for this imaginative game. All cards face up.

Begin by extricating all Fives, Sixes, and Jacks from both decks and place them on the table, coiled round to represent a snail's shell. Begin with the Jacks, spiralling them inwards, afterwards using the Sixes and ending with the Fives.

Shuffle the remainder of the two decks together and deal four cards, horizontally, beneath the layout as a reserve. (See below.) The snail is now complete.

The objects of the game are (a) to build down, in suit, on the Fives to the King (Five, Four, Three, Two, Ace, and King) and (b) to build up in suit on the Sixes, but ignoring the Jack, to the Queen (Six, Seven, Eight, Nine, Ten, and Queen).

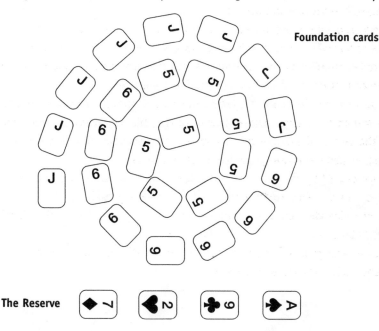

Foundation cards

The Reserve

SNAIL SOLITAIRE: **The layout—the Seven of Diamonds can be removed to a Foundation card immediately and replaced.**

The reserve quartet can be used at any time. Deal the cards in your hand one by one, building on a Foundation pile, hopefully.

Discard unplayable cards to a single heap, the top of which remains available.

Gaps made in the reserve are filled with either the next card taken from your hand or the top of that ever-present heap.

One redeal is permitted. A successful game will show a snail shell made entirely of face cards. But if you find this game too easy, deal the cards only once.

SNAKE SOLITAIRE

You will need two decks of cards for this game, which are to be well shuffled together.

Take out a complete sequence of cards, from the Ace up to the King, without any regard to suit, and lay them out in the form of the letter "S," beginning with the Seven as the end of the tail and Six as the snake's head.

Now deal out the rest of the cards, building up on the base cards (any Eight on the Seven of Diamonds and so on, any Jack on the Ten of Clubs, any Two on the Ace of Diamonds, etc.).

Obviously the first cards are easily placed, but as the game progresses some cards cannot find their correct position on the piles. Two heaps of whatever size can be made with these until they can be used; take care not to block cards that you will soon need. Also, a card placed on a Foundation pile cannot be moved onto another, so do not be tempted to build too quickly.

If the game works out successfully, the snake will be composed of an Ace as the tip of the tail, running in sequence up to the King as its head. (See the second "S" of the example below.) Each pile will contain eight cards.

If you yearn to give yourself a headache, you can make the game more difficult.

Lay out the Foundation cards in Diamonds. The second layer must consist of Spades, the third layer of Hearts, the fourth of Clubs, and so on. Since there are eight cards in the final piles, the top layer will be a sequence of Clubs.

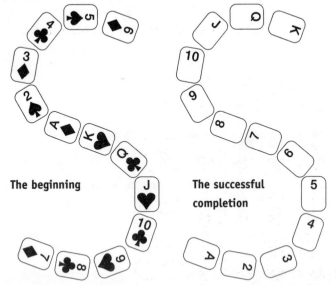

SNAKE SOLITAIRE.

The beginning

The successful completion

With this version, four heaps are allowed. Once you have dealt out all the cards, the heaps can be picked up, well and truly shuffled, and dealt out again. This may be done twice in the course of the game. However, it is still very difficult to avoid having cards hopelessly blocked. (Also, I find it extremely difficult to remember whether I am supposed to be laying down a red or black card when I am in full swing, but that is just me, probably!)

SPOILED SOLITAIRE

Again, a very simple Solitaire, but none the worse for that!

One deck of cards is required, with all the Twos, Threes, Fours, Fives, and Sixes removed. (This is sometimes called a piquet deck.)

Lay out four rows of seven cards each, face down, with a reserve of four cards placed to one side, also face down.

The four rows represent four different suits in the following order: first Diamonds, second Hearts, third Clubs, and the fourth row is Spades.

Take the first card in the reserve and put it in its correct place, face up. If it is an Ace it will be first in its own row, if a King the second, if a Ten the fifth, and so on.

(Let's assume that the first card in the reserve is the Jack of Clubs. Lift the concealed card lying in the place where the Jack of Clubs should be and put the Jack there. Put the card thus ousted into the correct place for it, removing the card lying there. Play on in the same way, placing and removing.)

Should you discover a Seven while doing this, for which there is no space available, place it horizontally at the end of the appropriate row and take a card from the reserve to continue the game.

If you turn over the fourth Seven while there are still cards face down, there is one last chance to make the game a success. Turn one of the remaining concealed cards and, if it is in the correct place, lay it down face up and turn another. This enables you to play on.

The game has failed if the card chosen was not where it should be: a Spoiled Solitaire.

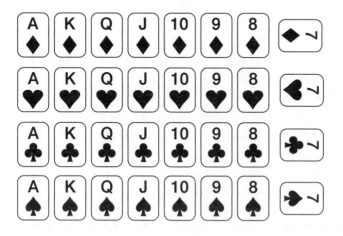

SPOILED SOLITAIRE: A successful Spoiled Solitaire game.

SQUARE SOLITAIRE

Two decks of cards, well shuffled together, are needed for this game.

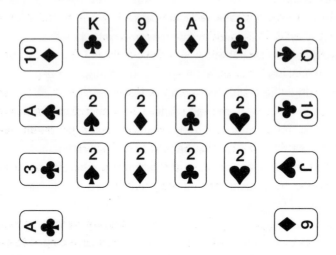

SQUARE SOLITAIRE.

Deal out twelve cards, face up, to make three sides of a square: four cards at the top and four at each side. This is the Tableau.

Remove the Twos as they emerge in play, placing them in two rows of four inside the confines of the square (face up, naturally).

The object of the game is to build up, in suit and sequence, until each Foundation is crowned by its respective Ace. (The sequence runs Two, Three, Four, Five, Six, Seven, Eight, Nine, Ten, Jack, Queen, King, and Ace.)

Deal out the cards you hold in your hand one by one. Build up on the Twos, if there are any available, or build down in suit on any suitable card in the Tableau (e.g., onto the Ace of Diamonds put the King, Queen, Jack, Ten, etc., of Diamonds) until these can be played to the Foundation piles. (If, when you deal out the Tableau at the start of the game, you have consecutively numbered cards in the same suit, you can, of course, build down on them and then deal other cards into any spaces.)

Unplayable cards are discarded face up to a single heap, the top card of which is always available. A space in the Tableau caused by the removal of a card or pile is filled with a card taken from the top of the heap.

I hope that all the Foundation piles are now topped with their Aces, no second deal of the heap being allowed.

A variant to this game, named Deuces, is a little less difficult. All the Foundation Twos are put in place before the game begins, but the columns of the Tableau to left and right have three cards in each, not four. The rest of the Solitaire is played in the same way, but this game does allow a redeal.

SQUARING THE CIRCLE SOLITAIRE

You will need two decks of cards for this game, together with a clear head. (At least all the cards face up ...)

Remove the four Aces from one deck—one of each suit—and put them in a square upon the table. These are the Foundation cards.

Now shuffle the two decks together very thoroughly and deal out a reserve of twelve cards, encircling the Aces.

Your object is to build simultaneously up and down upon each Ace, in suit, until the pile is topped by its twin, the second Ace. The sequence runs as follows: Ace, King, Two, Queen, Three, Jack, Four, Ten, Five, Nine, Six, Eight, Seven, Seven, Eight, Six, Nine, Five, Ten, Four, Jack, Three, Queen, Two, King and Ace.

Begin by removing anything suitable in the twelve-card reserve to a Foundation, filling spaces with the next card from those you hold.

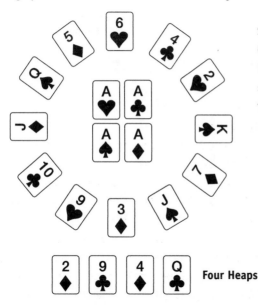

SQUARING THE CIRCLE SOLITAIRE: **The layout. The King of Spades is to be built upon the Ace of Spades, the space being filled by any top card from a heap.**

Four Heaps

When there is nothing more to be done (although the reserve cards are always eager to be used throughout the game), play out your cards one by one. Hopefully, some will find a home on the Foundation piles immediately. Discard unplayable cards to one of four heaps, piling these as you choose in the most judicious manner. The top card of each is available for use, but cannot be moved from heap to heap.

Fill any gap you make in the reserve from now on with the top card from a heap. If you are in the happy position of having made the heaps disappear in play, fill spaces again from the cards you hold.

Having exhausted the decks, gather up the four heaps from left to right and turn them over, dealing them out again as before. This is your last chance to square the circle...a mathematical conundrum which the ancient Greeks proved impossible, but not in our case.

STALACTITES SOLITAIRE

One deck is needed for this appropriately-named Solitaire. All cards must face up.

Begin by shuffling the deck, afterwards dealing four cards to the top of the table as Foundation cards. Turn them on their sides, so that you will have a constant visual reminder as to their value and where to stop! The other cards played onto these are piled in the usual way (i.e., upright).

The object of the game is to build up upon these horizontal cards, ignoring suits, until each pile contains thirteen cards. You may build in steps of one or two, but whatever you choose to do must apply to each of these Foundations.

In the example given below, I decided to build in twos, so the sequence on the first card will run as follows: Ten, Queen, Ace, Three, Five, Seven, Nine, Jack, King, Two, Four, Six, and Eight.

Deal out six rows of eight cards each, overlapping the rows so that the layout resembles eight upright columns.

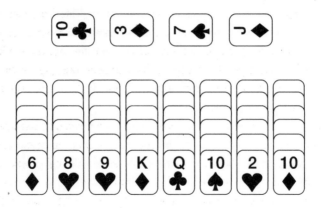

STALACTITES SOLITAIRE:

(All cards face up.)

(a) The Queen of Clubs can be removed to the first Foundation pile;

(b) The Nine of Hearts will be built upon the Seven of Spades;

(c) The Jack of Diamonds will gather the King of Diamonds to it, followed by the Two of Hearts. An excellent start.

Exposed cards at the base of each column are available for play; their removal frees the card above. A column emptied is not to be refilled.

While there is no building down on the Tableau, help is at hand. Two cards can be taken from anywhere in the columns and kept until they can be built onto a Foundation pile. This is invaluable in unblocking trapped cards, and can be repeated three times in all.

I hope this is of use. Stalactites Solitaire is not as easy as it appears at first glance.

STEP-UP SOLITAIRE

You will need two decks for this game. All cards face up.

Shuffle the deck and deal out a row of thirteen cards, from left to right, in the center of the table. This reserve is known as the "landing."

Take the next card from your hand and place it above the reserve. This card, of whatever value, is the first Foundation card.

Your object is to find the other seven cards of the same value as they emerge in play, putting them in a line beside the first; and to build up upon each of the eight Foundation cards, in sequence and suit, until each pile contains thirteen cards. For example: if the Foundation is a Queen, the sequence will run as follows—Queen, King, Ace, Two, Three, Four, Five, Six, Seven, Eight, Nine, Ten, and Jack.

Deal another row, of nine cards, below the landing reserve and call this the "staircase" or Tableau.

This game has a chain of command. Cards can be removed to a Foundation pile only from the landing reserve.

Found, or build on Foundations, using whatever is possible from here and fill the spaces with any card you choose, taken from the staircase Tableau. You don't have to fill a gap in the landing immediately it becomes vacant, nor do you have to fill a gap in the landing before you fill a gap in the staircase. But gaps in the staircase are immediately refilled with the next cards from the deck, or from the heap when this useful item comes into existence.

Cards in the staircase can also build down upon each other, in sequence and alternating colors, until they can step up onto the landing. Place the cards in such a way that their values can be seen. Cards must be moved singly, never in sequences. (Red King on black Ace, black Queen on red King, and so on...)

Begin to deal out the cards in your hand one by one. Build down on the staircase Tableau, if possible, or discard unplayable cards to a single heap, the top of which remains ever available.

(Please don't forget to remove suitable cards from the landing reserve to a Foundation pile when you can, filling the gap with any exposed card from the staircase!)

No redeal of the heap is allowed.

STONEWALL SOLITAIRE

One deck is needed for this austere little game, which was named as a compliment to Thomas J. Jackson, one of the Confederate generals of the American Civil War, who stood with his brigade "like a stone wall" at the Battle of Bull Run in 1861.

Shuffle the deck very thoroughly—an absolute necessity here—and deal out six rows of six cards each as the Tableau.

The first row, together with the third and fifth, must face down, while the second, fourth, and sixth rows face up. Overlap the rows so that they resemble six vertical columns.

The object of the game is to remove the four Aces to a row at the top of the table as they emerge in play, building up upon these Foundation cards, in sequence and in suit, to the King. Unfortunately, if you deal an Ace into any row except the sixth row of the Tableau, you have to wait until it can be released.

The remaining cards are dealt in two rows of eight, face up, beneath the Tableau. This is your reserve.

All sixteen cards here, together with exposed cards at the base of the columns, are available. (When a card which faces down is uncovered, turn it over and carry on.)

Move anything possible to a Foundation pile; with the remaining cards, build down on the Tableau in sequence and alternating colors until they can be played through.

A single card, or any length of sequence, can be transferred to the base of another column, provided the join is correct.

An empty column is filled with any available single card or sequence, but the reserve is not to be replaced.

I hope that you will not find this game too annoying! I always feel a great satisfaction when I bring it off, which is not often, I must admit.

STRATEGY SOLITAIRE

One deck is necessary to attempt this marvellously infuriating game, devised by Mr. A. Morehead and Mr. G. Mott-Smith.

Shuffle the deck very thoroughly, then begin to deal the cards (face up) as you decide, to any one of eight heaps.

Remove the four Aces to a row at the top of the table as they emerge in play.

The object of the game is to build up upon each Ace, in sequence and in suit, to the King.

No card can be built upon a Foundation Ace until the whole deck has been dealt.

Now your strategy (or, in my case, lack of it) in distributing the cards between the eight heaps is made clear.

With luck, you should be able to lay the exposed cards from each heap, freeing the card beneath as you remove the top one, on the Foundation cards up to the King, without becoming blocked.

To attain this happy state of affairs, it is wiser to keep one of the eight piles exclusively for the Kings and Queens and not to put a higher card upon a lower one unless forced to.

The only comfort I can give is that practice makes the game a little easier ...

SULTAN SOLITAIRE

You will need two decks of cards for this game, the aim of which is to surround the sultan, or King of Hearts, with his harem.

Remove the eight Kings and one Ace of Hearts and place them in three rows of three, face up, as follows:

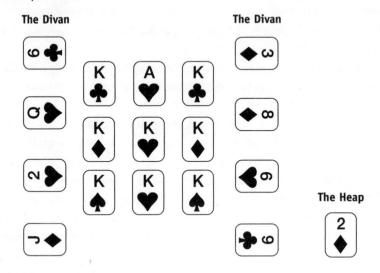

SULTAN SOLITAIRE: **Ready to begin.**

Top row: King of Clubs, Ace of Hearts, King of Clubs.
Middle row: King of Diamonds, King of Hearts (the sultan), King of Diamonds.
Bottom row: King of Spades, King of Hearts and King of Spades.

Give the rest of the cards a good shuffle, then deal out eight cards and place them face up at right angles, four to the left and four to the right of the square. These cards are called the "divan," the Turkish word for a long bench covered in cushions, much in evidence in Victorian paintings of the mysterious harem.

The King of Hearts in the center is not to be covered by any other card. The other Kings and the Ace of Hearts are to be built in suit up to their respective Queen. (The Ace is placed on the King, the Two on the Ace, etc. The Two of Hearts is placed upon the Ace of Hearts and so on.)

Use the cards in your hand to build if possible, or place them onto a single heap, the top card of which is always available.

When there is a suitable card in the divan, this must be used and the space filled from the top of the heap. (If there is no heap at that moment, use the next card from those you hold in your hand.)

All the cards having been used, the heap may be played twice without reshuffling.

If the game has come through successfully, the King of Hearts is to be seen surrounded by his eight Queens.

TRIPLE LINE SOLITAIRE

Two decks are needed for this plain, no-nonsense game. Begin by shuffling the decks together, afterwards dealing out, face up, three rows of twelve cards each, from left to right, as the Tableau. Overlap the rows so that the layout resembles twelve upright columns of three.

The object of the game is to take the eight Aces as they surface in play (putting them in a row at the top of the table), building up on these Foundation cards, in sequence and in suit, to the King.

Remove all Aces in the exposed cards (those in the bottom row of the Tableau with no other card upon them) and anything that can be built on them. Yes, this releases the card above for use!

Any single exposed card in the Tableau can be built down in suit onto another column until needed (Seven of Hearts onto the Eight of Hearts, Six of Hearts onto the Seven, and so on ...). The removal of sequences of cards would make this game easier, but is not allowed.

When nothing more can be done, play out the cards in your hand one by one, hopefully to a Foundation pile, otherwise building down in suit on the Tableau.

Discard useless cards to a single heap, the top of which remains available.

Should all the cards in a column have disappeared, fill the gap with a single card, taken either from the top of the heap or the next card from those in your hand.

The heap can be turned over and played through once more when all your cards are dealt. Despite this grudging second chance, the game is surprisingly difficult to finish successfully.

TRIPLETS SOLITAIRE

One deck of cards is necessary for this venerable Solitaire. All cards face up.

Deal sixteen groups of three cards, each trio overlapping one another in the shape of a fan. Four cards remain: use these to make two fans of two.

The aim of the game is not to build on a Foundation, but to eliminate all cards in numerical groups of three, ignoring suit, until just one card remains. (For example: Five, Six, Seven; or Queen, King, Ace; or King, Ace, Two; or Nine, Ten, Jack.)

Only the exposed card at the top of each fan, that with nothing upon it, is available for play and each card removed must be taken from a different fan. It is not permitted to dispose of an original fan in one fell swoop!

Some, of more heroic stature, make the game more difficult by removing one card from the deck before the game begins and attempting to empty the table completely.

WANING MOON SOLITAIRE

Two decks are needed for this most appropriately named game. All cards are to be dealt face up.

Shuffle the decks together very thoroughly and deal out thirteen piles in the shape of a semicircle, three cards to each pile. This Tableau represents the crescent moon.

Any Aces found during this deal are taken out (replaced by the next card in the deck) and used to form a curved row beneath the Tableau. (The remaining Aces will take their places later as they emerge in play.) These are the Foundation cards.

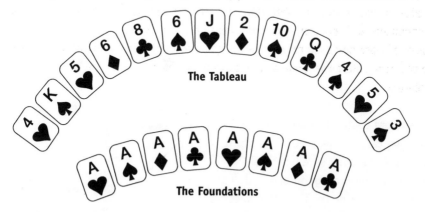

WANING MOON SOLITAIRE: (a) The Four of Hearts can be placed on top of the Five of Hearts in the Tableau. (b) The Three of Spades is placed on top of the Four of Spades.

The object of the game is to build up, in sequence and in suit on the Foundations, to the King.

The top card of each pile in the Tableau is available for use and removing cards frees those beneath.

When all available cards in the original layout have been removed to the Foundations, build down on the Tableau, in suit, until they can be played off. (For example, Seven of Hearts upon the Eight of Hearts, Four of Diamonds on the Five of Diamonds, and so on.) But please remember to keep the Tableau piles meticulously tidy. You don't wish to see the cards beneath the top card and cheat inadvertently, do you?

Now deal out the cards in your hand one by one; either to the Foundation piles or to the Tableau. Discard unplayable cards to a single heap, the top of which always remains available.

Move cards singly, not in groups, between piles. A gap in the Tableau is filled by any exposed card. You must decide whether it is wiser to choose the top card of the heap or the top card of a Tableau pile for this.

Since it is not permitted to play through the heap again, all cards having been dealt, a great deal of thought is needed to bring this game through. Should you have built correctly on each Foundation pile to the King, the crescent Tableau will have disappeared...the moon has waned.

WHEAT-EAR SOLITAIRE

Two decks are needed for this game. The wheat-ear was a very popular motif in Georgian and Victorian times, which certainly dates this Solitaire. The Crown Jewelry collection includes six fine diamond brooches of this design, dating from the days of William IV; but that is off the subject.

Shuffle the two decks together very thoroughly and deal out twenty cards in the shape of a wheat-ear (see diagram). The cards are to be placed face up, as are all in this game. Beside them place a further eight cards, four to each side, as a second reserve. The next card dealt, of whatever value, is a Foundation card. In the example given, it is a Four. Take the other seven cards of the same rank as they emerge in play and put them in a row beside the first. The object of the game is to build up on these Foundation cards in thirteen-card sequence, disregarding suit, arriving at a card one less in value to the base card (Four, Five, Six, Seven, Eight, Nine, Ten, Jack, Queen, King, Ace, Two, Three).

Play out the cards from your hand one by one, discarding unplayable cards to a single heap. The top of this remains available, as usual.

All eight cards of the side reserves can be used at any time. Gaps here are refilled with the top card from the heap or with the next card from the deck.

The wheat-ear reserve differs slightly. The cards available for play are those nearest to you at the bottom of the layout. Removing one frees the card above. The wheat-ear is not replaced and quickly vanishes.

When all your cards are gone, turn over the heap and play it through again once more. A successful game will find the table empty of all except eight neat piles of thirteen cards.

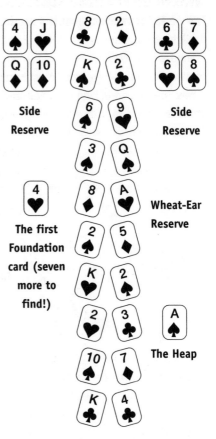

WHEAT-EAR SOLITAIRE: The Four of Spades, from the side reserve, and the Four of Clubs, at the base of the wheat-ear, can be removed to the Foundation row immediately.

WHEEL OF FORTUNE SOLITAIRE

Two decks of cards are required for this game, but they must not be shuffled together.

Begin by dealing out a circle of sixteen cards from the first deck. (All cards in this Solitaire face up.)

If there are any Kings or Aces, remove them to the center of the circle, putting them in two parallel lines as Foundation cards. Immediately fill any gaps made with the next cards from the deck. The other Kings and Aces are to be placed correctly as they emerge.

The object of the game is to build up on the four Aces, in sequence and in suit, to the Kings and to build down on the four Kings, in sequence and in suit, to the Aces.

Move whatever else you can from the Tableau to the Foundation cards, always refilling spaces from the cards in your hand.

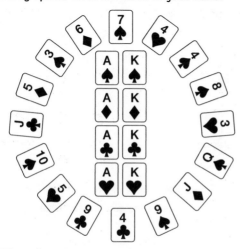

**WHEEL OF FORTUNE SOLITAIRE:
A demonstration of the Tableau,
all the Foundation cards having
emerged.**

When there is no more to be done, deal a second complete circle of sixteen cards upon the first. Use these cards to build up or down as before, remembering to remove Aces or Kings to the center. The taking of a card frees the one beneath for use. Again, a space made in the layout must be filled by the next card from those you hold.

Now deal out another complete circle of sixteen cards, continuing with the second deck when the first is exhausted, and play on in the same way. (Obviously, the Kings and Aces in the new deck are not to be placed in the center until needed to crown their respective Foundation piles.) Probably the very last deal will not have sixteen cards, but we will excuse it.

At the end two further chances are given, should the game not have worked out.

Cards can be transferred between Foundation piles if they agree in suit and sequence. For example, if the Ace of Hearts' pile has been built up to the Eight and the King of Hearts' pile has been built down to the Seven, one pile can build on to the other, if this means that the cards left in the wheel become of use.

Spaces caused by this play can be filled by any available card left in the Tableau. Hopefully this will free any blockage.

101

WINDMILL SOLITAIRE

Two decks are needed for this classic Solitaire.

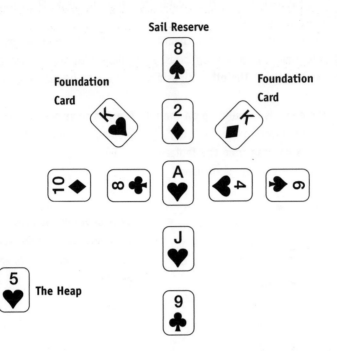

WINDMILL SOLITAIRE: The layout. Only two of the four Kings have emerged so far. The Two of Diamonds can be moved directly to the center Ace and the gap refilled from the heap.

Take an Ace, of any suit, placing it in the middle of the table. This is the first Foundation card.

Shuffle the two decks together and deal a reserve of eight cards (face up, as are all the cards in this game): put two above, two below, two to the right and two to the left of the Ace, representing the sails of the windmill.

As four Kings, of any suit, emerge in play, place one diagonally between each of the sails as Foundation cards. (See diagram above.)

The object of the game is (a) to build four sequences of thirteen cards upon the Ace in the center, ignoring suit, to finish with a King (Ace, Two, Three, Four, Five, Six, Seven, Eight, Nine, Ten, Jack, Queen, King, Ace, Two, Three, and so on; the numbering is continuous). And (b) to build down on each of the four Kings, ignoring suit, to the Ace (King, Queen, Jack, Ten, Nine, Eight, Seven, Six, Five, Four, Three, Two, and Ace).

Begin to play out the cards in your hand one by one, building wherever possible. Discard useless cards to a solitary heap, the top of which is there to be removed at any time.

All eight cards in the reserve are available. Spaces made here are to be filled from the top of the heap or, if that is exhausted or not yet begun, with the next card from the deck. It is permissible to transfer the top card of a King Foundation pile to the Ace Foundation pile, if you consider it advantageous, but never remove the base card. I am afraid the opposite is not allowed: cards placed upon the center Ace are not removed.

No redeal of the heap is allowed. If you have been successful, the final layout will be as follows:

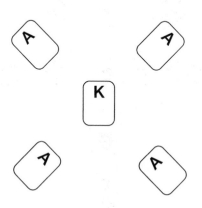

WINDMILL SOLITAIRE: The happy ending.

other games
for one

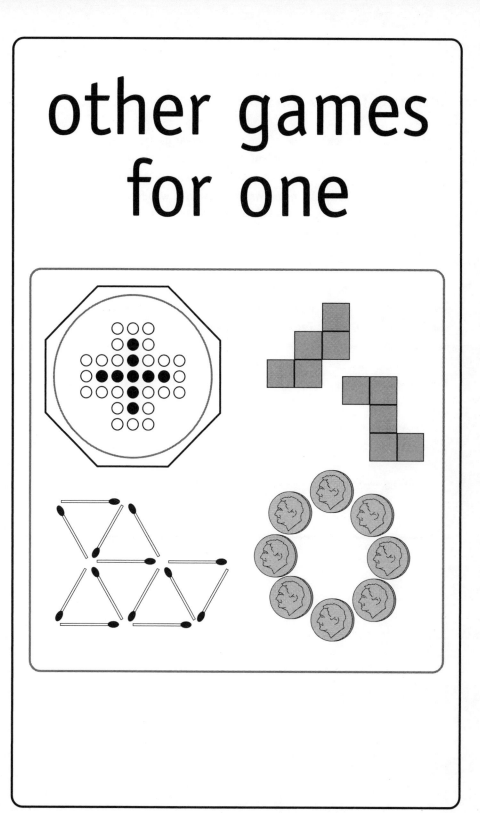

Solitaire (Board Version)

Solitaire (board version) is one of the most popular games for one of all time. There are two ways to play: either you try to remove all the pegs from the board leaving just one in the center, or you try to remove as many pegs as you possibly can. Originally the game was played on a wooden board with small depressions to hold the pegs (marbles are often used instead of pegs). You can, however, play without any special equipment. A "board" made out of paper and buttons instead of pegs will work just as well.

The rules could not be simpler. You can move a peg only by leaping over another one and into an empty place behind it. The peg that has been jumped is removed from the board. Pegs can move forwards, backwards or sideways, but not diagonally.

In all diagrams, black circles represent pegs and white ones are empty holes.

SIMPLE CROSS

The arrangement of pegs looks like a Christian cross. This is the easiest version of Peg Solitaire and it is a good training ground for beginners. But just because it is the simplest, don't get the idea that you'll complete the puzzle in a moment. You may find that a bit of thought has to go into the task.

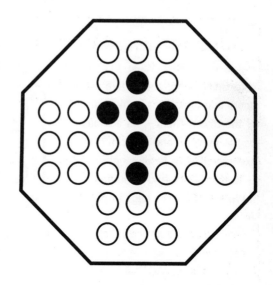

PLUS

This cross looks like a mathematical plus (+) sign. This is still a fairly simple game, but the skills you learned in playing the simple cross will stand you in good stead for this slightly more challenging version.

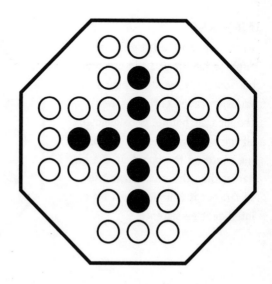

TOWER

In the Tower, you will see that one arm of the cross is filled and two pegs intrude into the middle of the board and look like the foundations of the tower. There is no obvious peg to leave in and you can experiment with various options. Is it possible to find a method of leaving each of the pegs in place? Try it!

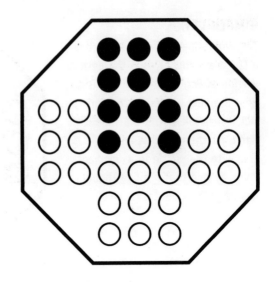

AIRPLANE

This setup looks a little like an airplane (and if you add one more horizontal row, you can play a variation called Christmas Tree). The idea, as before, is to remove all the pegs, leaving just one in the center of the board. It is a bit harder than those you have tried so far, but it will yield to a bit of intelligent persistence.

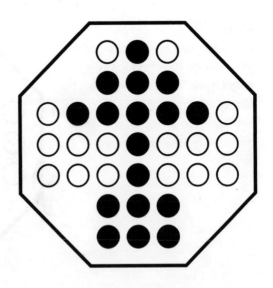

TRIANGLE

The Triangle is another puzzle that will require some cunning if you are to succeed. Trial and error is the only way though, by now, you should have a god idea of the tactics you need to employ.

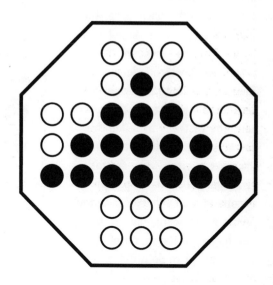

DIAMOND

This is the last of the lesser games. Once you have knocked off this one, you should be ready for the Classic Game itself.

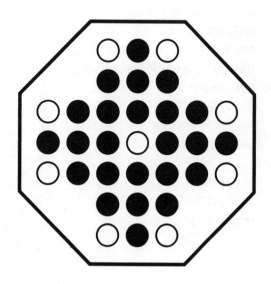

CLASSIC GAME

This is the best-known game. The object is simple: the whole board is filled with pegs except for the hole in the center, which is left vacant. The challenge is to remove all the pegs leaving just one in the center hole. The best way to tackle this puzzle is to deal with each arm of the cross in turn. If you do this just right you will end up with something resembling a "T" in the center of the board. You can then use the peg in the center of the horizontal bar to polish off the final superfluous pegs, leaving just one survivor. Before you try this, you might like to hone your skills on the easier games described below.

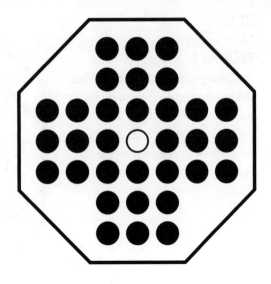

DOUBLE ARROW

Here is a puzzle that might keep you guessing for a while. It will eventually yield to a concerted attack but you might find that it takes quite a lot of thought to work out exactly how to rid yourself of all the pegs.

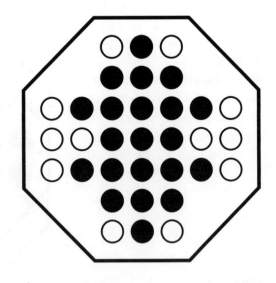

EIGHT

This is an apparently easy puzzle that might yet manage to cause you some problems. As with all the other problems the only method is trial and error. But don't let the simple design fool you. You will find that everything appears to be going well until you try to get rid of the last few pegs and that is where your troubles begin.

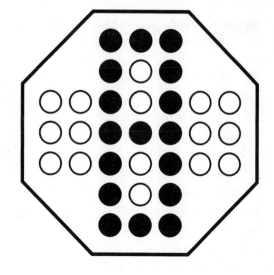

WEIGHTLIFTER

Again this is a simple design and, in truth, it is a puzzle that shouldn't detain you for long. It's quite good fun but won't tax your imagination.

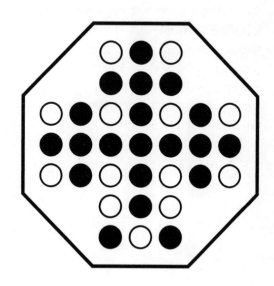

FINALLY

Remember that all the games can be played backwards. In other words, you can start with a board that has only one peg and then add pegs to each hole you jump over and thereby build up a pattern. This is a variation that will sharpen your wits and heighten your enjoyment of the puzzle.

Matchstick puzzles (for answers *see* pages 364 and 365)

1.   Move four matchsticks to make five triangles.

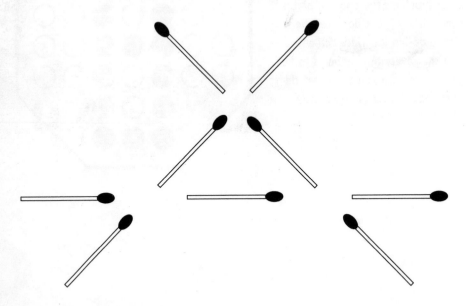

2.   Using the four matches, divide the large square into two parts of the same shape. No breaking or overlapping are allowed.

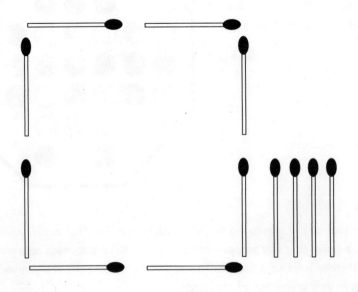

3. Move one matchstick to make the equation balance.

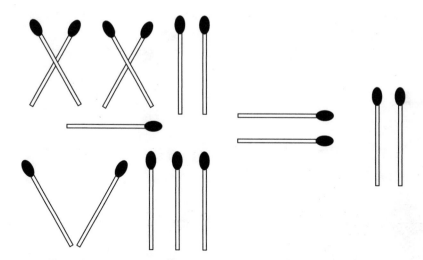

4. Move four matches to make two squares.

5. Move three matches to make two squares.

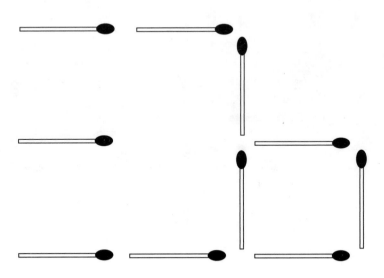

6. Moving only three matches, see if you can turn the fish around. You must use all the matches and overlapping is not allowed.

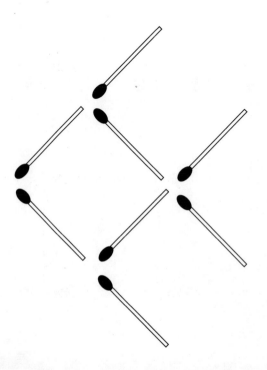

7. Make five triangles by moving just three matches.

8. Move two matches to get four squares. All the matches must be used and none may overlap.

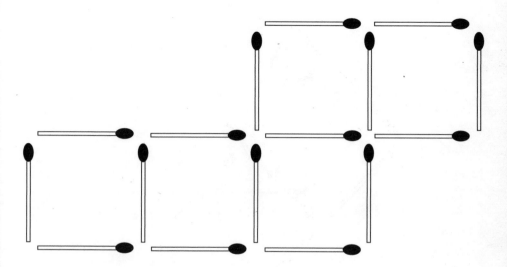

9.   By moving only three matches create four squares. All matches must be used and none may overlap.

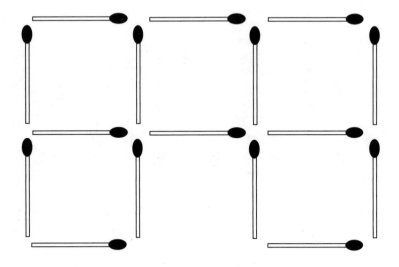

10. Move three matches to make four equilateral triangles. Overlapping is cheating.

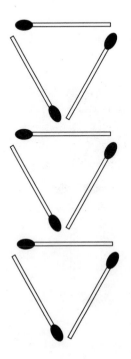

11. You start with nine matches. First, make a triangle from three of the matchsticks. Now, try to make three triangles from nine matches. Easy, isn't it? Now comes the hard part. Make four triangles from nine matches.

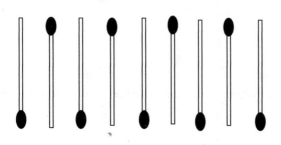

12. By moving only two matchsticks remake the glass so that so the ice cube is outside it.

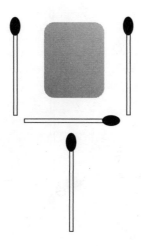

13. Set out the four matches as shown. Now, by moving only one match, make a square.

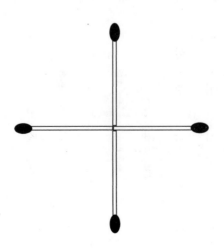

14. Use twelve matchsticks to make this pattern. Now move three matchsticks to produce three identical squares. There is more than one way to do this.

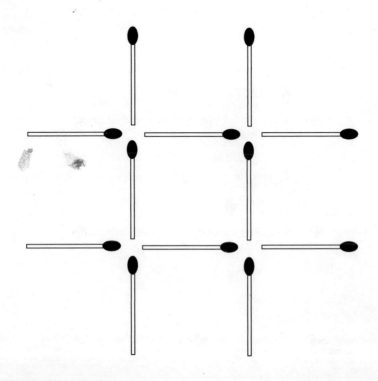

15. Move three matches and end up with three triangles.

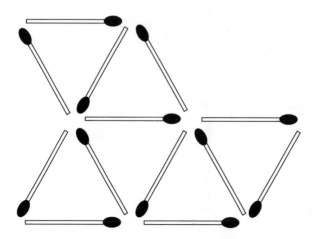

16. Try to move four matchsticks to form two squares.

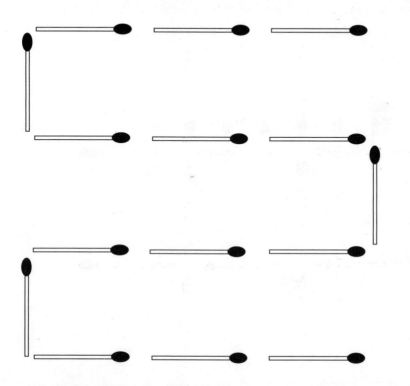

17. Turn the house from east to west by moving only one stick.

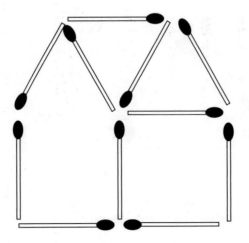

18. Remove one match and move two to leave nothing.

19. To these six matches you must add five to get nine.

20. Try to move four matchsticks to form two squares.

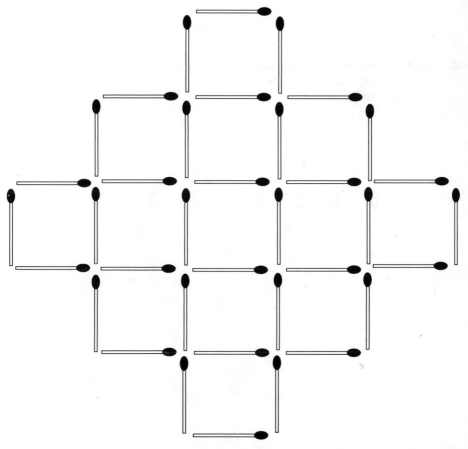

Coin Games (for answers *see* pages 366 and 367)

1. Take three identical coins and arrange them so that they all touch each other. Easy, isn't it? Now see just how many coins you can arrange so that each touches every other coin.

2. Look at this coin cross. Your challenge is to move one coin only once, to make two rows (in any direction) of four coins.

3. An empty bottle has been placed on top of a coin. The coin and bottle are near the the edge of the table. How do you remove the coin from under the bottle without touching the bottle or knocking it over?

4. You find a rare antique bottle (sealed with a cork) which contains an even rarer and more valuable coin. How do you get the coin out of the bottle without smashing the bottle or taking out the cork?

5. Place twelve coins on a sheet of paper as shown in the diagram. Now try to draw around them in such a way that you divide the paper into four parts, all identical in size and shape, so that each part contains three coins.

    Hint: You should accept help from a notorious dictator.

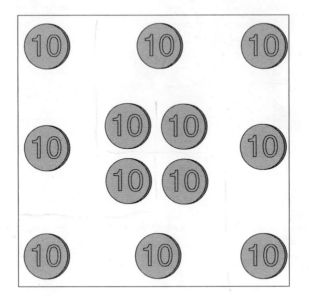

6. Take twelve coins and arrange them in a square as in the diagram. There are four coins along each side. Now rearrange them so that you have a square with five coins on each side.

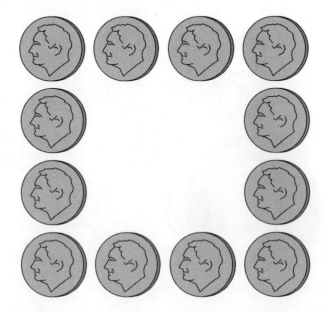

7. Lay out six coins as shown in the diagram:

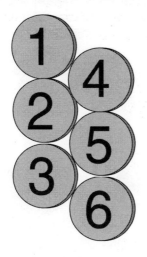

Now make a circle of coins in just three moves You can only move one coin at a time and once you have moved it to a new position it must be touching at least two other coins.

8. Lay out ten coins as shown in the diagram.

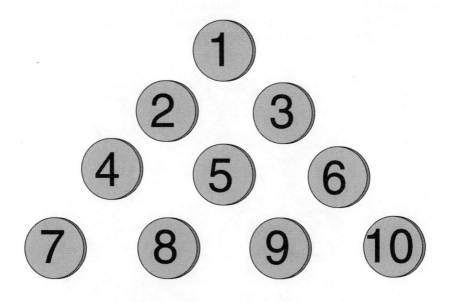

Move just three coins to turn the pyramid upside down.

9. With seven coins make an "H" as shown. If you count diagonal, vertical, and horizontal lines you have five rows with three coins in each row. Add two more coins so that you create ten rows with three coins in each.

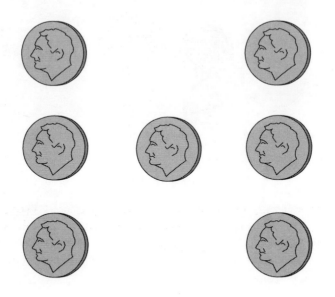

10. Use sixteen coins to make a pattern like the one shown with heads and tails alternating. Now rearrange the coins so that four vertical columns are alike. At the finish you must have a column of heads, a column of tails, another column of heads, and a final column of tails. Here's the tricky part: you are allowed to touch only two of the sixteen coins.

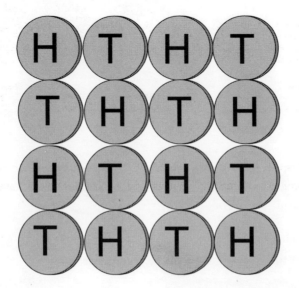

11. Take three small coins and three bigger ones and lay them out in a row as shown in the diagram:

In just three moves, and moving only two adjacent coins at a time, you must make a row of coins in which the large and small coins alternate without there being any gaps left between the coins.

12. Take four small coins and four large ones. Lay them out in a row as shown:

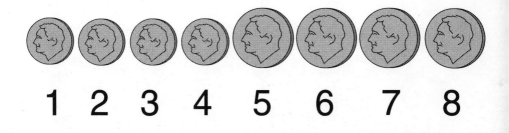

In four moves, moving only two adjacent coins at a time, you have to make a row in which the large and small coins alternate. You must leave no gaps.

13. Take eight coins and lay them out as shown in the diagram. You can start with any coin and, moving clockwise or counterclockwise, count 1, 2, 3, 4 and turn over the fourth coin so that it is tails up. Start again from any coin that is heads up and repeat the process. Keep going until all the coins but one are tails up.

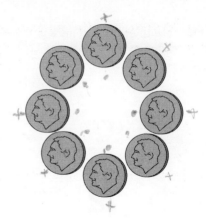

14. Using thirty-two coins make a square with nine coins on each side. Remove four coins and rearrange the remaining twenty-eight in such a way that there are still nine on each side of the square. Now take away another four coins and rearrange the remaining twenty-four so that there are still nine coins on each side. Now remove another four coins and rearrange the final twenty so that there are still nine coins on each side.

Pentominoes (for answers *see* pages 367 and 368)

Pentominoes were the invention of Solomon W. Golomb, a California mathematician. One pentomino consists of five small squares connected together. There are twelve separate ways you can do this and therefore a complete set consists of the following pieces:

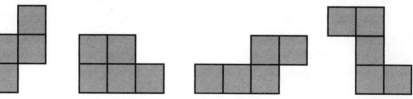

Once you have your pentominoes, the aim is to produce rectangles with them according to set rules. Use the templates provided to create your own set of pentominoes, and let the fun begin!

HERE IS THE CHALLENGE:

1. Using any four pentominoes make a 4 x 5 rectangle.

2. Using any five pentominoes make a 5 x 5 rectangle.

3. Using any six pentominoes make a 5 x 6 rectangle.

4. Using any seven pentominoes make a 5 x 7 rectangle.

5. Using any eight pentominoes make a 4 x 10 rectangle.

6. Using any nine pentominoes make a 3 x 15 rectangle.

7. Using all twelve pentominoes make a 4 x 15 rectangle.

8. Using all twelve pentominoes make a 8 x 8 rectangle with a 2 x 2 square hole in the middle.

9. Select any one of the pentominoes. Using nine pentominoes form a large-scale version of the selected pentomino, each dimension being three times greater than the original.

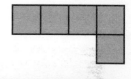
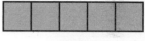
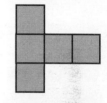
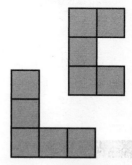
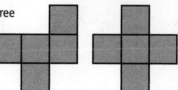

Tricks

SPINNING A COIN

Take any small copper coin and, using a sharp knife, make a small nick in one side of the edge. Watch your fingers! Now place the coin on its edge on a table and, with a quick snap of your fingers, set it spinning. You will find that you can now tell which side (head or tail) will be uppermost when the coin comes to rest. How? If you listen carefully you will hear that as it settles the coin makes a different sound depending on which side is uppermost.

COIN CATCHING TRICK

You'll have to do this quite a few times before you get it right. Bend your arm back as shown and place a small pile of coins on your elbow. Toss the coins into the air and catch them without dropping any. Once you can do it with a small pile of coins try adding more and more. What is the maximum number you can catch without dropping any?

DOLLAR BILL TRICK

Take a bill of any denomination and place paperclips on it as shown in the diagram. If you pull the ends of the note sharply, you'll find that the paperclips spring into the air and come down interlinked. Once you have the knack of doing it right every time, you can challenge your friends to do it.

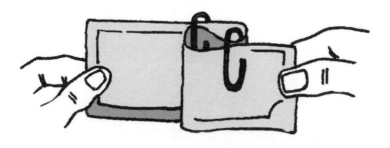

FINGER TRICK

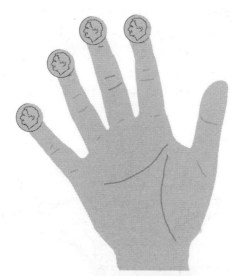

Take four coins of the same size and place one on the tip of each finger as shown in the picture. Now, without using your thumb or your free hand, manipulate the coins so that they all end up in a pile on your index finger. There is no easy way of doing this; you just have to keep at it until you get the knack. Once you can do it, try to make the pile on the end of your little finger. Hard? Oh, yes.

WINE GLASS TRICK

Take a *conical* wine glass (the trick won't work in a glass of any other shape) and place a small coin in the bottom of it. Now put in a large coin as shown in the picture. Can you extract the small coin without touching either coin or the glass? You'll find that if you blow strongly on the top coin it will flip over and propel the small coin out of the glass. If you blow with a little less force, you can flip the coins so that the smaller ends up on top of the larger.

BOTTLE BASH

Put a sheet of newspaper on a table and balance a bottle upside down on top of it as shown in the picture. Now you have to remove the paper without touching the bottle. What you have to do is hammer on the table with your fist and each time you make the bottle jump you take the opportunity to pull the paper towards you. This probably doesn't sound easy and, guess what? It isn't. It is, however, possible with practice.

NOSE NONSENSE

Cross your fingers and rub them along the bridge of your nose. It will feel as though you have two noses. You can also do this trick by putting the crossed fingers in your mouth and running them along your lower teeth. You will find a third set of teeth that runs under your tongue.

PAPER PROBLEM

Put a strip of paper on the table as shown in the picture. Now balance a coin on its edge on top of the paper strip. You will find that if you strike the paper sharply with a pencil it will get pulled out from under the coin but leave it undisturbed.

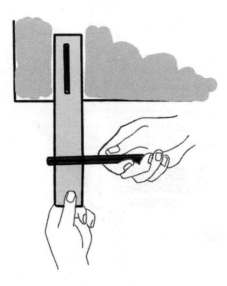

TUMBLER TRICK

Lay a small coin on a flat plate and pour in enough water to barely cover it. The challenge is to remove the coin with one finger without wetting it. The trick is to set a small candle in the dish and set light to it. You then cover the candle with a tumbler. As the candle burns up the oxygen inside the tumbler atmospheric pressure will force the water into the tumbler leaving the coin high and dry.

SAUCER SOMERSAULT

Place a saucer face down on the table with one edge protruding over the table edge. Place the backs of your fingers under the overhanging edge of the saucer and, with a quick upward flick, turn it over in mid air and catch it before it has time to touch the table. This is much easier than it looks (though maybe you should try it with an old saucer just in case).

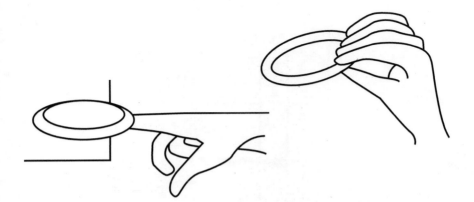

ROUND THE BROOMSTICK

Place a broomstick in the angle between the skirting board and the floor. Now grip the broomstick with both hands and try to lower your head and bring it up on the far side of the broomstick. At no time must you let go of the broomstick. There is no easy way of doing this; it depends entirely on whether you are supple enough to do it.

REVOLVING WATER

Here's a simple trick that, when perfected, will win you admiring glances. All you have to do is take a tumbler of water and whirl it around as shown in the picture. Once you have the knack you will be able to do this without spilling a drop. Until then maybe you should practice in the yard.

135

chess problems

(for answers *see* pages 368 and 369)

1. White to play and win.

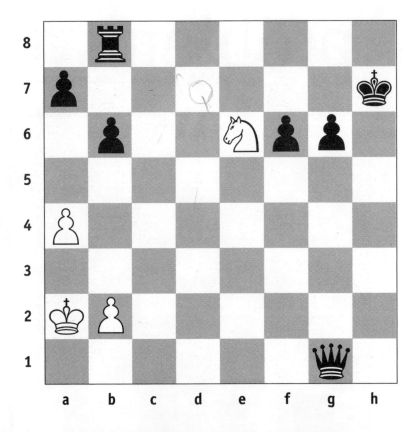

For those unfamiliar with chess, here is a brief summary of the pieces and what they can and cannot do. White pieces start on rows 1 (court) and 2 (pawns), Black on 7 (pawns) and 8 (court), respectively. Apart from their first move, when two is possible, pawns can only move forward one space and can only take an opposing piece that is one diagonal space ahead of it. Knights can move three squares only, but in any direction and in an "L" shape, two forward, one right or left. Bishops and rooks (castles) can move any number of squares, but the bishop only along a diagonal and rooks horizontally or vertically. The Queen can move in any direction, horizonaly, vertically, or diagonally for an unlimited number of squares, while the King can move only one square in any direction. There are other possibilities, such as castling, when a Rook can quickly come into play by jumping over his King. An explanation of chess notations follows on the next page.

2. White to play and win.

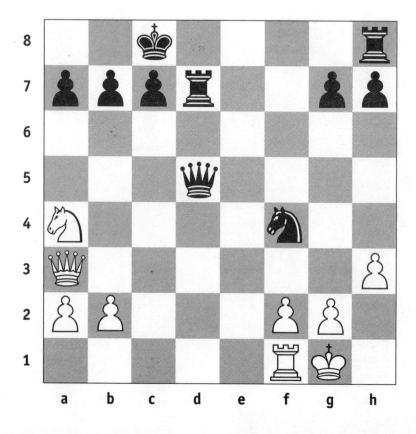

Chess moves are recorded in shorthand notation which looks complex, but is both simple and logical. A chessboard is viewed using a grid reference and is always read from White's perspective. The columns go from a to h, and rows from 1 to 8, with the White Queen's Rook being on a1 and King's Rook on h1. All moves are denoted in the same way with the grid reference being the square the piece moves to, e.g. "a4." When a court piece (Rook, kNight, Bishop, Queen, King) moves it prefixes the position it moves to. For example, if the first move of a phase has the White Queen moving from the home square diagonally to the "a" column would be "1. Qa4." A pawn move is shown only by the square it moves to, so a pawn moving two squares would be "1. a4." If a piece is captured, the move is described as "1. Qxa4," while a move forcing a check is "1. Qa4+." A promoted pawn is denoted as "1. a8=Q" (or R, N, B). Castling is shown as 0–0 (King's side) or 0–0–0 (Queen). White's moves are always noted first.

3. Black to play and win.

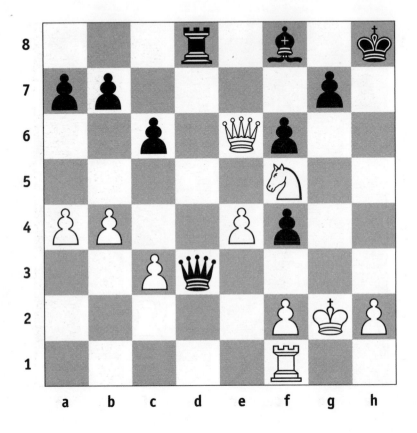

4.   Black to play and win.

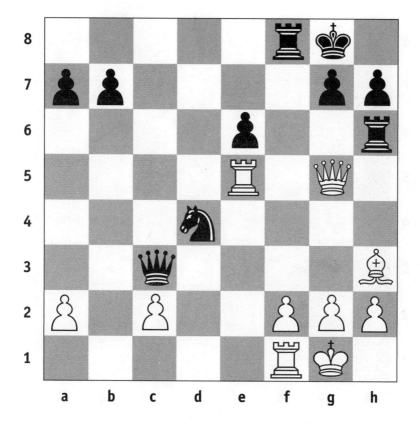

5.   White to play and win.

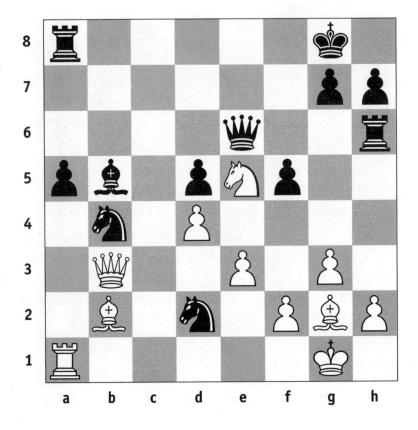

6. Black to play and win.

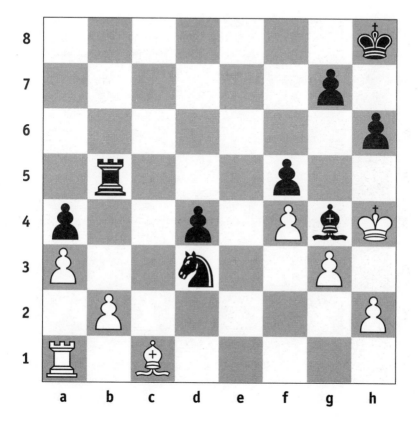

7. White to play and win.

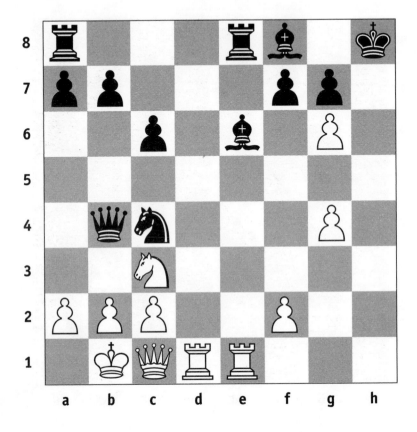

8. White to play and win.

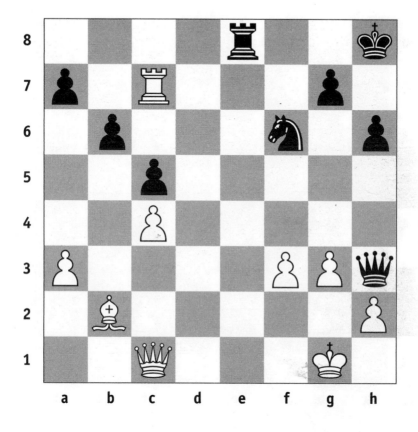

9. White to play and win.

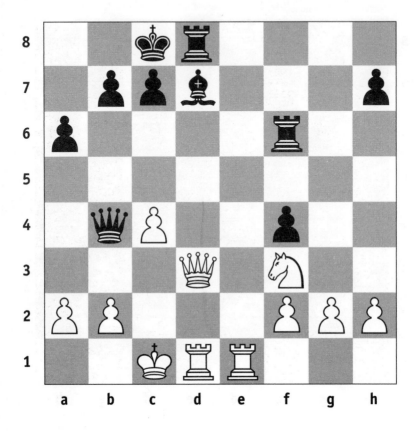

10. Black to play and win.

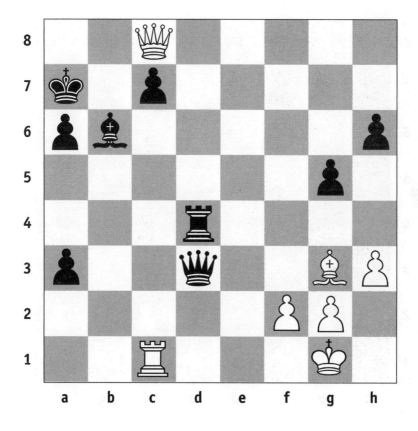

11.   White to play and win.

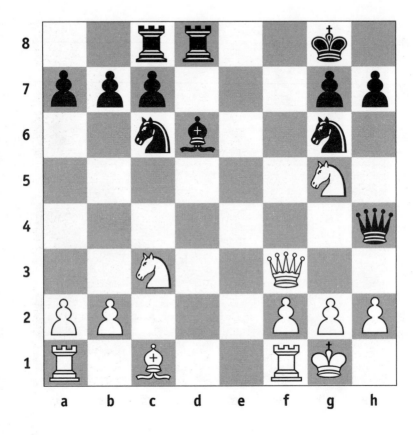

12. Black to play and win.

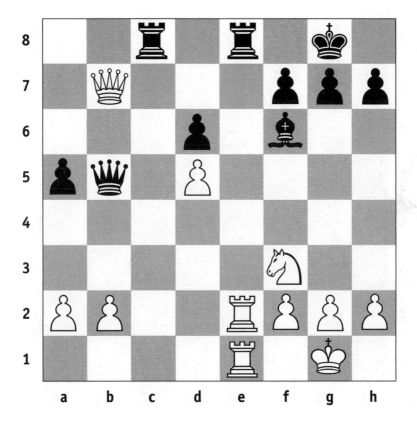

13. Black to play and win.

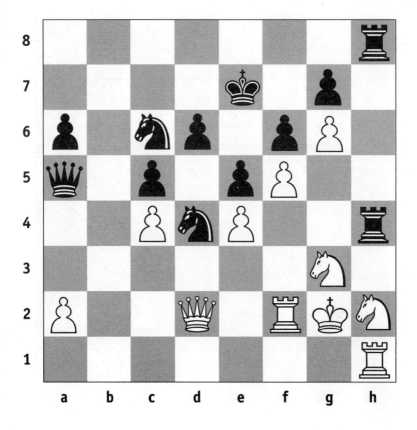

14. White to play and win.

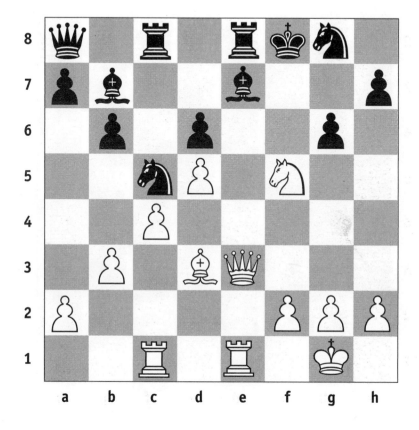

15.   White to play and win.

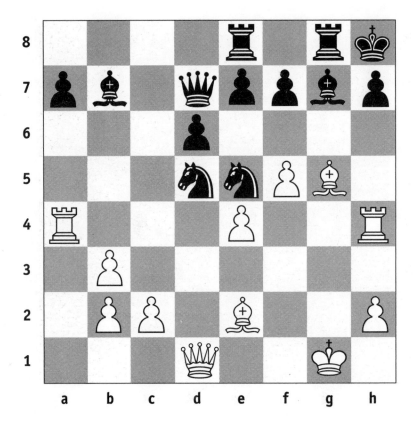

16.   White to play and mate in two moves.

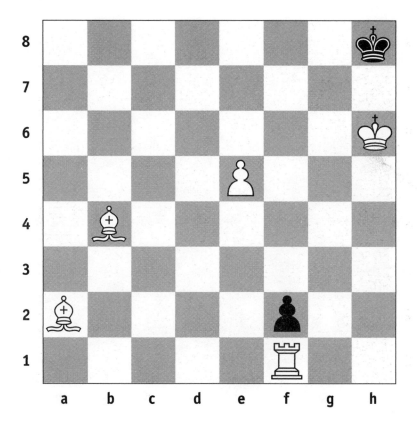

17.   White to play and mate in two moves.

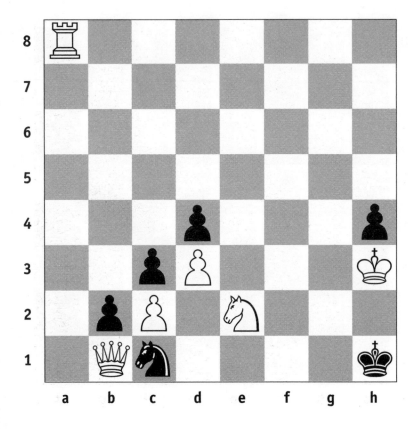

18.   White to play and mate in three moves.

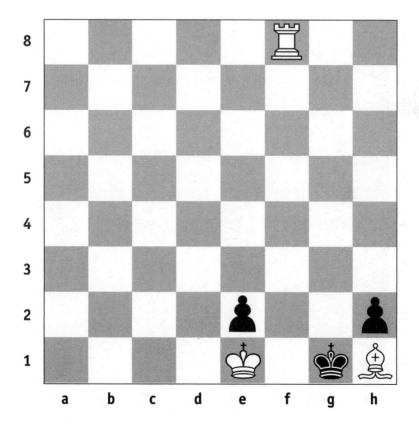

19.   White to play and mate in three moves.

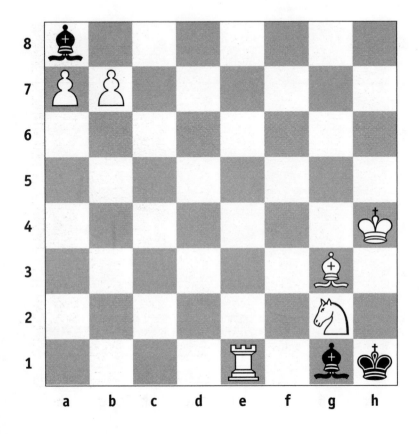

20.   White to play and mate in three moves.

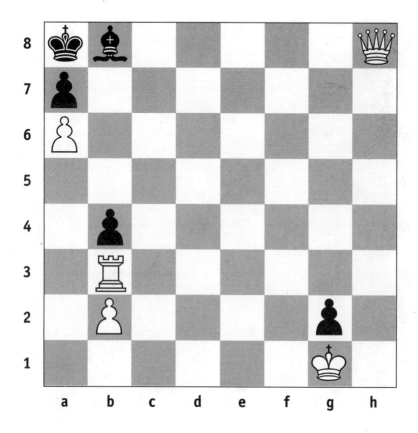

21. White to play and win.

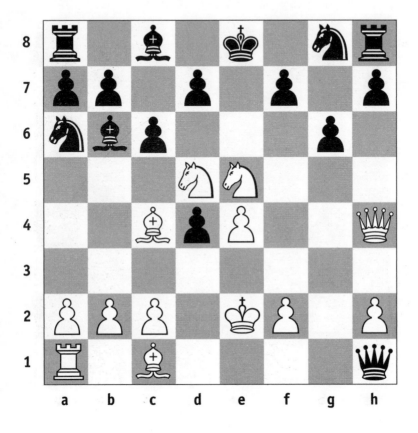

22. Black to play and win.

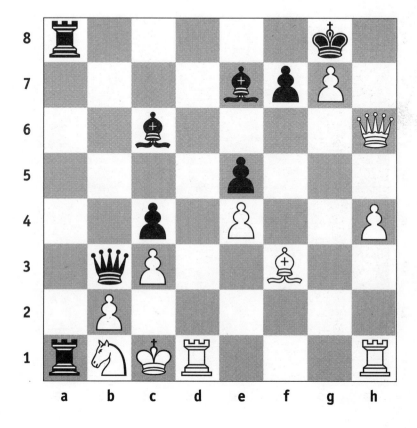

23. Black to play and win.

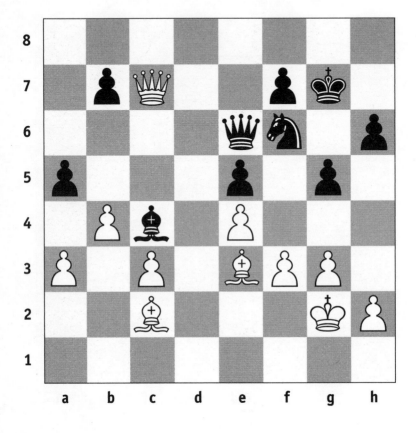

24. White to play and mate in three moves.

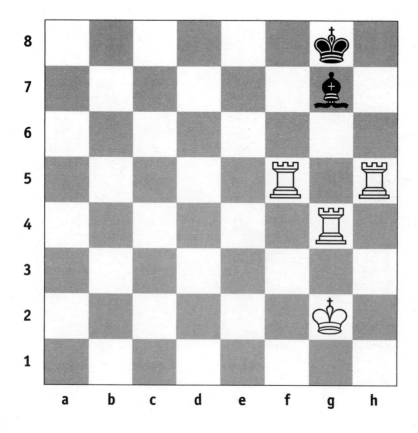

25.   White to play and win.

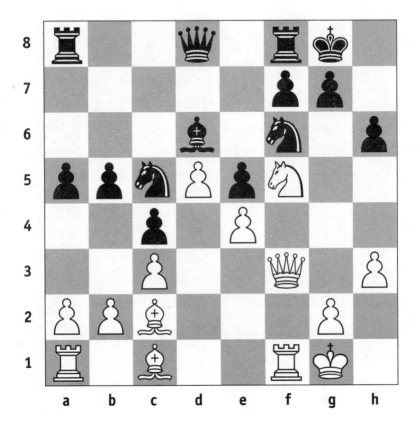

26. White to play and win.

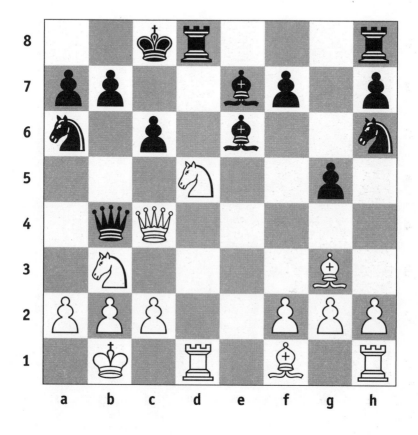

27.   White to play and win.

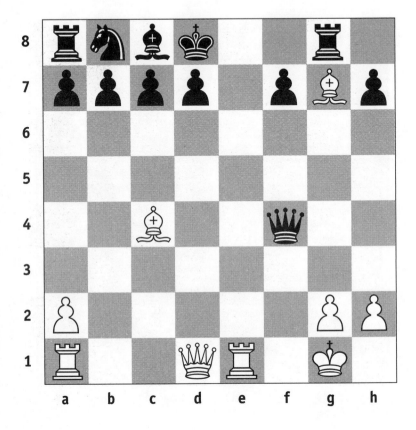

28. White to play and win.

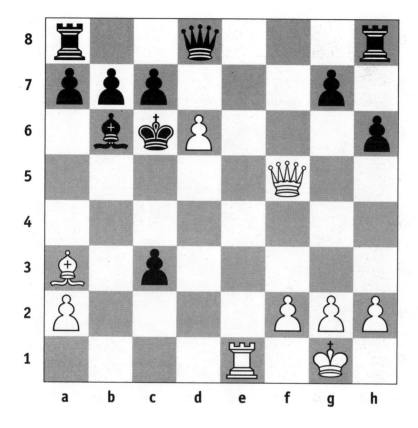

29.   White to play and win.

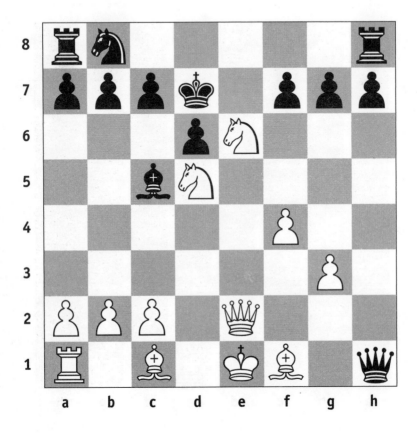

30. White to play and win.

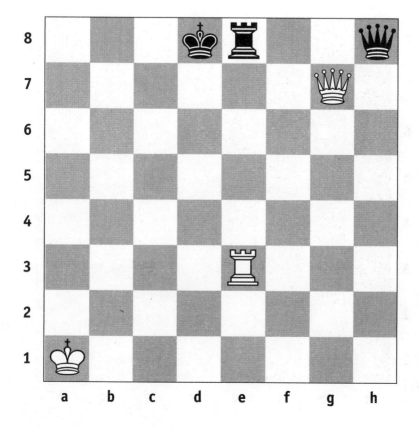

31. White to play and win.

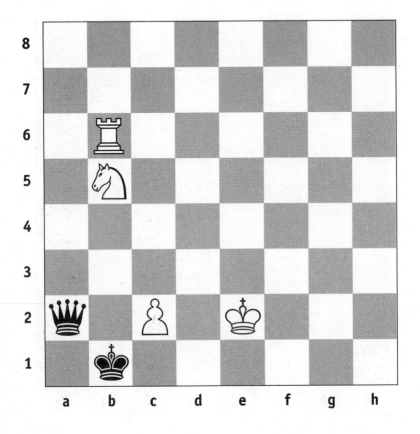

32.   White to play and win.

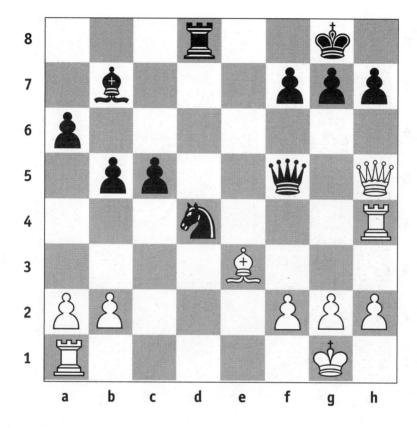

33.   White to play and mate in four moves.

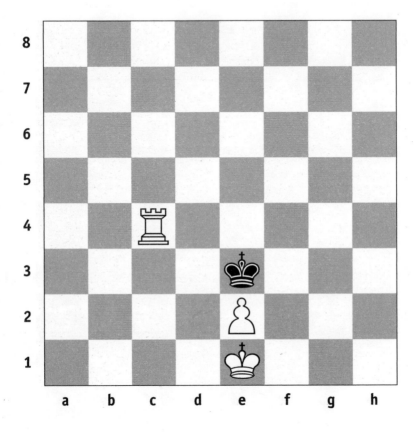

34.   White to play and mate in two moves.

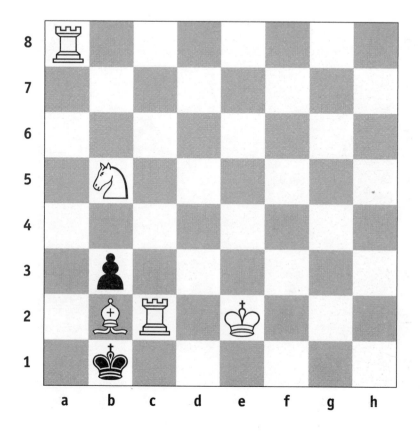

35.   White to play and mate in three moves.

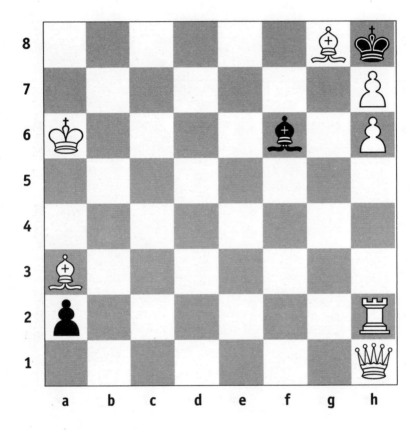

36.   White to play and mate in three moves.

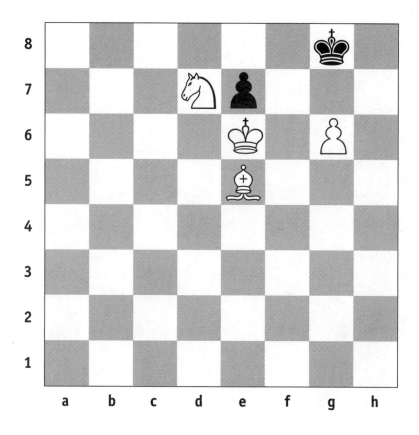

37. White to play and mate in three moves.

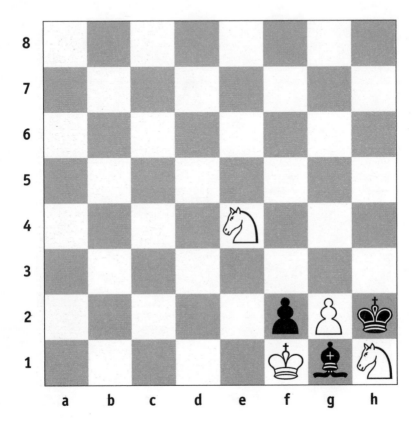

38. White to play and mate in two moves.

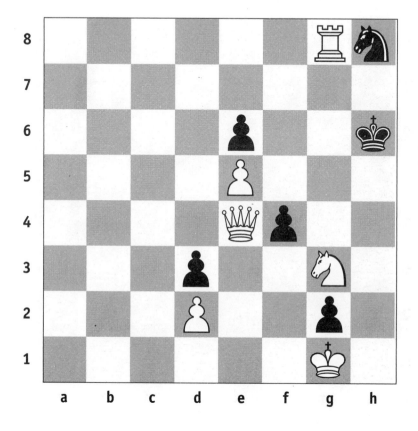

39. White to play and mate in two moves.

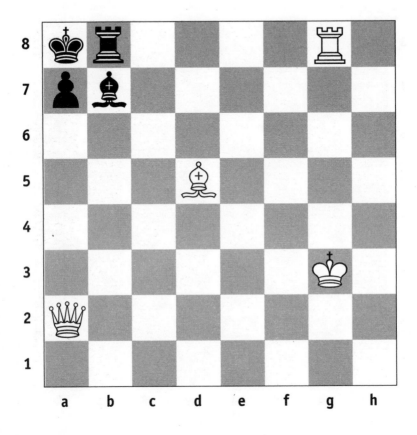

40.   White to play and mate in two moves.

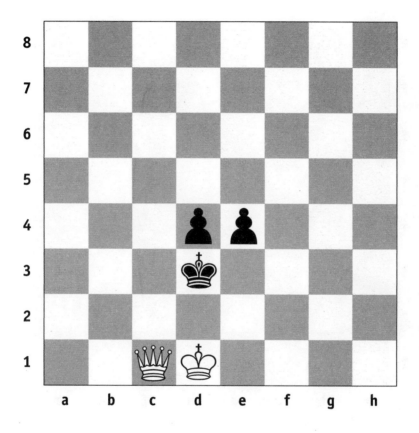

41. The quickest possible checkmate can be achieved in two moves. It is called "Fool's Mate" and requires suicidal play by White to lose. Can you work out how the game should go?

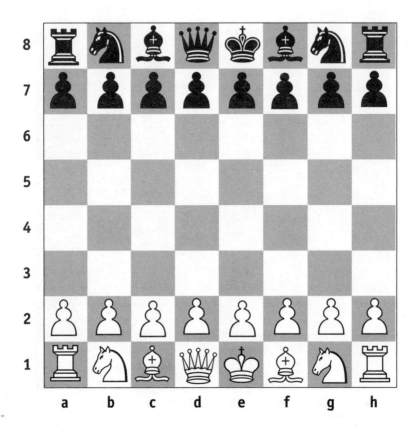

42. White to play and mate in two moves.

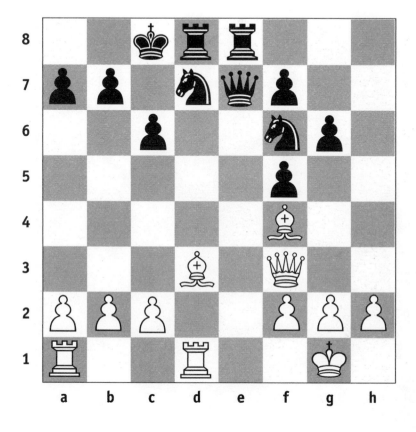

memory games

(for answers *see* page 370)

WHAT'S IN KIM'S HANDBAG? (for answers *see* page 370)

You have 30 seconds to memorize what Kim manages
to stuff into her handbag. Then cover up the page
and jot down everything you can remember. How many
of the 20 items did you get?

WHAT'S IN KEN'S SCHOOLBAG?

You have 30 seconds to memorize what Ken had in his bag when he got home from school. Then cover up the page and jot down everything you can remember. How many of the 20 items did you get?

WHAT'S IN KARL'S BACKPACK?

You have 30 seconds to memorize what Karl squeezed into his backpack to go on a trip up the mountains. Then cover up the page and jot down everything you can remember. How many of the 20 items did you get?

WHAT'S IN KIM'S BEACH BAG?

You have 30 seconds to memorize what Kim took with her to the beach. Then cover up the page and jot down everything you can remember. How many of the 20 items did you get?

WHAT'S IN GRANNY'S WHEELBARROW?

You have 30 seconds to memorize what Granny takes with her when she does some gardening. Then cover up the page and jot down everything you can remember. How many of the 20 items did you get?

WHAT'S IN BILL'S BRIEFCASE?

You have 30 seconds to memorize what Bill has in his briefcase after a hard day at the office. Then cover up the page and jot down everything you can remember. How many of the 20 items did you get?

WHAT'S IN KIM'S SHOPPING CART?

You have 30 seconds to memorize what Kim has in her shopping cart when she gets to the checkout. Then cover up the page and jot down everything you can remember. How many of the 20 items did you get?

WHAT'S IN SAM'S GOLF BAG?

You have 30 seconds to memorize what Sam has in his golf bag as he retires to the nineteenth hole. Then cover up the page and jot down everything you can remember. How many of the 20 items did you get?

MEMBERS *only*

WHAT'S IN KIM'S TOILET BAG?

You have 30 seconds to memorize what Kim takes with her for a weekend break in a hotel. Then cover up the page and jot down everything you can remember. How many of the 20 items did you get?

WHAT'S IN BOB'S TOOLBOX?

You have 30 seconds to memorize what Bob has in his toolbox to get the job done. Then cover up the page and jot down everything you can remember. How many of the 20 items did you get?

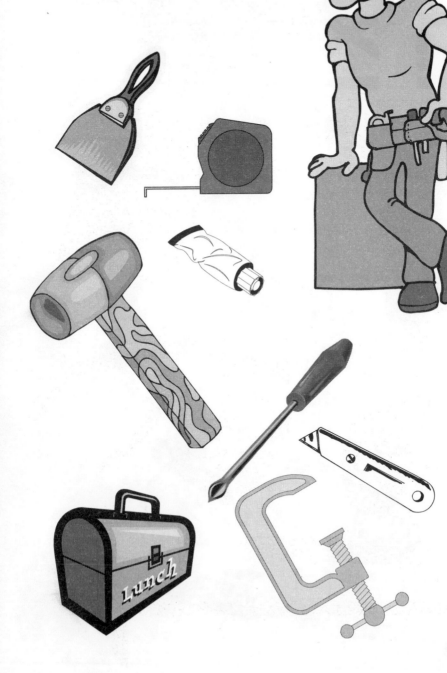

puzzles

Number puzzles (for answers *see* page 371)

1. My watch was correct at 2:00 a.m. but it gains fifty-one minutes per hour. It currently shows 11:15 a.m., but I know that it stopped exactly three hours ago. What is the correct time now?

2. What number should replace the question mark?

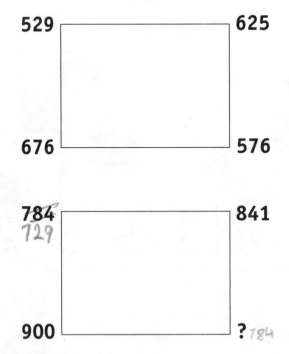

529   625

676   576

784   841
729

900   ? 784

3. I went out for a meal where the soup cost twice as much as the main course, and the wine cost twice as much as the soup. The meal cost $28 in total. How much did the soup cost?

4. Which number should replace the question mark?

| 7 | 9 | 6 | 3 | 5 | 5 | 2 | ? |

5. A cyclist cycled up a hill at 10mph and then down the other side—exactly the same distance—at 30mph. What was his average speed for the whole trip?

6. Which number should replace the question mark?

A	B	C	D	E
3	13	8	5	21
2	10	6	4	16
4	16	10	6	?

7. I saw this sign in the grocery store window:

ORANGES   33¢

PEARS   23¢

APPLES   30¢

How much did BANANAS cost?

8. Which number should replace the question mark?

| 1 | 5 | 7 | 13 | 21 | 35 | 57 | 93 | 151 | ? |

9. A businessman gave a Christmas bonus to each of his employees. Each staff member received the same amount, which was a round figure in dollars. There are more than seventy-eight employees but fewer than one hundred. He gave away a total of $2,156. How much did each employee receive?

10. Each like symbol has a like value. What number is represented by the question mark?

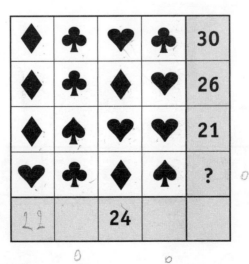

11. On a recent train journey I covered one-half of the total distance in the first hour. I then covered one-third of the remaining distance in the second hour. In the third hour I covered one-third of the remaining distance; and in the fourth hour I covered one-half of the remaining distance. At this point I was still twenty-eight miles away from my destination. How far had I already travelled?

12. Six years ago Angie was nine times as old as her daughter Ellie. Now Angie is only three times as old as Ellie. What are the present ages of Angie and Ellie?

13. It takes one faucet six minutes to fill a sink, while it takes the other three minutes to fill it. If the sink is filled and the plug is left out, it will empty in four minutes.

If both faucets are turned on but the plug is left out, how long will it take for the sink to fill up?

14. The grocer has a number of baskets, each containing the same number of apples. While displaying them in his shop he notices an odd thing: if he adds the number of baskets to the number of apples in a basket, reverses this number, and adds the difference between the number of apples in a basket and the number of baskets, he gets the same number as the total number of apples. The number of apples in a basket is greater than the number of baskets. There are fewer than fifteen apples in any basket. How many apples are there in a basket?

15. A man cashed a check in the bank but the clerk accidentally transposed the dollars and cents, giving the man much more cash than she should have done. On the way home the man gave two cents to a beggar, after which he had twice as much money as he should have had if he had been given the correct amount. How much money did the bank clerk give him?

16. A car went from Paris to Berlin at an average speed of 30mph. How fast would it have had to make the return journey in order to make the average speed for the journey 60mph?

17. Ann and Barbara went shopping with $33 between them. Ann started with $3 more than Barbara, but spent twice as much as her friend. Ann ended up with two-thirds as much money as Barbara. How much did Barbara spend?

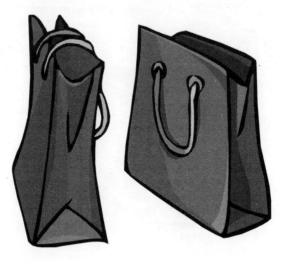

18. A man bought some pens, pencils and paperclips. Pens cost 10¢ each; pencils cost 5¢ each; paperclips cost 1¢ for two. If the man bought a total of one hundred items at a total cost of $1, how many of each item did he buy?

19. Replace the question marks at each end of this sequence with the correct numbers.

| ? | 32 | 33 | 34 | 35 | 36 | 38 | 39 | 40 | 42 | ? |

20. What number, when added to a number ten times as big, gives a number that, when its right-hand digit is multiplied by four and added to the result of the above, gives 1,000?

21. What is the next number in this sequence?

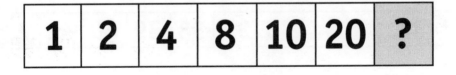

| 1 | 2 | 4 | 8 | 10 | 20 | ? |

22. Can you solve this equation?

Five armadillos = two pigs
One pig + one cat = one dog
One armadillo + one cat = one horse
Four pigs + two armadillos = two dogs
Four horses + three dogs = five cats + seven pigs + one armadillo

If armadillos are worth two, what are the values of dogs, horses, cats, and pigs?

23. The top two sets of scales balance. What is needed to make the third set balance?

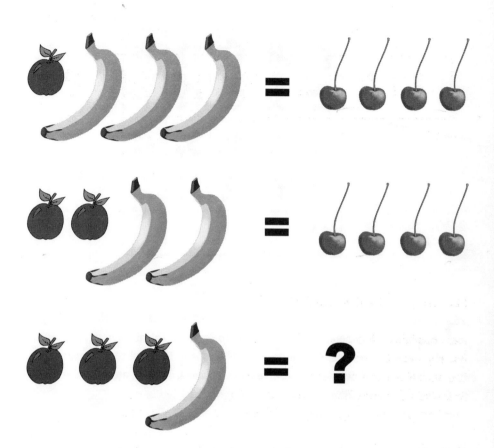

24. If two is added to both the top and bottom of a certain fraction, its value becomes one-half. If two is subtracted from both the top and bottom of the same fraction, its value becomes one-third. What is the fraction?

25. Each like symbol has a like value. What number is represented by the question mark?

26. I have a deck of cards from which some are missing. If I deal them equally between nine people, I have two cards to spare. If I deal them equally between four people, I have three cards to spare. If I deal them equally between seven people, I have five cards to spare. If there are normally 52 cards in a deck, how many are missing?

27. Here is a dartboard with the numbers 0, 2, 3, 5, 10, 12, 15, 20. You have three darts. How many ways are there to score 25? You may land more than one dart in the same segment, but you cannot use the same numbers in a different order. A miss counts as six.

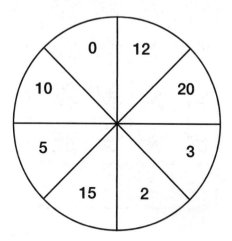

28. Jack is twelve years old. If Ben is three times as old as Jack was when Jack was a quarter as old as he is now, and Jack's brother is half the age of Ben's sister who is two-and-a-half times Ben's age, how old is Jack's brother in months?

29   It takes one faucet twelve minutes to fill a bathtub, while it takes the other thirteen and a half minutes to fill it. If the bathtub is filled and the plug left out, it will empty in fourteen minutes.

If both faucets are turned on but the plug is left out, how long (to the nearest second) will it take for the bathtub to fill up?

30.   An architect, after drawing plans for a room, finds that if he increases the length of the room by two units and reduces the width by one unit, while maintaining the same room height, the room will have the same volume. If the difference between the original dimensions was three units, what were the length and width of the room in the original drawing?

31. Which two numbers, when multiplied together, give a result that, when added to itself, produces a number that, when the digits are added together, has a solution that gives the same result as the original two numbers added together and, if doubled, produces the same result as the original two numbers multiplied together?

32. Each like symbol has a like value. What number is represented by the question mark?

				31
29	37	24	?	

33. What number should replace the question mark?

2	6	3	1	9	9	4	8	2
4	8	2	5	20	4	6	6	1
3	12	4	8	16	2	2	10	?

34. A rectangular plot of land is twenty-eight paces shorter on one side than on the other. If the longer side were reduced by thirty-four paces and the smaller side were lengthened by forty paces, the area contained within the plot would be unchanged. What are the lengths of the sides?

35. What number should replace the question mark?

6	3	5	?
9	7	7	8

36. Forty people took part in a freestyle race. Twenty people ran. Ten people dashed. Five people bolted and sprinted but did not run. Three people bolted, dashed, ran, and sprinted. Two people ran, bolted, and sprinted but did not dash. Five people ran and sprinted but did not bolt or dash. Two people dashed, ran, and sprinted but did not bolt. Twenty-two people sprinted. There was no person who bolted or dashed but did not sprint. There was no person who bolted and dashed but did not run. How many people neither dashed, ran, bolted, nor sprinted?

37. If you buy nine barrels of beer for $25 each, but you are given a 25% discount on the last four barrels, and you are given in change three times the cost of all the barrels less half the value that your discount would be if your discount were 25% more for the last two barrels than the discount you were actually given, what was the total cost of the barrels?

38. When a ball is dropped from a height of 9m, it bounces back two-thirds of the way. Assuming that the ball comes to rest after making a bounce which takes it less than 2mm high, how many times does it bounce?

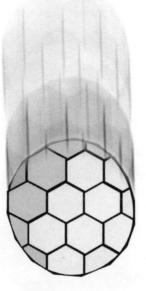

39. Which two-digit number, the values of which when added together total ten, will always divide exactly into any eight-digit number in which the first four digits are repeated in the second half in the same order?

40. What number, when you multiply it by 5 and add 6, then multiply that result by 4 and add 9, gives you a number that, when you multiply it by 5 and subtract 165, gives you a number that, when you knock off the last two digits, brings you back to your original number?

Visual reasoning puzzles (for answers *see* page 372)

1. Which is the not like the others?

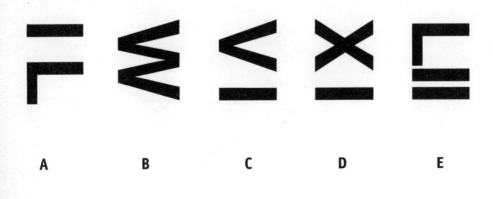

A   B   C   D   E

2. Which of the patterns makes up the cube?

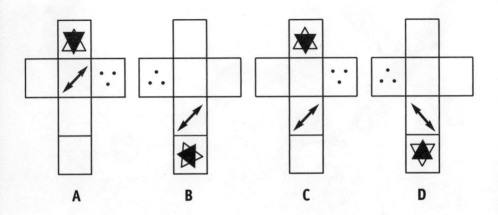

A   B   C   D

3. Which is the not like the others?

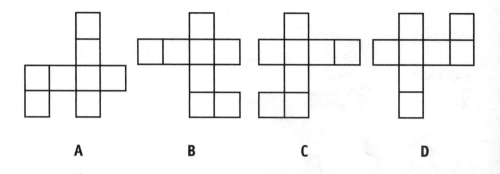

A   B   C   D

4. Following the directions of the arrows, how many different routes are there from A to B?

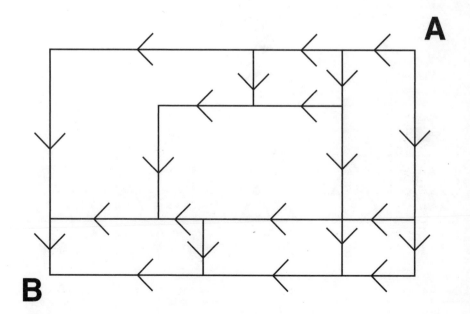

5. Which figure should replace the question mark?

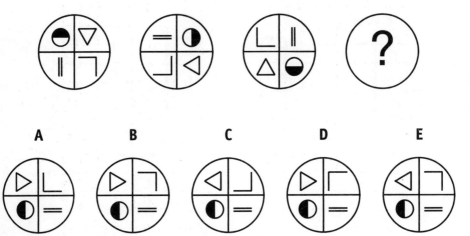

A   B   C   D   E

6. Which of the patterns makes up the pyramid?

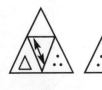

A   B   C   D   E   F

7. Which is the not like the others?

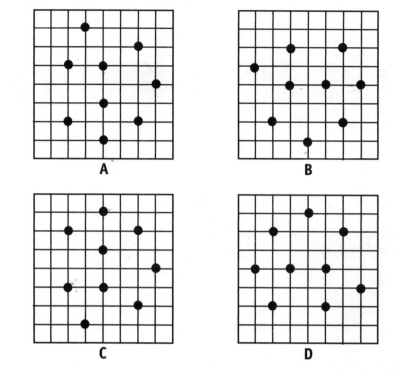

8. Following the directions of the arrows, how many different routes are there from A to B?

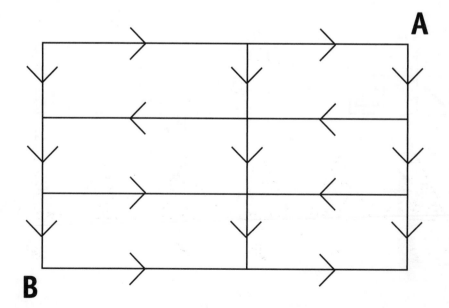

9. Which is the not like the others?

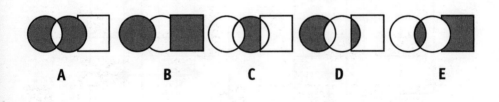

10. Which of these patterns makes up the cube?

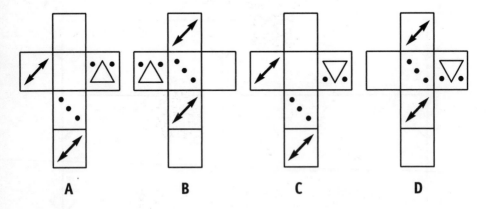

11. Which is the not like the others?

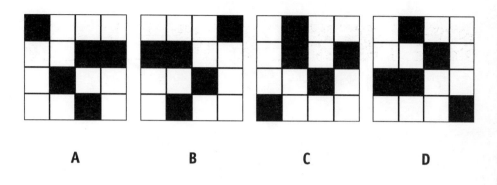

A   B   C   D

12. Which one of the cubes is made up from the pattern?

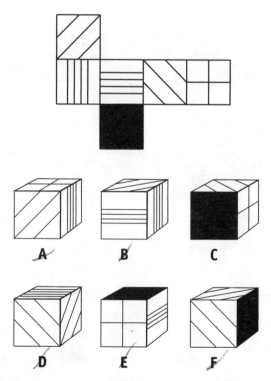

13. If no symbol is used more than on one side of the cube, which of these is not a view of the same box?

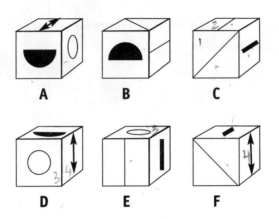

14. Which tile should replace the question mark?

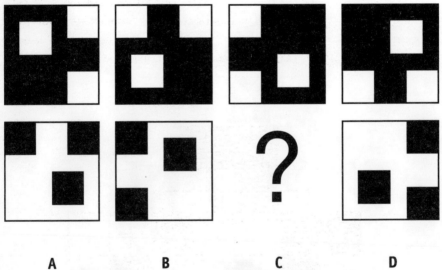

15. Which is the not like the others?

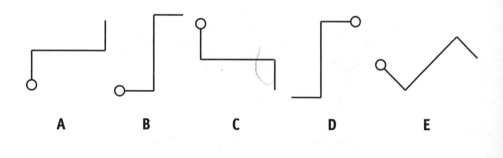

| A | B | C | D | E |

16. There are four different types of candy in this box and your task is to start in the middle and move out to the edge, collecting just one candy of each type. You may only move between two candies which are touching horizontally or vertically. How many ways are there to collect four different candies? You cannot pick up the same four candies using different routes.

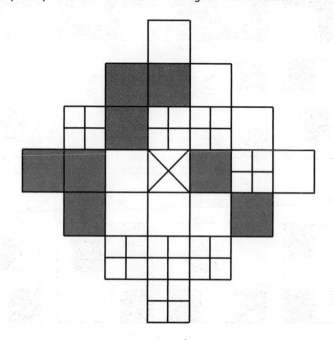

17. Which is the next image in the series?

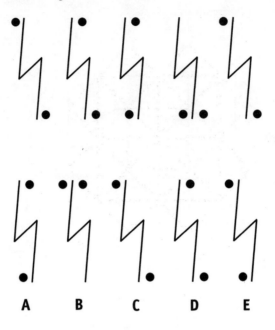

18. Which of the patterns makes up the pyramid?

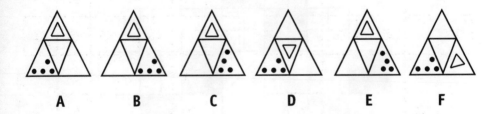

19. How many squares are there in this diagram?

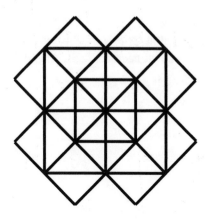

20. Which of the patterns makes up the cube?

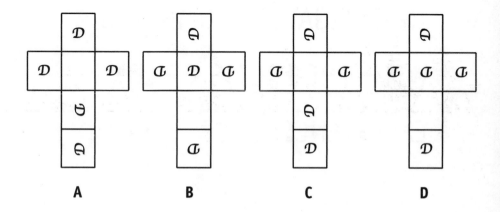

A   B   C   D

Lateral thinking puzzles (for answers *see* pages 372 to 373)

1. A man turned off the light and went to bed. The next morning he turned on the radio and heard of a dreadful tragedy in which more than 100 people had been killed. He realized it had all been his fault. Why? He did not wake in the night and he did not sleepwalk.

2. How many times does the letter "f" appear in the following sentence?

THE FANTASY FACTORY IS THE RESULT OF SCIENTIFIC INVESTIGATION COMBINED WITH THE FRUITS OF LONG EXPERIENCE.

3. How can you throw a ball with all your strength, and make it stop and come back to you, without it hitting a wall or any other obstruction, and without anything being attached to it?

4. A woman was walking down the street when she ran into an old friend whom she hadn't seen since school.

"Hello, I haven't seen you for twenty years," she said. "How are you?"
"Well, I got married ten years ago, and this is our son," was the response.
"Hello," said the woman to the boy, "and what is your name?"
"It's the same as Daddy's."
"Ah, then it's Michael," said the woman.

How could she have known this when the boy's name had not been mentioned?

5.   A certain room is steel-lined and has no entrances or exits other than a single solid door which fits flush in the jamb when closed. There is only one key to the room and it belongs to Ed. Ed locked Fred in the room and went away for an hour with the key in his pocket; when he came back the door was open and Fred had escaped. Fred had not picked the lock, since there is no keyhole on the inside of the door, and nothing in the room was damaged or disturbed. How did Fred get out?

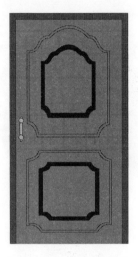

6.   Eric goes to school every morning but he rarely does homework and never achieves high grades in tests. There are thirty children in his class and twenty-nine of them are good students. Eric is not related to anyone at the school and is not a special student. Why does he never get into trouble?

7. A family planning a party had inflated a number of balloons with air and tied the ends so that they would not deflate. They left the balloons on the floor of their living room while they went shopping. When they came back, all the balloons were two inches above the floor. Why was this? The room and balloons were at the same temperature; the doors were firmly closed and had draft excluders fitted; there were no air currents involved; and the balloons did not contain any lighter-than-air gases.

8. A reel of cotton is 1.1 inches in diameter. The cotton is one-hundredth of an inch (0.01 inch) in thickness, and it is wound to a depth of 0.4 inches around the central spindle. What is the simplest way of determining the total length of cotton wound on the reel?

9. A night watchman once requested an urgent meeting with his company's CEO. The CEO was a busy man and was about to fly to a conference in Paris, but gave the employee five minutes of his time. The man nervously explained that he had woken after a terrible dream the previous night. He dreamed that the CEO's plane flying to France had crashed and everyone on board had been killed. He begged the CEO not to take the flight. The CEO thanked the employee for his concern but flew to the conference anyway. The plane did not crash and the conference was uneventful, but as soon as the CEO got back to the office he fired the night watchman. Why?

10. If rubber shoes are used in tennis, cleats in baseball, and spikes in running, in what sport are the shoes made entirely of metal?

11. My uncle eats two eggs for breakfast every morning, but he neither begs, borrows, steals, finds, nor buys the eggs. He doesn't keep chickens, and the eggs are not given to him; nor does he trade them for other goods. No hen comes into his garden and lays the eggs. How does my uncle get the eggs?

12. The housekeeper was distraught after she found Fred and Ginger lying dead on the floor. There was some broken glass near their bodies, and the carpet was damp. Neither of them was wearing any clothes. Who had killed Fred and Ginger?

13. A man charged through a crowd, ripped open a lady's blouse, punched her in the chest and carried her away with him. However, nobody, including two policemen who were nearby, tried to stop him. Why? The man was unarmed and was not a particularly imposing figure physically.

14. A father and son were in a dreadful car accident. The father was killed and the son terribly injured. The son was rushed to the hospital and straight into the operating room. On catching sight of the patient's face, the surgeon recoiled in shock, saying: "I can't possibly operate on this patient – he is my son!" How can this be?

15. While standing on a hard wooden floor, it is possible to drop an egg three feet without breaking the shell. Nothing can be used to break the fall. How is it done?

16. A policewoman stood and watched as a man tried to pick a lock to enter her house. He failed to do so, so he broke a window and gained access that way. The policewoman did not report the incident. Why?

17. How many hands does Big Ben—the famous one in London—have?

18. A family of four were going on a mountaineering trip. Sadly, on the second morning they were all found dead in their cabin, having died from drowning. The faucets had not been left on and the water system in the cabin was undamaged. There was no sign of foul play. What had caused them to drown? They were a mile from the nearest lake, it had not rained for two weeks, and there was no dam nearby.

19. A man married each of his three sisters. However he did nothing to offend against the laws of God or man. How could this be? He did not belong to a religious order which permitted multiple marriages.

20. Arthur and Barry were born on the same day and month of the same year in the same room. They have the same mother and the same father. Their appearance is identical. However, they are not twins. What is the simplest explanation for this?

Logic puzzles (for answers *see* pages 373 to 375)

1. How many male and female mice are there in a family if each female mouse has one fewer male relative than she has female relatives, and each male mouse has two fewer female relatives than twice the number of male relatives he has?

2. Four girls received different birthday presents from their parents this year.

   1. The daughter of Mr. & Mrs. Black is named Gemma.
   2. Rebecca is eleven years old.
   3. Mr. & Mrs. Brown gave their daughter a pony.
   4. Kelly received a bike from her parents.
   5. The daughter of Mr. & Mrs. Gray is two years younger than the girl who was given a CD player.
   6. The daughter of Mr. & Mrs. Green is ten years old.
   7. The nine-year-old was given a doll.

   What is the name of the eight-year-old?
   Which present did Tammy receive?

	Black	Brown	Gray	Green	Eight	Nine	Ten	Eleven	Bicycle	CD Player	Doll	Pony
Gemma												
Kelly												
Rebecca												
Tammy												
Bicycle												
CD Player												
Doll												
Pony												
Eight								
Nine								
Ten								
Eleven								

Girl	Family	Age	Gift

3. Two bicycles, initially 350 miles apart, are travelling toward each other at speeds of 15 mph and 20 mph respectively. A fly sets off from the front wheel of one bike and flies until it touches the front wheel of the other; then it immediately turns and flies back to the first bicycle. It continues to do this until the two bicycles meet and the unfortunate insect is crushed between the two front wheels. If the fly flies at a constant speed of 40 mph, how far does it travel altogether?

4. What is the next letter in this series?

O U E H R

5. A four-person rock group has a concert that starts in seventeen minutes and they must all cross a bridge to get there. All four members begin on the same side of the bridge. It is night. There is one flashlight. A maximum of two people can cross the bridge at one time, but each band member walks at a different speed and any pair must walk together at the rate of the slower member's pace. Any party which crosses, either one or two people, must have the flashlight with them and it must be walked back and forth; it cannot be thrown. How can all four members reach the stage in time?

The singer takes one minute to cross.
The guitarist takes two minutes to cross.
The bass player takes five minutes to cross.
The drummer takes ten minutes to cross.

(For example – if the singer and drummer cross the bridge first, ten minutes will have elapsed when they get to the other side. If the drummer then returns with the flashlight, a total of twenty minutes will have passed and the concert will be off.)

6. A young man claimed: "The day before yesterday I was sixteen, but I will be eighteen this year." Is this possible?

7. A lady walked up to a counter with two books. The assistant said: "That will be seven dollars, please." The lady handed over the money and walked away without the books. Why did she do that?

8. What is the next letter in this series?

A T G C L

9. A man has nine children born at regular intervals. The sum of the squares of their ages is equal to the square of his own. What are the ages of the children?

10. In a six-story apartment block, Steve lives three floors above Tim, and two floors above Bob. Daniel lives just above Steve. Tim lives above Richard but below Bob. On which floor does Ed live?

11. Four British friends have different careers, nationalities, and sporting hobbies.

1. Adam is the tennis fan.
2. Donna is the lawyer.
3. Billy is English.
4. The cycling fan, who is not Chloe, is Welsh.
5. The accountant is a Scotsman.
6. The baker is Irish and is not the cricket fan.

Who is the soccer fan?
Who is the nurse?

	English	Irish	Scottish	Welsh	Cricket	Cycling	Soccer	Tennis	Accountant	Baker	Lawyer	Nurse
Adam												
Billy												
Chloe												
Donna												
Accountant												
Baker												
Lawyer												
Nurse												
Cricket												
Cycling												
Soccer												
Tennis												

Friend	Nationality	Hobby	Career

12. What is the smallest number of checks needed to settle the following debts, if all debts are settled by check?

Mr. Smith owes Mr Jones $10.
Mr. Jones owes Mr Brown $20.
Mr. Brown owes Mr Johnson $30.
Mr. Johnson owes Mr Smith $40.

13. The barber in a certain town shaves all the men living in the town. By law, no man living in the town is permitted to shave himself. The barber lives in the town. The barber does not leave the town and nobody enters the town from outside. Who shaves the barber?

14. A man's right foot was facing due south and after one pace his left foot was facing due north. How was this possible? He took the pace in the direction of his right foot and did not turn in mid-stride. His feet both pointed in the same direction. His right foot had not been twisted around when he originally placed it on the ground.

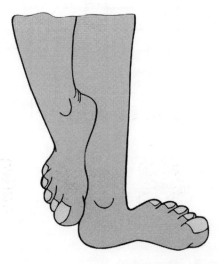

15. Six women are waiting in the bus line. Christine is ahead of Beth. Barbara is three places behind Sarah. Jane is directly behind Rebecca. Barbara is directly behind Beth. In what position is Jane?

16. What is the next letter in this sequence?

N B R R Y

17   A window cleaner was cleaning windows on the tenth floor of a skyscraper when he slipped and fell. He did not have his safety harness on, nothing slowed his fall, and yet he suffered only minor bruising. How was that possible?

18. A woman was aged between fifty and seventy. She calculated that each of her daughters had as many daughters as sisters, and that the combined number of her daughters and granddaughters was equal to her age. How old was she?

19. Four couples are celebrating their wedding anniversaries, which each fall on St. Valentine's Day! Here are some facts about them:

1. Sarah is married to Alan. They are not the couple celebrating fifteen years of wedded bliss.
2. Bob and his wife live in Maine.
3. Chester and his wife are celebrating their fifth anniversary. She is not Gina, who lives in Delaware.
4. The couple who live in Vermont are not the pair celebrating their twelfth anniversary.
5. David's wife is not Alice, who has been married for seven years.

Which couple lives in New Hampshire?
Who is married to Janet?

	Alice	Gina	Janet	Sarah	Fifth	Seventh	Twelfth	Fifteenth	Delaware	Maine	N Hampshire	Vermont
Alan												
Bob												
Chester												
David												
Delaware								
Maine								
N Hampshire								
Vermont								
Fifth				
Seventh				
Twelfth				
Fifteenth				

Husband	Wife	Anniversary	State

20. What is the next letter in this sequence?

R U T R E

Word Puzzles (for answers *see* pages 375 to 376)

1. Find the missing word that can go in front of the other words to form new ones.

JACK

SMITH

LEG

— — — — —   GUARD

BOARD

SPOT

2. Find the missing word that can go in front of the other words to form new ones.

MEN

SIDE

WAY

— — — —   WORTHY

MAP

RUNNER

3.   Find the missing word that can go in front of the other words to form new ones.

SHINE

SPOT

DIAL

— — —   BED

RISE

DRY

4.   Find the missing word that can go in front of the other words to form new ones.

WORD

FATHER

CAST

— — — —   MOST

GOING

LEG

5. Go down the ladder from WELL to SICK changing one letter at each step. Only proper English words can be used.

6. Go down the ladder from LOSE to FIND changing one letter at each step. Only proper English words can be used.

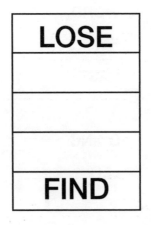

7. Go down the ladder from MEAT to FISH changing one letter at each step. Only proper English words can be used.

MEAT
FISH

8. Go down the ladder from FRESH to CRAMP changing one letter at each step. Only proper English words can be used.

FRESH
CRAMP

9. Reading clockwise, take one letter from each segment to form an eight-letter word.

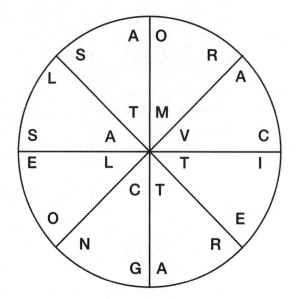

10. Reading clockwise, take one letter from each segment to form a country.

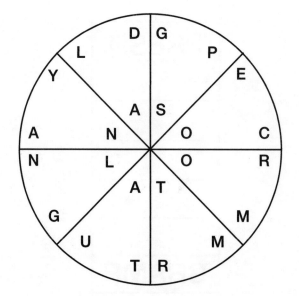

11. Reading clockwise, take one letter from each segment to form an eight-letter word.

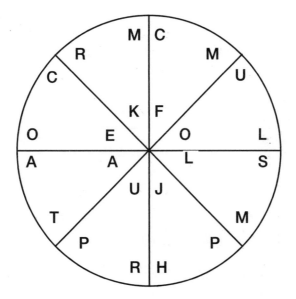

12. Reading clockwise, take one letter from each segment to form an eight-letter word.

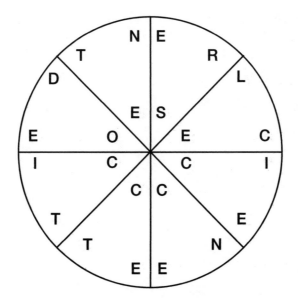

13. Find the missing word that can go at the end of the other words to form new ones.

CAR

POP

SNIP

PARA   — — —

PUP

WHIP

14. Find the missing word that can go at the end of the other words to form new ones.

PAPER

FULL

OUT

COME   — — — —

SLING

TALK

15. Find the missing word that can go at the end of the other words to form new ones.

CHIP

SWITCH

OVER

HEAD   — — — — —

CARD

SNOW

16. Find the missing word that can go at the end of the other words to form new ones.

BUCK

MUG

HOT

MAIL   — — — —

GUN

LONG

17. Hidden inside the grid are the names of three famous movie directors. The names may not be spelled in the same direction, but no letters are omitted or out of order. Who are they?

18. Hidden inside the grid are the names of three items of Italian cuisine. The names may not be spelled in the same direction, but no letters are omitted or out of order. What are they?

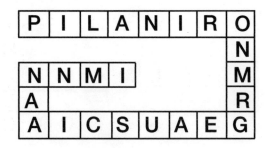

19. Hidden inside the grid are the names of three international cities. They may not be spelled in the same direction, but no letters are omitted or out of order. Which are they?

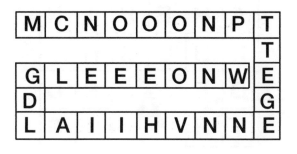

20. Hidden inside the grid are the names of three World War II leaders. The names may not be spelled in the same direction, but no letters are omitted or out of order. Who are they?

21. Start at the middle A and move from square to square, either up or down, but not diagonally to find a well-known phrase. Every letter is used once only.

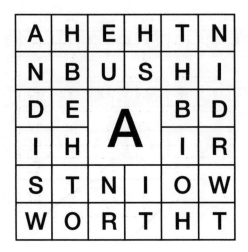

A	H	E	H	T	N
N	B	U	S	H	I
D	E	**A**		B	D
I	H			I	R
S	T	N	I	O	W
W	O	R	T	H	T

22. A funny science fantasy novel, together with its author, has been written in this grid. Find the starting point and move one square horizontally or vertically, not diagonally, to find them.

G	U	O	D	I	H	H
L	S	M	Y	K	E	C
A	D	A	X	A	R	T
S	A	G	A	L	S	I
T	H	E	I	U	G	H
O	T	E	D	T	H	E

23. A famous sporting quotation by legendary football coach Vince Lombardi has been written in this grid. Find the starting point and move one square horizontally or vertically, not diagonally, to find it.

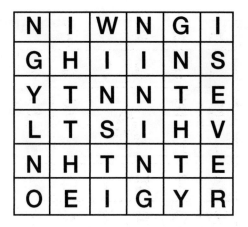

N	I	W	N	G	I
G	H	I	I	N	S
Y	T	N	N	T	E
L	T	S	I	H	V
N	H	T	N	T	E
O	E	I	G	Y	R

24. The opening lines of a Shakespearean soliloquy have been written in this grid. Find the starting point and move one square horizontally or vertically, not diagonally, to find it.

A	I	O	A	F	T	S	E	T	I
L	T	A	R	E	L	L	J	E	N
A	S	H	O	W	E	O	W	O	I
O	P	M	I	H	N	K	I	F	F
O	R	Y	O	R	I	C	K	I	N

25. Find the missing word that can go at the end of the four words to the left to form new ones and the beginning of the four words to the right to form other new ones.

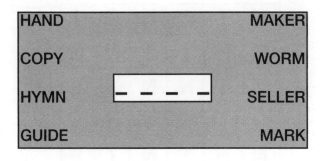

HAND		MAKER
COPY		WORM
HYMN	- - - -	SELLER
GUIDE		MARK

26. Find the missing word that can go at the end of the four words to the left to form new ones and the beginning of the four words to the right to form other new ones.

WAY		BOARD
TWIN		ION
SPOON	- - - -	POSTER
HORN		FOLD

27. Find the missing word that can go at the end of the four words to the left to form new ones and the beginning of the four words to the right to form other new ones.

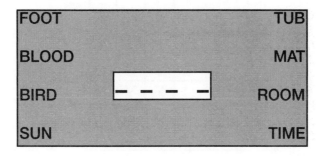

FOOT		TUB
BLOOD		MAT
BIRD	– – – –	ROOM
SUN		TIME

28. Find the missing word that can go at the end of the four words to the left to form new ones and the beginning of the four words to the right to form other new ones.

UNDER		SOME
BEFORE		MADE
BACK	– – – –	LING
SHORT		OFF

29. Create a sixteen-letter word by using the grid references supplied. However, to make things harder, one reference is a red herring.

	1	2	3	4	5	6
A	A	O	G	J	L	P
B	E	T	W	X	Z	S
C	K	C	I	V	B	U
D	M	Q	D	F	Y	H
E	N	R	I	O	E	T
F	A	P	D	S	C	R

A1	E3	C4	A6	E2	A2	F2	E4	A1	B2	C3	F3	E1	F1	B6	B1
D3	B4	F4	D6	F1	E1	D1	F5	F6	A1	C5	A2	D1	B4	B2	E6

30. Create a sixteen-letter word by using the grid references supplied. However, to make things harder, one reference is a red herring.

	1	2	3	4	5	6
A	Y	E	T	A	G	J
B	Z	M	K	D	F	V
C	P	D	S	C	B	R
D	L	I	P	E	T	W
E	X	U	N	H	I	O
F	A	N	O	Q	C	R

D2	F2	B1	D6	C3	A3	C6	B3	B6	A5	C1	D5	E5	B4	D1	D4
C2	B5	C4	F3	E3	E2	A4	E6	D3	A2	F6	F2	A1	C5	A6	B2

31. Create a sixteen-letter word by using the grid references supplied. However, to make things harder, one reference is a red herring.

	1	2	3	4	5	6
A	K	D	S	N	R	C
B	I	A	L	I	P	E
C	T	D	G	J	A	M
D	X	W	N	V	B	U
E	Z	S	Q	O	E	P
F	H	N	F	Y	O	T

D1	F3	E2	D6	D3	F5	D4	A5	A3	C5	D2	B3	A2	E6	F2	E5
C6	B1	F4	E1	E4	C2	B6	E3	D6	F6	B2	A4	D5	B4	C1	C3

32. Create a sixteen-letter word by using the grid references supplied. However, to make things harder, one reference is a red herring.

	1	2	3	4	5	6
A	U	M	Q	D	K	C
B	I	V	O	G	H	E
C	T	A	P	S	C	R
D	E	T	N	W	X	Z
E	R	I	J	L	F	B
F	O	S	A	P	D	Y

A4	C2	E1	F3	C6	A2	F6	D3	B2	D1	E4	B3	C4	D4	C4	D2
F4	B1	A1	D5	C3	F2	C1	A6	B5	F1	A3	C5	B4	E2	A5	B6

33. The five animals on the left side of the box have something in common. Will COW follow that logic?

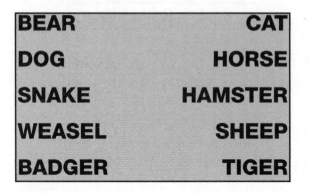

BEAR	CAT
DOG	HORSE
SNAKE	HAMSTER
WEASEL	SHEEP
BADGER	TIGER

34. The five words on the left side of the box are all linked, as are the five words on the right side. Will DIWALI follow the logic of the left or right side?

ROBUST	ISSUE
DONUT	PERUSAL
ALFALFA	BANJO
LESSON	ABBESS
DESIRE	NUTMEG

35. The five words on the left side of the box are all linked, as are the five on the right. On which side should FILLY go?

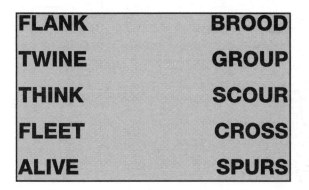

FLANK	BROOD
TWINE	GROUP
THINK	SCOUR
FLEET	CROSS
ALIVE	SPURS

36. The five words on the left side of the box are all linked, as are the five words on the right side. Will FORTY follow the logic of the left or right side?

ABORT	SPOKE
CHINTZ	PLIED
CHIPS	TONED
DIRTY	WOLFED
FIRST	WRONG

37. Can you put together the pieces below to form a five-letter word square?

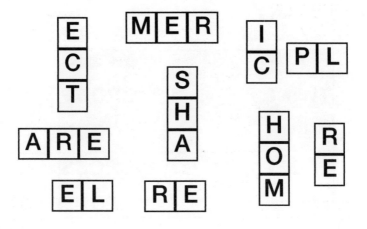

38. Can you put together the pieces below to form a five-letter word square?

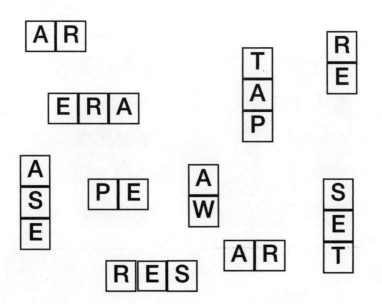

39. Can you put together the pieces below to form a five-letter word square?

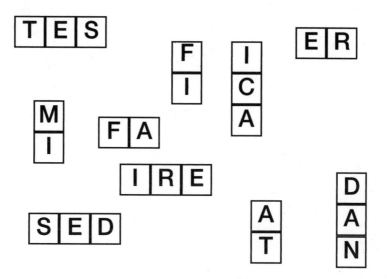

40. Can you put together the pieces below to form a five-letter word square?

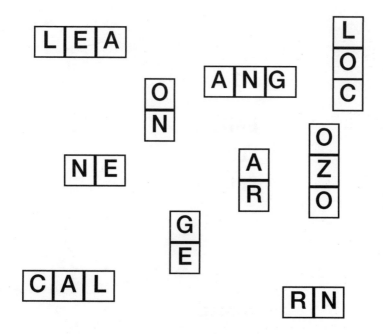

Rebus puzzles (for answers *see* page 376)

1.

S
T
O
R
Y

2.

Man
———
Board

3.

O
———
BAHons
LLB
PhD

4.

14 road

5.

MEAL

6.

7.

KNEE

SIGN

8.

CYCLE
CYCLE

9.

$$\frac{\text{STAND}}{\text{DO U}}$$

10.

O
V
A
T
I
O
N

11.

PRO **M** *ISE*

12.

~~**PRICE**~~

13.

$$\frac{\text{weather}}{\text{sensation}}$$

14.

cod
business
salmon

15.

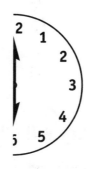

16.

HERE birthday NOW

17.

BRIDGE

A   E
W   R
  T

18.

C I 2 I

19.

PO/VER

20.

cry WILLOW

cry cry cry

cry cry cry

21.

GROTTO

22.

L(head heels)VE

23.

WAR AND PEA

24.

CCCCCCC

25.

ENTURY

26.

GBO

Jumble words (for answers *see* page 377)

With a few exceptions, each grid contains the jumbled names of two people or things, sometimes with their first names, sometimes without. All you have to do is to use the clue to help you discover the hidden words. Puzzles 1–4 are on former US Presidents, 5–8 on scientists and inventors, 9–16 recording artists, and 17–24 the world of movies.

1. One of them is also a car, the other preceded him.

F	N	D
I	R	X
N	O	O

2. The name of one of them means "monetary aid," the other succeeded Teddy Roosevelt.

T	A	F
N	T	R
T	G	A

3. One of them is almost human, the other is last in alphabetical order.

W	O	T
R	N	M
N	A	I
L	S	U

4. One of them really cleaned up, the other played his part in history.

V	H	R
G	E	O
A	A	E
R	O	N

5. One from Syracuse, Sicily, the other an astronomer from Poland.

A	P	M	C	C
R	U	S	C	S
E	E	R	O	I
H	E	N	I	D

6. There are three in this grid. One is relatively simple, another is connected with apples, and the third is connected with degrees.

I	C	U	W	I	N	S
E	S	S	E	L	O	N
T	N	T	N	E	E	I

7. Three more here: one was a star gazer, another an American inventor, and the other connected with milk.

L	A	D	S	L
I	O	T	S	E
R	U	G	E	P
N	A	E	O	I

8. One reminds you of birds of prey, the other sounds like a candy bar.

H	E	H	H	W
G	C	K	L	N
S	I	E	A	R

9. Two girls who are not normally so close.

C	I	A	R	R
L	S	I	P	U
B	E	A	G	R
I	S	H	R	T
A	E	Y	S	T
N	N	I	E	A

10. One of them reminds you of spring; the other is blushing slightly.

A	I	E	I
L	P	V	G
A	I	N	L
N	R	K	V

11. Both these guys are dead, despite rumors to the contrary.

E	N	H
E	J	O
N	N	L
N	O	L
S	V	I

12. The virgin and the writer.

S	I	D
N	A	N
O	I	W
A	A	T
A	N	M
N	H	A

13. One is from Australia, the other seems very affectionate.

K	C	Y	I	E	L
O	N	V	L	E	G
O	N	E	Y	R	U
I	T	O	M	U	E

14. Just one in this grid. She's an Aussie with a touch of Italian.

T	I	A	L
L	G	I	U
R	I	N	E
A	M	B	A

15. One sounds like a member of a cartoon family, the other is a New York-born, Texas-raised singer-songwriter.

J	N	S	O	S	N
E	C	N	R	O	O
S	J	H	E	S	A
P	S	A	I	M	I

16. Frankly, happy birthday to you.

S	K	W	R	I	A
N	O	T	I	E	V
R	D	F	N	A	T
N	A	S	E	E	R

17. A pretty woman and a tough cookie.

A	L	G	O	I
U	R	T	J	E
E	R	N	S	B
A	I	E	A	L
I	N	O	J	L

18. A knight and a guy in a tuxedo.

O	P	C	E	W
A	G	O	E	R
N	N	S	N	R
E	C	A	R	B
I	G	M	E	R

19. They both got involved with pirates.

L	I	T	I
K	A	N	Y
O	P	N	N
E	G	H	P
E	D	Y	K
J	R	H	E

20. An English rose and an American fruit.

A	O	E	A
Y	H	A	A
H	R	L	N
R	H	L	N
E	E	T	E
R	R	B	M
E	C	B	L

21. A wild one meets the original Alfie.

N	H	D	L	L	A
I	R	A	A	N	I
M	E	R	A	C	E
O	N	C	O	M	B

22. A girl from Swansea and a stiff-sounding guy from New York.

S	N	R	Y	J	T	T
E	W	A	N	N	D	E
H	L	L	C	E	O	A
Z	I	O	E	O	A	E

23. A duke and a rodent.

W	M	N	E	J
O	S	Y	U	K
C	Y	E	M	I
E	H	N	A	O

24. A Scot and a film fowl.

C	D	Y	N	L	U	O
A	N	K	C	S	D	E
E	N	R	N	D	O	A

quizzes

TRIVIA QUIZZES
(for answers *see* pages 377 to 379)

FASTEST AND SLOWEST

1. At which athletic event is the Paralympic record more than 40 minutes better than the able-bodied?

(a) 1,500 metres   (b) Marathon

(c) 5,000 metres   (d) 10,000 metres

2. Which is the fastest mammal on earth over short distances?

(a) Hare   (b) Racehorse

(c) Elephant   (d) Cheetah

3. What was the name of the vehicle that went supersonic when breaking the world land speed record in 1997?

(a) Blast MAC   (b) Sonikboom DFB

(c) Thrust SSC   (d) Zoomer SOK

4. Which is the slowest creature in the animal kingdom?

(a) Three-toed sloth   (b) Giant tortoise

(c) Snail   (d) Mule

5. In which English city did Roger Bannister become the world's first sub-four-minute miler?

(a) Cambridge   (b) Oxford

(c) London   (d) Manchester

6. Which is the slowest fish in the marine kingdom?

(a) Flounder   (b) Sea horse

(c) Guppy   (d) Koy carp

7. Whose world record of 19.32 seconds for the men's 200 meters in 1997 is, at 37.267km/h, the fastest recorded speed for a completed race?

(a) Carl Lewis   (b) Donovan Bailey

(c) Maurice Greene   (d) Michael Johnson

8. For how many years did Lee Evans hold the 400m world record, set in 1968?

(a) 18 months   (b) 20 years

(c) 16 years   (d) 25 years

9. What is the top speed of the *Shinkansen,* the Japanese Bullet Train, the world's fastest rail train?

(a) 290.4 km/h   (b) 259.4 km/h

(c) 272.6 km/h   (d) 261.8 km/h

10. When Paula Radcliffe set a new women's world Marathon record at the 2003 London Marathon, where would she have finished in the men's race?

(a) 1st   (b) 32nd

(c) 20th   (d) 15th

11. Which bird can dive at up to 90 meters per second?

(a) Sparrowhawk   (b) Bald eagle

(c) Peregrine falcon   (d) Condor

12. Which swimmer set, or was part of, seven world-record performances in a single Olympic Games?

(a) Ian Thorpe   (b) Matt Biondi

(c) Michael Phelps   (d) Mark Spitz

HIGHS AND LOWS

1. Which US state has no "mountain" higher than 345ft (105m)?

(a) Mississippi   (b) Florida

(c) Delaware   (d) Louisiana

2. Which sea is the furthest below sea level?

(a) Red Sea   (b) Yellow Sea

(c) Black Sea   (d) Dead Sea

3. Which mountain range contains the world's highest peaks?

(a) Urals   (b) Himalayas

(c) Alps   (d) Rockies

4. In which country is the world's highest active volcano?

(a) Argentina   (b) Peru

(c) Ecuador   (d) Chile

5. Which US city, with a population of more than 1 million, is actually below sea level?

(a) Dallas   (b) Minneapolis

(c) New Orleans   (d) Chicago

6. In which country is the world's tallest tower at 1,815ft (553m)?

(a) Indonesia   (b) Taiwan

(c) Malaysia   (d) Canada

7. Which is the highest peak in Europe?

(a) Mount Elbrus   (b) Mont Blanc

(c) Mount Eiger   (d) Ben Nevis

8. What is the highest peak in Great Britain?

(a) Mount Snowdon   (b) Ben Lomond

(c) Ben Nevis   (d) Old Man of Hoy

9. In which state is the highest peak in North America, Mount McKinley?

(a) Alabama   (b) Alaska

(c) Arkansas   (d) Arizona

10. In which decade was the peak of Mount Everest first officially reached?

(a) 1920s   (b) 1970s

(c) 1950s   (d) 1930s

11. What is the deepest valley in the United States?

(a) Death Valley, Arizona

(b) Death Valley, South Carolina

(c) Grand Canyon, Arizona

(d) Hell's Valley, Oregon/Idaho

12. Which waterfall is the world's highest above sea level?

(a) Victoria Falls

(b) Niagara Falls

(c) Suligad Falls

(d) Reichenbach Falls

HITS AND MISSES

1. Who wrote Whitney Houston's global hit "I Will Always Love You?"

(a) Bryan Adams   (b) Phil Spector

(c) Quincy Adams   (d) Dolly Parton

2. When first released in 1956, how high did Elvis Presley's "Blue Suede Shoes" reach in the Billboard Top 20?

(a) 1   (b) 17

(c) 20   (d) 4

3. Paul McCartney has not recorded a hit with which of the following?

(a) Stevie Wonder   (b) Wings

(c) The Beatles   (d) Cliff Richard

4. At what number did Robbie Williams' *Sing When You're Winning* album enter the Billboard charts in 2000?

(a) 110   (b) 1

(c) 12   (d) 57

5. Which husband and wife first went to No. 1 with "I Got You, Babe?"

(a) Ike and Tina Turner

(b) Sonny and Cher

(c) Paul and Linda McCartney

(d) Buddy and Julie Miller

6. Which bandleader went to No. 1 with the "Theme to *The Good, the Bad and the Ugly*?"

(a) Glenn Miller

(b) Geoff Love

(c) Hugo Montenegro

(d) Count Basie

7. Which Michael Jackson recording is the biggest-selling music video of all time?

(a) "Thriller"   (b) "Moonwalking"

(c) "Bad"   (d) "Billie Jean"

8. What was the highest position the Righteous Brothers reached with their version of "Unchained Melody" in the US Top 40?

(a) 1   (b) 12

(c) 7   (d) 4

9. Which Chuck Berry No. 1 was banned by the BBC?

(a) "Johnny B. Goode"

(b) "My Ding-a-Ling"

(c) "Reelin' and Rockin'"

(d) "Promised Land"

10. Which Canadian singer won the Eurovision Song Contest representing France?

(a) Avril Lavigne

(b) Alanis Morissette

(c) Diana Krall

(d) Celine Dion

11. Who played the lead role in the movie *Grease* and had a hit with a song from it?

(a) John Travolta   (b) Michael J. Fox

(c) Michael Douglas   (d) Mel Gibson

12. "Jean Genie" was a UK No. 2 in 1972, but how far did it go in the US Top 100?

(a) No. 1   (b) No. 32

(c) No. 71   (d) No. 96

KINGS AND QUEENS

1. Which British king was on the throne when the United States gained independence in 1776?

(a) Henry VIII   (b) Richard I

(c) Edward VII   (d) George III

2. Which country returned to a monarchy after the death of its military dictator in the 1970s?

(a) Sweden   (b) Spain

(c) Belgium   (d) Netherlands

3. Who was known as the Virgin Queen?

(a) Mary Queen of Scots

(b) Queen Victoria

(c) Queen Elizabeth I

(d) Queen Anne

4. Which French queen is reputed to have said, "Let them eat cake" during a famine?

(a) Anne de Bretagne

(b) Catherine de Medici

(c) Marie Antoinette

(d) Berthe

5. The royal family of which European principality has the name Grimaldi?

(a) Monaco   (b) Andorra

(c) Wales   (d) Liechtenstein

6. Who, in 1991, became King of Norway?

(a) Olav V   (b) Harald V

(c) Oscar II   (d) Haakon VII

7. How many Dutch monarchs died in office during the twentieth century?

(a) None   (b) Four

(c) Two   (d) Three

8. What was the first name of the sleuth Queen in American whodunit novels of the 1960s and 70s?

(a) Edgar   (b) Elrick

(c) Ellery   (d) Eldon

9. Which King was granted a patent for the first safety razor in 1904?

(a) Gillette   (b) Remington

(c) Parker   (d) Brown

10. Who was the last British monarch to celebrate 50 years on the throne?

(a) Queen Victoria

(b) King Edward VII

(c) King George VI

(d) Queen Elizabeth II

11. Who is the Prince of Wales?

(a) Philip   (b) Edward

(c) Charles   (d) Harry

12. Which of these countries is a constitutional monarchy?

(a) Malaysia   (b) Philippines

(c) Indonesia   (d) Thailand

HUSBANDS AND WIVES

1. Which movie star responded to the question, "How many husbands have you had?" with the question, "You mean apart from my own?"

(a) Zsa-Zsa Gabor　　(b) Elizabeth Taylor

(c) Bette Davis　　(d) Marilyn Monroe

2. With which band did David Beckham's wife Victoria rise to prominence?

(a) Hear' Say　　(b) Girl Power

(c) Spice Girls　　(d) Destiny's Child

3. Ex-baseball star David Justice was married to which star of the movie *Catwoman*?

(a) Sharon Stone　　(b) Halle Berry

(c) Kim Smith　　(d) Frances Conroy

4. What was the maiden name of the wife of Prince Andrew, the Duke of York?

(a) Diana Spencer

(b) Sophie Rhys-Jones

(c) Anne Windsor

(d) Sarah Ferguson

5. Actress Rhea Perlman was married to which fellow diminutive comedy actor when she was starring in *Cheers*?

(a) Dom DeLuise　　(b) Gene Wilder

(c) Danny De Vito　　(d) Martin Short

6. What was the name of presidential candidate Al Gore's wife?

(a) Tani　　(b) Tipper

(c) Tiffy　　(d) Teresa

7. Baseball legend Joe DiMaggio was married to which movie legend in the 1950s?

(a) Jean Harlow　　(b) Bette Davis

(c) Jayne Mansfield　　(d) Marilyn Monroe

8. Who did the woman born Cherilyn Sarkisian marry in 1969?

(a) Sonny Bono　　(b) Roman Polanski

(c) Jerry Garcia　　(d) Ike Turner

9. Elizabeth Taylor has had many husbands, but which one did she marry twice?

(a) Michael Wilding　　(b) Richard Burton

(c) Mike Todd　　(d) Eddie Fisher

10. Which couple were the male and female stars of the movie *Husbands and Wives*?

(a) Sydney Pollack and Judy Davis

(b) Woody Allen and Mia Farrow

(c) Liam Neeson and Juliette Lewis

(d) Timothy Jerome and Lysette Anthony

11. Who was President of the US when the First Lady was Lady Bird?

(a) Richard Nixon　　(b) Gerald Ford

(c) Lyndon Johnson　　(d) Jimmy Carter

12. Which First Lady gave her name to a famous drug and alcohol rehabilitation clinic?

(a) Betty Ford　　(b) Nancy Reagan

(c) Laura Bush　　(d) Hillary Clinton

BROTHERS AND SISTERS

1. Which singing family contained brothers and sister, Jay, Alan, Donny, Marie, and Jimmy?

(a) The Cassidys   (b) The Jacksons

(c) The Osmonds   (d) The Osbournes

2. Which two US states in the 1990s had brothers as Governor?

(a) Florida and Texas

(b) North Carolina and South Carolina

(c) North Dakota and South Dakota

(d) Arkansas and Oklahoma

3. Which pair of twins are NFL starters for Tampa Bay and the New York Giants, respectively?

(a) Anthony and Chris Davis

(b) Kenyatta and Greg Walker

(c) Ronde and Tiki Barber

(d) Will and Kenderick Allen

4. What are the names of the two children of Anne, the Princess Royal?

(a) Harry and Beatrice

(b) William and Eugenie

(c) Peter and Zara

(d) Andrew and Diana

5. Which actor is the brother of Emilio Estevez?

(a) Charlie Sheen   (b) Joe Estevez

(c) Taylor Estevez   (d) Martin Sheen

6. Who is Lorna Luft's Oscar-winning sister?

(a) Meryl Streep

(b) Liza Minnelli

(c) Sharon Stone

(d) Ingrid Bergman

7. Which post-World War II US President appointed his brother Attorney General?

(a) Dwight Eisenhower

(b) Jimmy Carter

(c) George Bush, Sr.

(d) John F. Kennedy

8. Which of these recording groups were actually full blood brothers?

(a) Doobie Brothers

(b) Righteous Brothers

(c) Everly Brothers

(d) Blues Brothers

9. Which two members of the Fonda family are siblings?

(a) Jane and Peter

(b) Henry and Peter

(c) Jane and Bridget

(d) Henry and Bridget

10. What are the names of the Williams sisters, world No. 1 tennis players in 2002?

(a) Justine and Kim

(b) Venus and Serena

(c) Maria and Elena

(d) Anna and Martina

11. Which Marx brother used to begin after dinner speeches with, "Unaccustomed as I am to public speaking?"

(a) Chico   (b) Zeppo

(c) Groucho   (d) Harpo

12. In which country were recording stars/actresses Kylie and Dannii Minogue born?

(a) New Zealand   (b) Australia

(c) England   (d) Canada

PARENTS AND CHILDREN

1. Who was the youngest daughter of Queen Elizabeth The Queen Mother?

(a) Elizabeth (b) Alice

(c) Anne (d) Margaret

2. What is the name of the second son of George Herbert Walker Bush?

(a) George Walker (b) John Ellis

(c) Neil Mallon (d) Marvin Pierce

3. Sean and Jason Connery have both played which character?

(a) James Bond

(b) Inspector Clouseau

(c) Robin Hood

(d) Macbeth

4. Jamie Lee Curtis is the daughter of which actress?

(a) Vivien Leigh

(b) Janet Leigh

(c) Pattie Leigh

(d) Chyler Leigh

5. Which father and son have hit the most runs in major league baseball?

(a) Bobby and Barry Bonds

(b) Julian and Stan Javier

(c) Maury and Bump Wills

(d) Ken Griffey Sr. and Jr.

6. Who wrote the novel *Fathers and Sons*?

(a) Leo Tolstoy (b) Ivan Turgenev

(c) Anton Chekhov (d) Boris Pasternak

7. Who are Daughters of the Moon?

(a) A 1970s British punk rock band

(b) A prostitutes' collective in Montana

(c) A group of female cosmonauts

(d) A global spiritualist organisation

8. What was the family name of the first father and son to be US President?

(a) Roosevelt (b) Adams

(c) Bush (d) Johnson

9. What did John Henry Williams do to his father, legendary baseball player Ted Williams, after he died in 2002?

(a) Sold the rights for the funeral photos to a Hollywood magazine

(b) Filmed the burial and offered it for view on the internet

(c) Had his body cryogenically frozen

(d) Spread his ashes over the home plate at Yankee Stadium

10. What number car did Dale Earnhardt, Sr., father of Dale, Jr., drive in NASCAR?

(a) 27 (b) 3

(c) 8 (d) 26

11. Singer Marvin Gaye was murdered by his father, but what was his name?

(a) Mervyn (b) Martin

(c) Mark (d) Marvin

12. Emmy-nominated actress Blythe Danner has a more famous daughter. Who is she?

(a) Sandra Bullock

(b) Angelina Jolie

(c) Gwyneth Paltrow

(d) Cameron Diaz

TRAINS AND PLANES

1. What is the only English station on the Eurostar line between Waterloo and France?

(a) Clapham Junction

(b) Gatwick Airport

(c) Ashford International

(d) Dover Priory

2. What is the name of the main airport in Tokyo?

(a) Oita   (b) Narita

(c) Itami   (d) Toyama

3. What is the main Amtrak rail station in New York City?

(a) Pennsylvania

(b) Madison Street

(c) Port Authority

(d) Grand Central

4. Where is John Wayne Airport?

(a) Orange County, California

(b) Houston, Texas

(c) Burbank, California

(d) El Paso, Texas

5. What is the name of the fastest train in Europe?

(a) Train à Grand Vitesse

(b) Thalys

(c) Sehrschnell

(d) Molto Velocemente

6. After which French president is a Parisian airport named?

(a) Jacques Chirac

(b) Georges Pompidou

(c) Charles de Gaulle

(d) Valéry Giscard-d'Estaing

7. Going by train from Sydney to Perth in Australia involves how many nights aboard?

(a) 5   (b) 3

(c) 4   (d) 2

8. The New Orleans airport is named for which famous musician?

(a) Louis Armstrong

(b) Elvis Presley

(c) Duke Ellington

(d) Cab Calloway

9. William Huskisson, the first victim of a passenger rail crash, had which occupation?

(a) Miner   (b) Driver

(c) Farmer   (d) Politician

10. Dulles Airport serves which major city?

(a) Dallas   (b) Washington

(c) Philadelphia   (d) Los Angeles

11. Which legendary American railroadman was the subject of a 1950s and '60s children's TV series?

(a) Joe Lewis

(b) Sim Webb

(c) Casey Jones

(d) Memphis Belle

12. In which city is there a Sky Harbor airport?

(a) Baku   (b) Cairo

(c) Phoenix   (d) Kathmandu

REDS AND BLUES

1. A Red Admiral is what type of creature?

(a) Moth   (b) Butterfly

(c) Cicada   (d) Beetle

2. Someone who is blue-blooded is said to be what?

(a) Born into nobility

(b) Always depressed

(c) A risqué comedian

(d) Overweight

3. Which two nations' flags are identical, being top half red, bottom half white?

(a) Malta and Poland

(b) Qatar and Bahrain

(c) Monaco and Indonesia

(d) Singapore and Yemen

4. Who painted the *Blue Boy*?

(a) Thomas Gainsborough

(b) J.M.W. Turner

(c) John Constable

(d) Joshua Reynolds

5. Who investigated the Red-Headed League?

(a) Hercule Poirot

(b) Columbo

(c) Jessica Fletcher

(d) Sherlock Holmes

6. Which is known as the blue planet?

(a) Uranus

(b) Mercury

(c) Earth

(d) Venus

7. What is the maximum number of red cards that can be dealt to one person in a bridge hand?

(a) 13   (b) 10

(c) 4   (d) 8

8. In which city was *The Blues Brothers* set?

(a) Philadelphia   (b) New Orleans

(c) Memphis   (d) Chicago

9. "Red" Adair was famous in which field?

(a) Mathematics   (b) Sport

(c) Oil   (d) Politics

10. Who was the lyricist for "Blue Moon?"

(a) Richard Rodgers

(b) Lorenz Hart

(c) Oscar Hammerstein

(d) Irving Berlin

11. With which British royal family is the red rose linked?

(a) York   (b) Windsor

(c) Gloucester   (d) Lancaster

12. In Tom Sharpe's comic novel of the same name, what was a Porterhouse Blue?

(a) A steak cooked with mushrooms and wine

(b) A stroke brought on by overeating

(c) A sporting honor won by a student

(d) A punishment for missing an examination

SWORD AND SORCERY

1. Who was the queen of King Arthur?

(a) Guinevere   (b) Genevieve

(c) Geena   (d) Geneva

2. In which century did the Crusades begin?

(a) Tenth   (b) Thirteenth

(c) Twelfth   (d) Eleventh

3. In *The Wizard of Oz*, where did Dorothy call "home?"

(a) Arkansas   (b) Kansas

(c) Oklahoma   (d) Missouri

4. In which New England town were there famous witchcraft trials in 1692?

(a) Boston   (b) Hartford

(c) Salem   (d) Cambridge

5. What was the magical train that took Harry Potter to school?

(a) Mugwumps Express

(b) Hogwarts Express

(c) Azkaban Express

(d) Voldemort Express

6. In the Hansel and Gretel fairy tale, out of what was the witch's cottage made?

(a) Straw   (b) Brick

(c) Glass   (d) Gingerbread

7. Which goddess caused Hercules to kill his wife and children?

(a) Athena   (b) Hera

(c) Hebe   (d) Omphale

8. Who was the magician in Arthurian legend?

(a) Marlin   (b) Marlon

(c) Merlin   (d) Mervyn

9. How was it that a witch was proved guilty after she was ducked?

(a) If she was able to escape from her bonds

(b) If she survived the ducking

(c) If she drowned during the ducking

(d) If the water reversed its flow

10. Which card is the most valuable in the secondary market for *Magic The Gathering*?

(a) Ancestral Recall

(b) Black Lotus

(c) Time Warp

(d) Birds of Paradise

11. Who was the leader of the 1970s British glam-rock group Wizzard?

(a) Roy Wood   (b) Noddy Holder

(c) Marc Bolan   (d) Brian Connolly

12. A centaur was half-human and half of what other animal?

(a) Lion   (b) Elephant

(c) Horse   (d) Dog

ACTRESSES AND BISHOPS

1. Which Hollywood star had affairs with both the US President and Attorney General?

(a) Jayne Mansfield

(b) Jean Harlow

(c) Kim Basinger

(d) Marilyn Monroe

2. Who was the woman whose affair led to the ruin of TV evangelist Jim Bakker?

(a) Paula Hahn   (b) Echo Johnson

(c) Tammi Baker   (d) Jessica Hahn

3. Which cardinal was head of the Manila diocese in 2000?

(a) Cardinal Red   (b) Cardinal Bird

(c) Cardinal Sin   (d) Cardinal St. Louis

4. For what "crime" were Hollywood actors blacklisted in the 1950s?

(a) Having "communist" beliefs

(b) Making silent movies

(c) Refusing to serve in the armed forces

(d) Not paying Teamster union dues

5. Who was the actress who leapt to her death from the Hollywood sign in 1932?

(a) Ida Lupino   (b) Peg Entwistle

(c) Billie Burke   (d) Irene Dunn

6. How was Roberto Calvi, the chairman of Banco Ambrosiano who died in mysterious circumstances in London in 1982, nicknamed?

(a) Father Money

(b) The Pope's Exchequer

(c) Cardinal Cash

(d) God's Banker

7. Where in Los Angeles was John Belushi found dead of a drug overdose?

(a) Chateau Marchmont Hotel

(b) Hollywood Hilton and Towers

(c) Planet Hollywood

(d) Los Angeles Coliseum

8. Who was the Boston Catholic priest accused of abusing young men in his parish?

(a) George J. Johnson

(b) John J. Geoghan

(c) Graham G. George

(d) Gordon J. Jones

9. For what crime was Heidi Fleiss jailed in 1996?

(a) Gun-running in Nicaragua

(b) Drug deals in Colombia

(c) Running prostitutes in Hollywood

(d) Illegal immigration from Mexico

10. How was Joan of Arc executed?

(a) Hung, drawn and quartered

(b) By guillotine

(c) Beheaded

(d) Burned at the stake

11. Who was the actress wife of baseball pitcher Chuck Finley charged with spousal abuse on him?

(a) Tawny Kitaen   (b) Susan Sarandon

(c) Kitten Natividad   (d) Traci Lords

12. Who was the leader of the gang who murdered actress Sharon Tate?

(a) Charles Manson

(b) Lynette Fromme

(c) Gary Hinman

(d) Charles Watson

WET AND DRY

1. Chicago is known as "The Windy City," but what is the windiest city in the USA?

(a) Cleveland, Ohio

(b) Dallas, Texas

(c) Flagstaff, Arizona

(d) Buffalo, New York

2. The hottest day in British history was recorded in Gravesend, Kent, in 2003, with what temperature?

(a) 98.8°F (37.1°C)

(b) 100.6°F (38.1°C)

(c) 99.7°F (37.6°C)

(d) 100.2°F (37.9°C)

3. The wettest year on record occurred in 1861 when 1,042 inches (86.83 feet, almost 29 yards) of rain fell. Where was it?

(a) Manchester, England

(b) Seattle, Washington

(c) Cherrapunji, India

(d) Amazon Rain Forest, Brazil

4. How long was the driest spell in Chile?

(a) 11 years, 2 months

(b) 12 years, 2 months

(c) 13 years, 2 months

(d) 14 years, 2 months

5. The hottest day in the US occurred at Death Valley, California, in 1913. How hot was it?

(a) 130°F (54.4°C)   (b) 138°F (58.9°C)

(c) 134 °F (56.7°C)   (d) 146°F (63.3°C)

6. Since 1983, how often has there been air frost in Tel Aviv, Israel?

(a) Never   (b) 21 times

(c) 14 times   (d) Nine times

7. How low was the temperature on the coldest day ever recorded, in Antarctica in 1983?

(a) −89.2°C (−128.6°F)

(b) −112.2°C (−170°F)

(c) −93.6°C (−136.2°F)

(d) −98.4°C (−145.2°F)

8. What scale is used to measure wind speeds?

(a) Richter Scale   (b) Monsoon Scale

(c) Hurricane Scale   (d) Beaufort Scale

9. Groundhog Day has a meteorological background, but what date is it?

(a) March 13   (b) August 14

(c) February 2   (d) January 11

10. What is the name of the weather pattern that keeps the UK climate temperate?

(a) Gulf Stream   (b) Atlantic Stream

(c) Euro Stream   (d) Channel Stream

11. How many days per year is the average temperature below freezing point in the Arctic?

(a) 289   (b) 319

(c) 364   (d) 337

12. On average how many days per year is the temperature over 80°F (26°C) in Rio?

(a) 149   (b) 341

(c) 275   (d) 83

SWEET AND SOUR

1. What is the base ingredient of a Napoli sauce?

(a) Meat   (b) Fish

(c) Tomato   (d) Cream

2. What mainly Japanese delicacy can be deadly if not cooked in a certain way?

(a) Puffer or Tiger blowfish

(b) Coelacanth

(c) Cobra meat

(d) Scorpion

3. Which of these is actually accurate?

(a) Bombay duck

(b) Chicken Maryland

(c) Buffalo wings

(d) Fish fingers

4. What ingredient in absinthe was thought to send drinkers mad?

(a) Anis   (b) Rye

(c) Sandalwood   (d) Wormwood

5. What is the hottest curry type?

(a) Vindaloo   (b) Madras

(c) Phal   (d) Jalfrezi

6. Which fruit juice is recommended to those people suffering from urinary infections?

(a) Apple   (b) Cranberry

(c) Orange   (d) Tomato

7. What is the South African delicacy biltong?

(a) Garlic shrimp

(b) Processed ham and cheese

(c) An indigenous fruit

(d) Dried meat

8. Why is it impossible to drink American champagne?

(a) Champagne can only be made in the Champagne region in France

(b) Champagne grapes cannot survive the American climate

(c) The storing and bottling system is unique to Europe

(d) The bubbles don't last long enough

9. What is a smorgasbord?

(a) Norwegian herring

(b) Danish pastry

(c) Finnish elk steak

(d) Swedish buffet

10. How long is a steak tartare cooked?

(a) 2 minutes each side

(b) 1 minute each side

(c) It is not actually cooked

(d) Four minutes each side

11. Which varieties of Pimm's were manufactured in the 1940s?

(a) gin, scotch, brandy, rum, rye, vodka

(b) gin, brandy, rum, rye, vodka

(c) gin, scotch, rye, vodka

(d) gin, scotch, brandy, rum, vodka

12. From what organ does pâté de foie gras come?

(a) Stomach   (b) Kidney

(c) Heart   (d) Liver

CATS AND DOGS

1. What is the name of Bart's dog in *The Simpsons*?

(a) Widget

(b) Santa's Little Helper

(c) Pippin

(d) Kaia

2. In *Tom & Jerry*, by what name is Tom summoned by the terrified or furious maid?

(a) Thomas   (b) Tom

(c) Tommy   (d) Tomcat

3. Which 1970s thriller was set around the assassination attempt on Charles De Gaulle?

(a) *The Dogs of War*

(b) *The Killer is a Fox*

(c) *The Day of the Jackal*

(d) *The Lone Wolf*

4. What animal was Bagheera in *The Jungle Book*?

(a) Lion   (b) Tiger

(c) Cheetah   (d) Panther

5. In which novel and movie does Cruella de Vil appear?

(a) *101 Dalmatians*   (b) *The Lion King*

(c) *Dumbo*   (d) *The Jungle Book*

6. Jane Fonda and Lee Marvin co-starred in which 1965 movie?

(a) *Cat on a Hot Tin Roof*

(b) *Faster! Pussycat! Kill Kill!*

(c) *Cat Ballou*

(d) *That Darn Cat*

7. What was the name of the Darlings' dog in *Peter Pan*?

(a) Buster   (b) Nana

(c) Patch   (d) Suki

8. Which animated TV series was set in Hoagy's Alley?

(a) *Top Cat*

(b) *Huckleberry Hound*

(c) *Marmaduke Jinks*

(d) *Deputy Dawg*

9. What is the name of the large dog in *Tom & Jerry*?

(a) Buster

(b) Bruno

(c) Boy

(d) Butch

10. Tweety-Pie was the main prey for which cartoon character?

(a) Sylvester

(b) Daffy

(c) Pepe le Pew

(d) Elmer

11. Who was the dog in *The Wacky Races*?

(a) Meekley

(b) Blubber

(c) Muttley

(d) Sawtooth

12. What was the name of Josie's backing group?

(a) The Tomcats

(b) The Kittiecats

(c) The Little Kittens

(d) The Pussycats

MR. SMITH AND MRS. JONES

1. What is rapper Jay-Z's given name?
(a) John Zimmerman
(b) Anthony Hamilton
(c) Jeffrey Johnstone
(d) Shawn Carter

2. By what name did Archibald Alexander Leach gain Hollywood fame?
(a) Erroll Flynn
(b) James Dean
(c) Jimmy Durante
(d) Cary Grant

3. What was Tina Turner's original name?
(a) Alana Barrow
(b) Anna Mae Bullock
(c) Alicia Bourne
(d) Anita Bullough

4. Robert Zimmerman found fame under what name?
(a) Boris Pickett
(b) Bob Marley
(c) Bob Dylan
(d) Bob Probert

5. Norma Jean Mortensen became which Hollywood legend?
(a) Marilyn Monroe
(b) Audrey Hepburn
(c) Sandra Bullock
(d) Doris Day

6. By which name did actor/director Melvin Kaminsky become famous?
(a) Mel Olaes
(b) Mel Gibson
(c) Mel Brooks
(d) Mel Blanc

7. Rugby-playing Richard Walter Jenkins found greater fame as which movie star?
(a) Richard Rogers
(b) Richard Dreyfus
(c) Richard Pryor
(d) Richard Burton

8. What was Judy Garland's name before she became a movie star?
(a) Frances Gumm
(b) Mary Jane Gumm
(c) Lorna Luft
(d) Virginia Gumm

9. What is Vincent Furnier's stage name?
(a) Noddy Holder
(b) Alice Cooper
(c) Eric Clapton
(d) Tommy Steele

10. Marion Morrison became which very masculine movie star?
(a) John Wayne
(b) Gary Cooper
(c) Alan Ladd
(d) Errol Flynn

11. Marshall Bruce Mathers III is better know by which single name?
(a) Eminem
(b) Nelly
(c) Jaheim
(d) Ashanti

12. Allen Konigsberg is better known by which name?
(a) Alan Alda
(b) Alan Arkin
(c) Woody Allen
(d) Tim Allen

ROMEO AND JULIET

1. What was Juliet's family name in the Shakespeare tragedy *Romeo and Juliet*?

(a) Montagu   (b) Duncan

(c) Capulet   (d) Laurence

2. How long were Brooke Shields and Andre Agassi married before their annulment?

(a) 720 days   (b) 620 days

(c) 820 days   (d) 520 days

3. Which was King Lear's favorite daughter?

(a) Megan   (b) Regan

(c) Cordelia   (d) Goneril

4. To which playwright was Marilyn Monroe married?

(a) Michael Frayn   (b) Arthur Miller

(c) Tom Stoppard   (d) Sean O'Casey

5. Who were the central lovers in *The Merchant of Venice*?

(a) Antonio and Portia

(b) Bassanio and Nerissa

(c) Lorenzo and Jessica

(d) Leonardo and Salerna

6. To whom was Mike Tyson first married?

(a) Sheila Ferguson

(b) Desiree Washington

(c) Robin Givens

(d) Zena Garrison

7. In *The Merry Wives of Windsor*, who does Mistress Quickly marry?

(a) Nym   (b) Pistol

(c) Falstaff   (d) Bardolph

8. To whom was Britney Spears married for less than 72 hours in 2004?

(a) Michael Richards

(b) Richard Fancy

(c) Len Lesser

(d) Jason Alexander

9. Who were the central characters in *The Tempest*?

(a) Caliban and Sebastiana

(b) Banquo and Adriana

(c) Prospero and Miranda

(d) Alonza and Francesca

10. Who are the two tragic lovers in Emily Brontë's novel *Wuthering Heights*?

(a) Heathcliff and Catherine Earnshaw

(b) Lockwood and Nelly Dean

(c) Edgar Linton and Isabella

(d) Hareton Earnshaw and Catherine Linton

11. For whom does Malvolio have unrequited passion in *Twelfth Night*?

(a) Maria   (b) Viola

(c) Olivia   (d) Antonia

12. Which D.H. Lawrence novel was banned from sale in the 1920s and 1930s?

(a) *Sons and Lovers*

(b) *Lady Chatterley's Lover*

(c) *Women In Love*

(d) *The Lost Girl*

LITTLE AND LARGE

1. Danny De Vito played whose twin in the movie comedy *Twins*?

(a) Mel Gibson

(b) Arnold Schwarzenegger

(c) Tom Selleck

(d) Steven Seagall

2. Robert Wadlow is the tallest man ever recorded, but how tall was he?

(a) 8 ft, 11.1 in (2.72 m)

(b) 8 ft, 7.4 in (2.63 m)

(c) 9 ft, 3.2 in (2.82 m)

(d) 8 ft, 9.8 in (2.69 m)

3. Born in Corsica, who was "the Little General" who died in St. Helena in 1821?

(a) Jean Valjean

(b) Napoleon Bonaparte

(c) General Garibaldi

(d) Louis Moilanen

4. In which country was 7 ft, 7 in (2.3 m) NBA player Manute Bol born?

(a) Germany   (b) Nigeria

(c) USA   (d) Sudan

5. Which actor played Tattoo in the TV series *Fantasy Island*?

(a) Felix Silla

(b) Arturo Gil

(c) Hervé Villechaize

(d) Verne Troyer

6. Standing 6 ft, 9 in (2.1 m), Dallas Cowboys footballer Ed Jones had what nickname?

(a) Too Tall   (b) Longfellow

(c) The Stick   (d) Master Blaster

7. Who was "The Little Sparrow," a famous singer around World War II?

(a) Judy Garland

(b) Sally Bowles

(c) Edith Piaf

(d) Vera Lynn

8. Who was Britain's tallest prime minister at 6 ft, 3 in (1.9 m)?

(a) Harold Wilson

(b) Edward Heath

(c) John Major

(d) James Callaghan

9. Who was the first woman jockey to win a US Triple Crown horse race?

(a) Muriel Tufnell

(b) Julie Krone

(c) Donna Barton

(d) Diane Nelson

10. After which *Sesame Street* character was 6 ft, 8 in (2.1 m) cricketer Joel Garner nicknamed?

(a) Big Bird

(b) Elmo

(c) Cookie Monster

(d) Grover

11. How tall was nineteenth-century Parisian artist Henri de Toulouse-Lautrec?

(a) 5 ft, 2 in (1.6 m)

(b) 3 ft, 3 in (1 m)

(c) 4 ft, 4 in (1.4 m)

(d) 4 ft, 11 in (1.5 m)

12. Who or what was 7 ft, 3 in (2.2 m) Peter Mayhew's part in *Star Wars*?

(a) C-3PO   (b) Darth Vader

(c) Chewbacca   (d) R2-D2

BEAUTY AND THE BEAST

1. Who won the Junior Miss Georgia title in 1970?

(a) Susan Sarandon   (b) Jane Fonda

(c) Goldie Hawn   (d) Kim Basinger

2. What sea creature has scared Japanese moviegoers for more than half a century?

(a) King Ghidorah   (b) Mothra

(c) Godzilla   (d) Baragon

3. Which dance group did Terry Hall, Jerry's twin, join in 1963, their inaugural season?

(a) Dallas Cowboy Cheerleaders

(b) Playboy Playmates

(c) Ballet Rambert

(d) Dallas Ballet

4. Who played the possessed little girl in the 1973 movie *The Exorcist*?

(a) Katie Winn   (b) Linda Blair

(c) Ellen Burstyn   (d) Gina Petrushka

5. How many Grand Slam tennis double titles did Anna Kournikova win?

(a) Six   (b) None

(c) Two   (d) Four

6. Whose nightmare visitations were at the heart of the *Nightmare on Elm Street* series?

(a) Corne Krieger   (b) David Kreig

(c) Olivier Krug   (d) Freddie Krueger

7. In which movie did Cameron Diaz fall in love with NFL star Brett Favre?

(a) *Any Given Sunday*

(b) *Minority Report*

(c) *My Best Friend's Wedding*

(d) *There's Something About Mary*

8. When does Jason Voorhees create mayhem?

(a) Thanksgiving Day

(b) Groundhog Day

(c) Friday the 13th

(d) Independence Day

9. Which model married rock star Rod Stewart in 1990?

(a) Elle Macpherson   (b) Naomi Campbell

(c) Rachel Hunter   (d) Heidi Klum

10. Who was the bellringer in Victor Hugo's novel *The Hunchback of Notre Dame*?

(a) Quasimodo   (b) Frollo

(c) Phoebus   (d) Gringoire

11. With which character did Heidi Klum have an affair in the TV series *Spin City*?

(a) Paul Lassiter

(b) Mayor Winston

(c) Michael Flaherty

(d) Carter Heywood

12. Which murderous character was a human incarnation of a vampire bat?

(a) Nosferatu   (b) Lord Greystoke

(c) Frankenstein   (d) Count Dracula

UPS AND DOWNS

1. What was the name of the British mission to Mars that disappeared in 2004?

(a) Retriever I   (b) Beagle II

(c) Labrador II   (d) Pointer I

2. What was the name of marine scientist Jacques Cousteau's boat?

(a) *Calypso*   (b) *Deep Blue Sea*

(c) *Marine I*   (d) *Rumba*

3. How did Phineas Fogg cross the Alps in *Around the World in 80 Days*?

(a) He skied

(b) He went by train

(c) He flew in a balloon

(d) He rode a herd of elephants

4. What fish can be found in its natural habitat at 660 ft (200 m) deep in the ocean?

(a) Marlin   (b) Swordfish

(c) Shark   (d) Coelacanth

5. Which French brothers devised the first hot air balloon?

(a) Canard   (b) Avion

(c) Oiseau   (d) Montgolfier

6. In what plane did Charles Lindbergh become the first transatlantic pilot?

(a) *Spirit of St. Louis*

(b) *Pride of Pittsburgh*

(c) *Wonder of Washington*

(d) *Charm of Chicago*

7. How did submarine captains survey the sea aound them before sonar?

(a) Gyroscope   (b) Periscope

(c) Arthroscope   (d) Telescope

8. Near to which North Carolina town did the first manned flight take place?

(a) Durham   (b) Charlotte

(c) Kittyhawk   (d) Statesville

9. What is used to measure the depth of oceans at their deepest points?

(a) Fathometer   (b) Anemometer

(c) Barometer   (d) Thermometer

10. While still remaining on land, how high is it possible to go?

(a) 32,990 ft (10 km)

(b) 29,028 ft (8.9 km)

(c) 17,935 ft (5.5 m)

(d) 24,623 ft (7.6 km)

11. What was the name of the first submarine, a one-man craft built in 1775?

(a) *Lobster*

(b) *Sea-Beetle*

(c) *Turtle*

(d) *Crab*

12. Which capital city is at the highest altitude?

(a) Mexico City

(b) La Paz

(c) Brasilia

(d) Montevideo

YIN AND YANG

1. Which world boxing champion doesn't have a daughter who has boxed professionally?

(a) Joe Frazier

(b) George Foreman

(c) Mike Tyson

(d) Muhammad Ali

2. Who was the world's first woman prime minister?

(a) Mrs. Margaret Thatcher

(b) Mrs. Sirimavo Bandaranaika

(c) Mrs. Golda Meir

(d) Mrs. Indira Gandhi

3. Which summer Olympic sport is open to men and women in the same contest?

(a) Hockey   (b) Mountain biking

(c) Show-jumping   (d) Rowing

4. Which British era was also the title of a 1989 movie about a messy separation?

(a) War of the Roses

(b) Peterloo Massacre

(c) Profumo Affair

(d) Norman Conquest

5. Which drag artist duetted with Elton John on the 1994 cover of "Don't Go Breaking My Heart?"

(a) Lily Savage   (b) Rupaul

(c) Tedi Bear   (d) Alexis Miranda

6. In which species of animal does the female attempt to kill the male after mating?

(a) Squid   (b) Shark

(c) Snake   (d) Spider

7. Who was the first woman to play in an NHL hockey game, albeit an exhibition?

(a) Pam Postema

(b) Manon Rhaume

(c) Shirley Babashoff

(d) Irina Rodnina

8. Which English king got rid of a wife because she did not bear male children?

(a) George III   (b) Charles I

(c) Henry VIII   (d) Edward V

9. In what year were women jockeys licensed to ride by Britain's Jockey Club?

(a) 1905   (b) 1972

(c) 1937   (d) 2003

10. Which regulation forced US colleges to have sexual equality in classes and in sport?

(a) Title IV   (b) Title XI

(c) Title VI   (d) Title IX

11. When did women vote in all Swiss local and national elections?

(a) 1994   (b) 1912

(c) 1946   (d) 1804

12. Rebecca Felton was the first woman senator in the US, but how long did she serve?

(a) 4 months   (b) 21 years

(c) one day   (d) five weeks

True or False Quizzes (for answers *see* pages 380 to 382)

IN THE SCIENCE LAB

1. Nitrogen is the most common gas on Earth. ☐T ☐F
2. H_2SO_4 is the compound for water. ☐T ☐F
3. A bunsen burner can only be lit using helium gas. ☐T ☐F
4. Louis and Marie Pasteur invented electricity. ☐T ☐F
5. The study of insects is etymology. ☐T ☐F
6. Archimedes discovered his theory of measuring volume taking a bath. ☐T ☐F
7. Einstein's Theory of Relativity can be expressed by the equation $E=MC^2$. ☐T ☐F
8. Chemistry using carbon substances is called inorganic. ☐T ☐F
9. Air pressure is measured on a barometer. ☐T ☐F
10. Anatomists study the human form. ☐T ☐F
11. The higher the altitude the harder it is to breathe. ☐T ☐F
12. Carbon monoxide makes drinks bubbly. ☐T ☐F
13. The chemical symbol for gold is Au. ☐T ☐F
14. The lowest possible temperature, called Absolute Zero, is −954°F (−723°C). ☐T ☐F
15. An astrologer studies the stars and the galaxy. ☐T ☐F
16. Doctors must take the Hippocratic Oath before they can practice. ☐T ☐F
17. Dynamite was invented by Alfred Nobel. ☐T ☐F
18. The boiling point of all substances is 212°F (100°C). ☐T ☐F
19. Thomas Alva Edison was born in the nineteenth century. ☐T ☐F
20. The study of mammals is herpetology. ☐T ☐F
21. Lead is the heaviest element in the Periodic Table. ☐T ☐F
22. Wind is measured in isobars. ☐T ☐F
23. Humans exhale nitrogen. ☐T ☐F
24. Iridology involves studying part of the human eye. ☐T ☐F
25. A calendar year is exactly 365 days. ☐T ☐F
26. Isaac Newton's theory of gravity came when he was hit on the head by a falling apple. ☐T ☐F
27. The Kelvin scale of temperature measurement begins at Absolute Zero. ☐T ☐F
28. Penicillin was discovered in the seventeenth century, but not used on humans for 200 years. ☐T ☐F
29. The chemical symbol for chlorine is Cl. ☐T ☐F
30. Botany is the study of bays. ☐T ☐F

ON THE SPORTS FIELD

1. A javelin is thrown from within a circle. ☐T ☐F
2. All bats used in Major League baseball must be made of wood. ☐T ☐F
3. The original basketball net was actually a peach basket and not a net. ☐T ☐F
4. A *dohyo* is a Japanese sumo wrestling ring. ☐T ☐F
5. A bookmaker must accept a bet at the odds quoted. ☐T ☐F
6. All the spikes on an athlete's shoe are the same height. ☐T ☐F
7. A triple salchow is an ice-skating routine. ☐T ☐F
8. Boxers practice on a pommel-horse. ☐T ☐F
9. There is no live ammunition in a track and field starter's gun. ☐T ☐F
10. Only the cox in a rowing eight looks in the direction the boat is going. ☐T ☐F
11. The only common apparatus in men's and women's gymnastics is the floor. ☐T ☐F
12. Jockeys in trotting races sit in a sulky. ☐T ☐F
13. A Canadian football field is 30 yards longer, including end-zones, than an NFL field. ☐T ☐F
14. The foil is one of three weapons used in fencing. ☐T ☐F
15. Dressage is a show-jumping discipline. ☐T ☐F
16. Field and ice hockey use the same ball. ☐T ☐F
17. An ippon is a wrestling hold. ☐T ☐F
18. Ribbons and hoops are all used in different rhythmic gymnastics disciplines. ☐T ☐F
19. A baseball diamond is actually a rhombus. ☐T ☐F
20. A behind is a score in Australian rules football. ☐T ☐F
21. Curling and hurling are the same sports, just native to Scotland and Ireland. ☐T ☐F
22. The target ball in bowls is called a jack. ☐T ☐F
23. A limiter forces racing cars to slow down entering the pits. ☐T ☐F
24. The biathlon combines downhill skiing and ski-jumping. ☐T ☐F
25. Not all basketball fouls result in free throws. ☐T ☐F
26. Referees must wear black or black and white stripes in all ball sports. ☐T ☐F
27. A tsukohara is a type of gymnastic vault. ☐T ☐F
28. A baseball foul line ends at the foul pole. ☐T ☐F
29. A triple toe lutz is a type of karate kick. ☐T ☐F
30. An albatross or double-eagle cannot be achieved on a par-three golf hole. ☐T ☐F

AT THE MOVIES

1. Walt Disney Studios has never won an Oscar in any category. T F
2. "Springtime for Hitler" was a song from *The Producers*. T F
3. *The Great Escape* was set in a World War II prisoner-of-war camp. T F
4. Jack and Millwood were the Blues brothers in the movie of the same name. T F
5. *The Godfather* was based on a novel by Don Corleone. T F
6. The character Robin did not appear in the 1989 movie *Batman*. T F
7. The Oscar ceremony always takes place at Graumann's Theatre in Hollywood. T F
8. Mime artist Marcel Marceau has the only spoken role in 1976's *Silent Movie*. T F
9. "Take My Breath Away" is the theme song to *Top Gun*. T F
10. Gary Cooper won an Oscar for his role in *High Noon*. T F
11. Eddie Murphy starred with Chevy Chase in *Trading Places*. T F
12. *The Hunt for Red October* is about a Soviet nuclear submarine. T F
13. Leni Riefenstahl directed the movie of the 1936 Olympic Games, *Olympia*. T F
14. John Shaft was played by Richard Roundtree in the 1971 movie *Shaft*. T F
15. *Cabaret* was set during World War I. T F
16. "In space, no-one can hear you scream" was the tagline for *Space Balls*. T F
17. Alfred Hitchcock directed the 1963 movie *The Birds*. T F
18. *The Italian Job* had Michael Caine as the criminal mastermind in prison. T F
19. "Can't act. Can't sing. Balding. Can dance a little," was the unkind comment on Fred Astaire's first screen test. T F
20. The *Back to the Future* movie trilogy was in strict chronological order. T F
21. The theme tune to *The Sting* was "Raindrops Keep Falling On My Head." T F
22. Sergio Leone was the leading director of the Spaghetti Western genre. T F
23. *Glen Or Glenda* was the last movie Bela Lugosi starred in. T F
24. Ronald Reagan played the lead role in the biopic *Knute Rockne: All American*. T F
25. Tobe Cooper directed the original *The Texas Chainsaw Massacre* in 1974. T F
26. Whoopi Goldberg starred as a singing nun in *Sister Act*. T F
27. Robin Williams was nominated for an Oscar for his role in *Mrs. Doubtfire*. T F
28. Dom DeLuise plays Chief Inspector Dreyfus in the *Pink Panther* movies. T F
29. Peter Cushing was a regular cast member in Hammer horror movies. T F
30. *Gone With The Wind* was set in Georgia in the 1840s. T F

IN THE ART GALLERY

1. Rodin's first name was Auguste. **T F**
2. The Sistine Chapel has been on display away from The Vatican twice. **T F**
3. Andy Warhol was at the heart of the Pop-Art movement. **T F**
4. Perspective Painter Paolo Uccello belonged to the Renaissance Movement. **T F**
5. Thomas Chipperfield was a great eighteenth-century furniture-maker. **T F**
6. Manet's *Strawberries* is displayed at New York's Metropolitan Museum of Art. **T F**
7. The Prado Museum and Art Gallery is in Milan. **T F**
8. Michaelangelo painted *The Last Supper*. **T F**
9. Rembrandt was a Dutch master. **T F**
10. Salvador Dali painted in the nineteenth century. **T F**
11. Pieter Brueghel painted *The Tower of Babel* in the sixteenth century. **T F**
12. Surrealism was a twentieth-century art movement. **T F**
13. The biggest family of Russian nesting dolls (each fitting in the next largest one) is 84. **T F**
14. Artist René Lalique gave his name to a range of jewelry. **T F**
15. Berthe Morisot was the only woman in the Renaissance Artists' school. **T F**
16. Impressionist artists met in France in the nineteenth century. **T F**
17. J.M.W. Turner was famous for painting "matchstick" men and women. **T F**
18. Paul Gauguin was living in Haiti when he painted *On the Beach* in 1891. **T F**
19. René Descartes painted *The Waterlilies*. **T F**
20. The *Mona Lisa* is on display at The Louvre. **T F**
21. Rodin carved *The Thinker* in the seventeenth century. **T F**
22. Rembrandt painted seven self-portraits between 1629 and 1669. **T F**
23. Vincent van Gogh painted *Sunflowers* in 1889, ten years before his death. **T F**
24. Robert Mapplethorpe was a controversial late-twentieth-century photographer. **T F**
25. Claude Monet painted numerous London scenes. **T F**
26. Sandro Botticelli was an early Italian Renaissance painter. **T F**
27. Michaelangelo's sculpture *Bust of David* is made from clay. **T F**
28. Leonardo Da Vinci painted *The Last Supper* and the *Mona Lisa*. **T F**
29. Pablo Picasso was the greatest Italian artist of the twentieth century. **T F**
30. Fabergé eggs were created for the Russian court in the nineteenth century. **T F**

IN OUTER SPACE

1. Sirius is also known as the Dog Star. ☐T ☐F
2. The space shuttle orbits the Earth 16 times per day. ☐T ☐F
3. The Sun has two moons. ☐T ☐F
4. The rings of Saturn are bands of vanadium. ☐T ☐F
5. A solar eclipse occurs when another planet moves across the Sun. ☐T ☐F
6. The core temperature of the Sun is around 27 million°F (15 million°C) ☐T ☐F
7. The *Voyager I* craft discovered that there are rings around Jupiter. ☐T ☐F
8. Ursa Major is known as the Little Bear. ☐T ☐F
9. American astronomer Eric Halley discovered the comet bearing his name. ☐T ☐F
10. The night sky remains the same irrespective of where you are on Earth. ☐T ☐F
11. Our solar system has nine planets. ☐T ☐F
12. The Sun is further away from Earth than the nearest constellation. ☐T ☐F
13. A light year is the distance travelled in a lightship in 12 months. ☐T ☐F
14. Pluto was not discovered until 1930. ☐T ☐F
15. A meteor is a smaller version of a meteorite. ☐T ☐F
16. It takes Neptune around 165 Earth years to make a complete orbit
    of the Sun. ☐T ☐F
17. Phobos is one of the two moons of Mars. ☐T ☐F
18. Uranus was the planet most recently discovered. ☐T ☐F
19. Earth lies between Venus and Mercury in the Solar System. ☐T ☐F
20. Moons are satellites orbiting around a planet. ☐T ☐F
21. Jupiter is the planet closest to the Sun. ☐T ☐F
22. The Moon is larger than Pluto. ☐T ☐F
23. The moons of Uranus are named after female characters
    in William Shakespeare plays. ☐T ☐F
24. A comet is always visible with the naked eye every 65 years. ☐T ☐F
25. The first lunar landing, *Apollo XI*, was in the Sea of Tranquility. ☐T ☐F
26. The climate of Mars is warmer than that of Earth. ☐T ☐F
27. A year on Mercury is around 88 Earth days. ☐T ☐F
28. Italian Galileo Galilei was the first astronomer to use a telescope to
    study stars. ☐T ☐F
29. Distances to other constellations in the galaxy are measured in
    light years. ☐T ☐F
30. Venus is the only planet in the Solar System without a moon. ☐T ☐F

UNDERNEATH THE SEA

1. Plankton are the smallest of all water creatures. T F
2. A great white shark can attack prey at 150 mph (240 k/h). T F
3. Whales are not fish but mammals. T F
4. The first modern diving bell dates back to the sixteenth century. T F
5. Saltwater crocodiles can also be found in freshwater. T F
6. All forms of marine life are carnivores (eat only meat). T F
7. The Pacific Ocean is the world's largest body of water. T F
8. Atlantic salmon also live in the Pacific Ocean. T F
9. Tuna are the world's largest freshwater fishes. T F
10. Dolphins are mammals. T F
11. The average piranha weighs in excess of 44 lb (20 kg). T F
12. The Great Barrier Reef off the Australian coast is the world's largest coral. T F
13. The killer whale is a species of dolphin. T F
14. The Loch Ness Monster is a giant conger eel. T F
15. Octopi use their tentacles to trap food. T F
16. Sea snakes are varieties of eel. T F
17. Barnacles that attach themselves to boats feed on the metal of the hull. T F
18. Not all species of shark are man-eaters. T F
19. Sea anemones trap food on their tentacles. T F
20. The heaviest recorded lobster weighed 22 lb (10 kg). T F
21. The Arctic Ocean is the world's most southerly body of water. T F
22. North Atlantic cod is a popular food fish. T F
23. A shark will only attack if its dorsal fin is above the waterline. T F
24. Seahorses belong to the *hippocampus* family. T F
25. Marine turtles can drown. T F
26. A female killer whale has a life expectancy of 30 years and a male 20 years. T F
27. The poison from a stone fish can be fatal to humans. T F
28. A decompression chamber will help a deep-sea diver avoid the bends. T F
29. More than twenty species of fish live in the Dead Sea. T F
30. The world's longest-surviving breed of fish is the coelacanth. T F

IN THE EYE OF THE STORM

1. All hurricanes are given names that follow in alphabetical order.   T F
2. Extreme weather has never closed Minneapolis-St. Paul airport.   T F
3. A monsoon is a type of wind in India.   T F
4. The strongest winds on Mount Everest were measured at 50 mph (80 k/h). T F
5. Los Angeles, California, has had temperatures of 115°F (46°C)
   in September.   T F
6. Severe foggy conditions are very common in Italy's Po Valley.   T F
7. A tsunami is exclusively a Pacific tropical rainstorm.   T F
8. Some of the world's worst maritime weather conditions are off Cape Horn. T F
9. It has never snowed in Florida.   T F
10. Extreme heat or cold can cause railway tracks to crack and buckle.   T F
11. Around 95 percent of Mumbai's annual rain falls in June–September.   T F
12. A typhoon is a tornado which twists in a clockwise direction.   T F
13. The lowest recorded temperature in Vorkuta, Russia, is −58°F (−46.8°F).   T F
14. In an average year in Hammarfest, Norway, it rains on 364 days.   T F
15. Bad weather caused a sporting event at Houston's indoor
    Astrodome stadium to be postponed.   T F
16. Avalanches are invariably caused by local thunderstorms.   T F
17. A tropical storm becomes a hurricane if it lasts more than two hours.   T F
18. During the hottest summer on record, the icecap of
    Mount Kilimanjaro melted.   T F
19. It is impossible to forecast the exact path of a hurricane at its fiercest.   T F
20. The volcanic eruption of Mount Etna in 2000 was caused
    by a lightning bolt.   T F
21. Pea-souper fog was a problem in London until smokeless
    fuel became popular.   T F
22. Tropical cyclones only form if the ocean temperature exceeds 80°F (27°C). T F
23. The worst snowstorm to hit the US dropped 59 in (1.5 m)
    in 24 hours in 1992.   T F
24. The world's three worst outbreaks of flooding were reported in China.   T F
25. Tornadoes are inland versions of hurricanes and never hit coastal regions. T F
26. In 218 BC, Hannibal lost 18,000 men and 2,000 horses and elephants
    in avalanches as he crossed the Alps to fight the Romans.   T F
27. Nazret in Ethiopia had more than 4,000 days with rainfall 1990–2004.   T F
28. Extreme smog in New York City killed around 400 people in
    November 1966.   T F
29. A Category 1 hurricane is more devastating than a Category 5 hurricane.   T F
30. All hurricanes reach land during the night hours.   T F

IN THE RESTAURANT

1. Bouillabaisse is a fried fish dish. ☐T ☐F
2. Queen Elizabeth so enjoyed a steak banquet that she dubbed it "Sir Loin." ☐T ☐F
3. Tofu is meat-free soya produce. ☐T ☐F
4. Calamari is a dish of fried squid. ☐T ☐F
5. Calzone is a normal pizza only folded in half before baking. ☐T ☐F
6. Spam was invented in the 1930s as spiced ham. ☐T ☐F
7. Kosher cuisine in the Jewish faith forbids shellfish. ☐T ☐F
8. Taramasalata is pink because of the raspberries blended into it. ☐T ☐F
9. Poppadums and nan bread are side orders in a curry house. ☐T ☐F
10. Zucchini and aubergine are the same vegetable. ☐T ☐F
11. Sunny, easy is a hard-boiled egg with the shell removed and quartered. ☐T ☐F
12. Chow mein is Chinese noodles, served with either meats, or vegetables, or both. ☐T ☐F
13. Pollo sorpreso is a chicken kiev only using dark meat not white. ☐T ☐F
14. Gravadlax is a Scandinavian dish of smoked salmon smoked with dill. ☐T ☐F
15. Peanut sauce is commonly served with Thai dishes. ☐T ☐F
16. The Muslim diet requires meat to be prepared in the Halal method. ☐T ☐F
17. Kedgeree is eggs, rice, and chicken fried in tomato juice. ☐T ☐F
18. Apfel strudel is a German delicacy of roast apple halves with a honey coulis. ☐T ☐F
19. Fusilli are pasta parcels filled with meat or vegetables. ☐T ☐F
20. South Indian curries are normally milder than those served in the north. ☐T ☐F
21. Welsh rarebit is a dessert with fruit and cheese. ☐T ☐F
22. Goulash is a Hungarian meat dish. ☐T ☐F
23. The meat used in a classic shish kebab is lamb. ☐T ☐F
24. Soya beans are baked beans boiled in soy sauce. ☐T ☐F
25. A churro is a cinammon-coated sweetbread from Mexico. ☐T ☐F
26. A napoli dish in Italy is one served with tomato sauce. ☐T ☐F
27. Sauerkraut is red cabbage stewed overnight with molasses and beetroot. ☐T ☐F
28. In orthodox Hindu cuisine, beef and veal dishes are forbidden. ☐T ☐F
29. A Poor Boy is a Louisiana soup with meat and vegetables. ☐T ☐F
30. Beef Wellington is steak or a beef joint baked inside a pastry crust. ☐T ☐F

ON THE TELEVISION

1. *M*A*S*H* was set during the Korean War. T F
2. In the sitcom *Cheers*, "Mayday" Malone's name was Sal. T F
3. *The Monty Python's Flying Circus* team first met
   at the University of London. T F
4. Colin Firth played Mr. Darcy in the 1995 version of *Pride and Prejudice*. T F
5. *The Third Rock From The Sun* refers to Earth's position in the
   Solar System. T F
6. *Red Dwarf* is set on a Jupiter Mining Ship. T F
7. Frasier Crane was married to Carla Tortelli before returning to Seattle. T F
8. Joey and Monica in *Friends* were brother and sister. T F
9. The main Cable News Network studios are in Atlanta, Georgia. T F
10. Hanna Barbera produced historical dramas in the 1960s. T F
11. Ricky Gervais played David Trent in the comedy series *The Office*. T F
12. The spoof soap *Soap* revolved around the Tate and Campbell families. T F
13. Pamela Anderson Lee appeared in early episodes of *Home Improvement*. T F
14. *The Golden Girls* was set in Orlando, Florida. T F
15. The late British actor John Thaw played a police sergeant, police
    inspector, and a judge. T F
16. In the first series of *Roseanne*, Roseanne Barr was dating
    John Goodman. T F
17. The bookshop where Ellen DeGeneres was manager in *Ellen* was Read On. T F
18. The original *CSI Crime Scene Investigation* was set in Las Vegas. T F
19. Dick Rowan and Dean Martin teamed up for the comedy show *Laugh In*. T F
20. Yogi Bear lives in Jellystone National Park. T F
21. Each of the four *Blackadder* series was set in a different historical era. T F
22. *Who Wants To Be A Millionaire?* was first broadcast in 1994. T F
23. County General Hospital is the setting for *ER*. T F
24. The Ewings' family home in *Dallas* was South Park Ranch. T F
25. Peter Falk was the murder detective in the long-running *Columbo* series. T F
26. David Letterman replaced Johnny Carson as the host of
    The Tonight Show. T F
27. *The Phil Silvers Show* portrayed the life of Sergeant Ernest Bilko. T F
28. Calista Flockhart had a big part in *Sex and the City*. T F
29. Sabrina in *Sabrina, The Teenage Witch* has two aunts, Hilda and Zelda. T F
30. *Law & Order: Special Victims Unit* is set in Los Angeles. T F

ON THE CATWALK

1. Donna Karan's first collection came out in 1984. T F
2. Mary Quant used to model her own creations. T F
3. Dolce & Gabanna are based in Venice, Italy. T F
4. After Gianni Versace's 1997 murder, his sister Sandra took over the company. T F
5. Paris is at the heart of the French fashion industry. T F
6. Richard Burton began the Burton menswear chain in 1964. T F
7. The mini-skirt craze was a feature of the 1960s and early 1970s. T F
8. French designers Benetton displayed their first collection in 1996. T F
9. Jean-Claude Gaultier's collections are famous for being risqué. T F
10. Heidi Klum was the face of Victoria's Secret in 2004. T F
11. Vivienne Westwood designed punk rock fashion in the 1970s. T F
12. Nino Cerutti worked for Giorgio Armani during 1961–1964. T F
13. René Lacoste was a top tennis player before moving into fashion. T F
14. Christian Dior celebrated its 50th anniversary in 1997. T F
15. Milan Prada is the chief designer at Prada. T F
16. Ralph Lauren invented the polo-neck shirt. T F
17. Jasper Conran's mother wrote the best-selling book *Superwoman*. T F
18. Kate Moss was the face of Christian Dior in the 1990s. T F
19. Karl Lagerfeld moved to France from Germany at the age of 14. T F
20. Twiggy was the face of the Swinging Sixties in London. T F
21. Naomi Campbell went to stage school before becoming a model. T F
22. Stella McCartney is the daughter of former Beatle Paul McCartney. T F
23. Tommy Hilfiger didn't enter the fashion world until he was 34 years old. T F
24. Claudia Schiffer was the face of Chanel in the early 1990s. T F
25. Paul Smith's first shirt collection was shown in 1982. T F
26. Before becoming a designer, Yves St. Laurent was France's top jockey. T F
27. In the 1985 movie *Back To The Future* Michael J. Fox's character wore Calvin Klein underwear. T F
28. Linda Evangelista once claimed she didn't get out of bed for less than $100,000. T F
29. Louis Vuitton has stores in more than 90 countries around the world. T F
30. Hugo Boss models were ball girls at the 2004 Madrid Tennis Open. T F

wordsearches

```
L N G N O K G N I K A R B L A E A M
T O O F G I B L Y P R A H N R R L O
N D C E W T A U R M S S T I E Y L G
O A A H S O D A R I N F A F M M I S
G L L I N K R O L R A W B F I A Z E
R I Y C A E D D E R E N U I H N D D
O T D H O N S K S L P I E R C T O Y
G E O R L K R S N E Y E R G A H G C
S Y N Y L O S O M N A M P H M I O R
U A I S U P M A C O P R I H E A L O
S N A A U N G H T I N C C Y L N E H
A D N O F G Q L Y Y N S B H O B M P
G I B R B D R Y A D R U T J P O E H
E H O M E R M A I D R X V E A A R O
P C A F L E P R E C H A U N R R M E
C E R B E R U S P O L C Y C D M E N
W E R E W O L F K R U A T O N I M I
L E V I A T H A N E R I S P H I N X
```

(for answers *see* pages 383 to 392)

US PRESIDENTS

The forty-two Presidents of the United States (and 2004 Democratic candidate Kerry) are listed at the bottom of the page and hidden in the grid below. They are written in a straight line, without gaps, forward, back, up, down or diagonal. Can you find them all?

```
T G E O R G E B U S H S R V K J T G J
A H A R T H U R O L Y A T L O L N W A
F W E N G R E A G A N S O H E L O I C
M I J O O R E C R E I P N V J R T L K
O L E S D X A T A F T A E G O J N L S
N S F N H O I N R O D S B A H H I I O
R O F H A E R N T A O U E R N S L A N
O N E O R S R E M O C S D F A U C M Y
E E R J D O P S R H N N R I D B O H R
R R S W I O J N A O A S O E A E O A R
O U O E G R I N T L O S F L M G L R E
M B N R T L A G E O O S E D S R I R K
I N E D K N N V H O O V E R S O D I M
L A E N H I E T R U M A N V R E G S A
L V A A H L M C K I N L E Y E G E O D
I R Y S C E I S E N H O W E R L T N I
F E A L Y N D O N J O H N S O N T O S
S W B E N J A M I N H A R R I S O N O
Y D E N N E K R E L Y T L I N C O L N
```

JOHN ADAMS JR	HARDING	NIXON
JOHN ADAMS SR	BENJAMIN HARRISON	PIERCE
ARTHUR	WILLIAM HARRISON	POLK
BUCHANAN	HAYES	REAGAN
GEORGE BUSH JR	HOOVER	FRANKLIN ROOSEVELT
GEORGE BUSH SR	JACKSON	THEODORE ROOSEVELT
CARTER	JEFFERSON	TAFT
CLEVELAND	ANDREW JOHNSON	TAYLOR
CLINTON	LYNDON JOHNSON	TRUMAN
COOLIDGE	KENNEDY	TYLER
FORD	KERRY	VAN BUREN
EISENHOWER	LINCOLN	WASHINGTON
FILLMORE	MADISON	WILSON
GARFIELD	MCKINLEY	
GRANT	MONROE	

POP STARS

Here are the names of forty-one recording artists. They are also hidden in the grid at the bottom of the page, but their names are written horizontally, vertically or diagonally, forward or back, always in a straight line without breaks. U2 is spelled out in words and omitted forenames are in brackets. Can you find them all?

AKON	JOJO	N.O.R.E.
BLACK EYED PEAS	JUVENILE WACKO	NELLY
BOWLING FOR SOUP	AND SKIP	SEETHER
RYAN CABRERA	ALICIA KEYS	NINA SKY
CIARA	(AVRIL) LAVIGNE	SNOOP DOGG
KELLY CLARKSON	LIL FLIP	(GEORGE) STRAIT
DESTINY'S CHILD	LIL SCRAPPY	SWITCHFOOT
EMINEM	LIL WAYNE	TERROR SQUAD
SARA EVANS	LINKIN PARK	TRICK DADDY
FABOLOUS	LL COOL J	U TWO
ANTHONY HAMILTON	LOS LONELY BOYS	(KEITH) URBAN
HOOBASTANK	(KEVIN) LYTTLE	USHER
HOUSTON	MASE	(KANYE) WEST
JADAKISS	CHRISTINA MILIAN	GRETCHEN WILSON

```
J U V E N I L E W A C K O A N D S K I P
Y D D A D K C I R T L J L O O C L L J U
Y K N A T S A B O O H I T I M P Y N F O
L R O R I A O J O J A L C N S T O I A S
L A R E A S E S A R I T O I T J W N B R
E P E H R H E D E M E S L L A O T A O O
N N S T T L A R A R L I E W O K U S L F
S I A E S K B H R I L A V I G N E K O G
N K M E I A Y O W E N Y A W L I L Y U N
A N F S C N R N M T O O F H C T I W S I
V I S N O S E S Y O B E L E N O L S O L
E L A H Q H N O S K R A L C Y L L E K W
A Y T U C H R I S T I N A M I L I A N O
R N A T S E W S A E P D E Y E K C A L B
A D E S T I N Y S C H I L D M E N I M E
S R E H S U P I L F L I L S C R A P P Y
G G O D P O O N S U R B A N O T S U O H
```

US GENERALS

Here are the names of forty-two US Army Generals who saw action in World War II. They are also hidden in the grid at the bottom of the page, but their names are written horizontally, vertically or diagonally, forward or back, always in a straight line without breaks. Can you find them all?

ANDERSON	FORT	MCBRIDE
BARTH	GARDNER	MCCORNACK
BOUDINOT	GARLINGTON	MCNAIR
BRANN	GIBBONS	MURRAY
BRAUN	GODFREY	NEWGARDEN
BUCKNER	HOLLAND	PATCH
CARRINGTON	HYDE	PATRICK
CHAMBERLIN	JACKSON	PATTON
CRAIG	KEERANS	PRATT
DALTON	LAYMAN	ROOSEVELT
DARBY	LIM	ROSE
DAVISON	LYMAN	WATSON
EASLEY	MAHIN	WHARTON
EMERY	MAYNARD	WING

```
G A R L I N G T O N L B P A T C H
I B N U A R B L K C I R T A P A Y
A R O D R Y R E M E M A Y N A R D
R A T R E N L V E N O S K C A J E
C N G O R R O E P B S N A R E E K
F N N L I M S S D A O I T F T S N
L N I E A U B O I N T U I G O O O
H I R D N R O O N V A C D R N R T
K L R A C R R R N Y A L H I E S T
C R A L M A H I N E E D L N N N A
A E C T O Y E N P O D R D O M O P
N B M O E D A A R L M R F W H B T
R M O N I N S M A Y A H A D G B O
O A M R E R L Y T G T T O G O I F
C H B E L A E A T R S L N A W G M
C C E N A M Y L A O I I N D E E S
M R E N K C U B N E W H A R T O N
```

SUPERMODELS

Here are the names of sixty-two supermodels. They are also hidden in the grid below, but their names are written horizontally, vertically or diagonally, forward or back, always in a straight line without breaks. Can you find them all?

```
A B L U M E B U N D C H E N A R A M H E
L R L E G N E H A L L Y D A Y Z A E V V
T I E L L I O T T R P A T I T Z L E M A
B N B R S V R B U O E J R F Z E R H S N
A K P E S A E W R M S T E A N H S A C G
N L M D O L V V L I T R L A A V S U H E
K E A L M E I E I J O E Y R O T G A I L
S Y C U L T R N N N V G T N R H U V F I
B E L M T T K D G G A G G E D R P O F S
E K T E G A N E T C D E K W I W Y L E T
N A L N B S W L O N R B E D J D H A R A
I S D C E O P A N K N N K S C S T I U H
T S I M S U N L A O O J W C A C R V D A
E R E E C E F N S T A A O Y U R A A N L
Z H T E E L B R S W L D M V D B C Z A L
I F D B M N E R R A W Y D G O Q C F L V
H O A U M H E S M A I L L I W V M O E S
A R V C P V E L A S Q U E Z G U I U R A
R D D C L J K D E N O S R E D N A C I D
Z E A I M R S V R I A V O K E R A V H A
A M S O C S A M A R U O M Y E S O R R N
I U I K L E I N H R O L Y A T D F E A A
D H E R T Z I G O V A C S A M O H T I C
```

(CAROL) ALT
(JULIE) ANDERSON
(TYRA) BANKS
(ELSA) BENITEZ
(YASMINE) BLEETH
(VERONICA) BLUME
(CHRISTIE) BRINKLEY
(SYBIL) BUCK
(GISELE) BUNDCHEN
(NAOMI) CAMPBELL
(ESTHER) CANADAS
(GIA) CARANGI
(LAETITIA) CASTA
(YAMILA) DIAZ-RAHI
(NICOLE) EGGERT
(GAIL) ELLIOTT
(LONNEKE) ENGEL
(LINDA) EVANGELISTA
(ANGIE) EVERHART
(PATRICIA) FORD
(DAISY) FUENTES
(YASMEEN) GHAURI

(BRIDGET) HALL
(ESTELLE) HALLYDAY
HELENA
(EVA) HERTZIGOVA
(KIRSTY) HUME
(KATHY) IRELAND
(MILLA) JOVOVICH
(CARMEN) KASS
(MARTINA) KLEIN
(HEIDI) KLUM
(YASMIN) LE BON
(JENNY) MCCARTHY
(ELLE) MACPHERSON
(JOSIE) MARAN
(JUDITH) MASCO
(VALERIA) MAZZA
(KATE) MOSS
(KAREN) MULDER
(SARAH) O'HARE
(TATJANA) PATITZ
(DANIELA) PESTOVA
(AISHWARYA) RAI

(GABRIELLE) REECE
(INES) RIVERO
(REBECCA) ROMIJN
(INES) SASTRE
(CLAUDIA) SCHIFFER
(STEPHANIE) SEYMOUR
(ALICIA) SILVERSTONE
(MOLLY) SIMS
(KIM) SMITH
(NIKI) TAYLOR
(SARAH) THOMAS
(CHRISTY) TURLINGTON
(LIV) TYLER
(AMBER) VALETTA
(VERONICA) VAREKOVA
(PATRICIA) VELASQUEZ
VENDELA
(MANON) VON GERKAN
(ESTELLA) WARREN
(STACEY) WILLIAMS
(TATIANA) ZAVIALOVA

MYTHOLOGICAL CREATURES

Here are the names of forty-five creatures from mythology, whether ancient or modern. They are also hidden in the grid below, but their names are written horizontally, vertically or diagonally, forward or back, always in a straight line without breaks. Can you find them all?

```
L N G N O K G N I K A R B L A E A M
T O O F G I B L Y P R A H N R R L O
N D C E N T A U R M S S T I E Y L G
O A A H S I D A R I N F A F M M I S
G L L I N K C O L R A W B F I A Z E
R I Y C A E D I E R E N U I H N D D
O T D H O N S K E L P I E R C T O Y
G E O R L K R S N O Y E R G A H G C
S Y N Y L O S O M N Y M P H M I O R
U A I S U P M A C O P P I H E A L O
S N A A U N G H T I N C H Y L N E H
A D N O F G Q L Y Y N S B L O B M P
G I B R B D R Y A D R U T J P O E H
E H O M E R M A I D R X V E A A R O
P C A F L E P R E C H A U N R R M E
C E R B E R U S P O L C Y C D M E N
W E R E W O L F K R U A T O N I M I
L E V I A T H A N E R I S P H I N X
```

ARGUS	FAFNIR	MERMAID
BASILISK	GODZILLA	MINOTAUR
BIGFOOT	GOLEM	NAIAD
BLOB	GORGON	NEREID
CALYDONIAN BOAR	GREYON	NYMPH
CAMELOPARD	GRIFFIN	PEGASUS
CENTAUR	HARPY	PHOENIX
CERBERUS	HIPPOCAMPUS	PHORCYDES
CHIMERA	HYDRA	SATYR
CHRYSAOR	KELPIE	SIREN
CYCLOPS	KING KONG	SPHINX
DRYAD	LADON	UNICORN
ECHIDNA	LEPRECHAUN	WEREWOLF
ERYMANTHIAN BOAR	LEVIATHAN	WARLOCK
ELF	LOCH NESS MONSTER	YETI

HOLLYWOOD IDOLS

Here are the names of sixty Hollywood legends. They are also hidden in the grid at the bottom of the page, but their names are written horizontally, vertically or diagonally, forward or back, always in a straight line without breaks. Can you find them all?

BASINGER	DIAZ	HOPE	PENN
BOW	EASTWOOD	JACKSON	PHOENIX
BOGART	FLYNN	LEE	POWER
BRANDO	FONDA	LEMMON	REAVES
CHAPLIN	FORD	LONG	REDFORD
CLOONEY	GABLE	LORRE	REEVE
CONNERY	GARBO	MANSFIELD	RUSSELL
COOPER	GARDNER	MARX	SINATRA
CROSBY	GARLAND	MATTHAU	STONE
CROWE	GIBSON	MCQUEEN	STREEP
CRUISE	GOLDBERG	MONROE	TURNER
CURTIS	HANKS	MOORE	VALENTINO
DAVIS	HARDY	MURPHY	WASHINGTON
DEAN	HAYWORTH	NEWMAN	WAYNE
DE NIRO	HEPBURN	O'HARA	WINGER

```
N R U B P E H B T F O N D A V I S
D L E I F S N A M G A R D N E R K
J G P E E R T S S E V A E R M W N
Y R I L S Y N I L P A H C U U A A
E G A B L E I N A N S T D S R S H
N S E I S R E G N I W E I S P H M
O A R A H O V E T K A A A E H I C
O L E M M O N R O N R J Z L Y N Q
L D B Q R M U G H T G N O L D G U
C R O W E C C D A D E N I R O T E
F O U R E O Y N G R E W O P O O E
O F Q V O R I R T R B R H W W N N
R D E P E S E F Y B S O R C T O V
D E E N Y B L B O W E O L E S C A
R R N D D Y A M O N R O E K A R L
A O R L N S F U I G R B C G E U E
C A O N M A R X R R A A R G G I N
H G T U R N E R E E J R S A D S T
O H T R O W Y A H P L S T O N E I
P E N N A M W E N G A R L A N D N
E N Y A W P M A T T H A U L E E O
```

ANIMALS

Here are the names of fifty-two animals. They are also hidden in the grid below, but their names are written horizontally, vertically or diagonally, forward or back, always in a straight line without breaks. Can you find them all?

```
O  M  A  L  P  A  C  A  W  R  A  U  G  A  J  H  K
G  A  O  R  Y  X  Y  R  E  M  U  L  D  S  I  C  A
N  C  A  E  R  S  Y  A  A  K  K  N  L  P  A  R  Y
I  A  L  S  I  E  E  A  S  L  A  O  P  I  R  O  K
D  Q  L  I  P  A  K  O  E  P  T  O  E  P  R  C  A
R  U  I  O  A  H  N  W  L  H  P  U  L  U  E  O  N
A  E  H  T  T  O  O  F  A  O  D  N  I  F  T  D  G
E  A  C  R  V  R  M  I  T  L  D  C  C  F  T  I  A
B  S  N  O  B  S  A  A  L  A  R  E  A  I  O  L  R
R  O  I  T  L  E  M  H  E  I  M  U  N  N  E  E  O
A  R  H  N  I  U  G  N  E  P  R  A  S  U  N  G  O
L  E  C  H  S  E  A  L  I  O  N  D  R  A  Z  I  L
O  C  C  H  I  M  P  A  N  Z  E  E  N  I  D  O  H
P  O  T  I  G  E  R  B  E  A  R  N  F  O  N  A  O
T  N  G  O  S  N  A  K  E  L  N  T  B  A  T  R  N
A  I  I  N  L  T  L  C  I  L  E  T  W  E  U  B  O
K  H  B  B  I  H  O  O  P  L  A  O  E  N  E  E  O
R  R  B  J  Y  M  N  A  L  K  L  H  P  A  R  Z  B
E  U  O  E  Y  W  A  D  T  F  C  R  S  A  T  E  A
E  U  N  A  M  A  L  L  I  G  A  T  O  R  R  E  B
M  A  R  T  E  N  E  F  F  I  R  A  G  S  D  D  R
```

ALLIGATOR	GNU	MEERKAT	SLOTH
ALPACA	GORILLA	MONKEY	SNAKE
ANTEATER	HIPPOPOTAMUS	OKAPI	STOAT
BABOON	HYENA	ORYX	TAMARIN
BEAR	JAGUAR	OTTER	TAPIR
CHEETAH	KANGAROO	PANDA	TIGER
CHIMPANZEE	LEMUR	PELICAN	TORTOISE
CHINCHILLA	LEOPARD	PENGUIN	TURTLE
CROCODILE	LION	POLAR BEAR	WALRUS
DINGO	LIZARD	PUFFIN	WEASEL
FLAMINGO	LLAMA	RHINOCEROS	WOLF
GIBBON	MACAQUE	SEAHORSE	YAK
GIRAFFE	MARTEN	SEALION	ZEBRA

NOVELISTS

Here are the names of sixty famous novelists. They are also hidden in the grid at the bottom of the page, but their names are written horizontally, vertically or diagonally, forward or back, always in a straight line without breaks. Can you find them all?

ALCOTT	DAHL	HEMINGWAY	NAIPAUL
AMIS	DEFOE	HUXLEY	ORWELL
AUSTEN	DICKENS	ISHIGURO	PROUST
BAINBRIDGE	DOSTOEVSKY	JAMES	RUSHDIE
BECKETT	DUMAS	JEROME	SHAW
BELLOW	ELIOT	JOYCE	SPARK
BRONTE	FAULKNER	KAFKA	STEVENSON
BUCHAN	FITZGERALD	KEROUAC	SWIFT
BUNYAN	FLAUBERT	KING	THACKERAY
CAMUS	FORSTER	LAWRENCE	TOLKIEN
CARROLL	GRASS	LE CARRE	TROLLOPE
CERVANTES	GREENE	LONDON	TWAIN
CHANDLER	HARDY	MARQUEZ	WAUGH
COLLINS	HAWTHORNE	MAILER	WILDE
CONRAD	HELLER	NABOKOV	WOOLF

```
H S S A R G O R W E L L U A P I A N B
A U T F I W S K R A P S T W A I N R T
W M T E T H A D E N E I K L O T O U R
T A O E V Z E U Q R A M S V A N L S O
H C C C L E O M G F L F Y H T H P H L
O D L L E C N A I H A L W E I E R D L
R E A K O R F S H A W A Y E T G O I O
N D I N M O V I O A R U A E F H U E P
E N R A R E F A N N E B D T L J S R E
G A E S E Q B P N M N E G T K X T H O
D D T D L W U U W T C R E N K L U A F
I E E D L I W D N B E T F L O O W H E
R H E M I N G W A Y K S V E O T S O D
B E L L O W M A S A A C C A R R O L L
N E H F T O F U D R J N L U E R U Q A
I N A N O D N O L E E L L B L K C W R
A E D I C K E N S K R B A Y D R A H E
B E C K E T T A C O L L I N S U E G
A R B O O K S F D A M T O F A N O L Z
M G N A B O K O V H E H E N H D R L T
I R E L I A M N E T S U A D C O E E I
S E M A J O Y C E E R R A C E L K R F
```

BIRDS

Here are sixty-eight birds. They are also hidden in the grid at the bottom of the page, but their names are written horizontally, vertically or diagonally, forward or back, always in a straight line without breaks. Can you find them all?

ALBATROSS	EGRET	MOCKINGBIRD	PTARMIGAN
BIRD OF PARADISE	FALCON	MOORHEN	PUFFIN
BITTERN	FLAMINGO	MYNAH	QUAIL
BLACKBIRD	GANNET	NIGHTJAR	RAVEN
BLUEBIRD	GOOSE	NUTHATCH	ROBIN
BLUE JAY	GROUSE	ORIOLE	SANDPIPER
BUNTING	HERON	OSPREY	SNIPE
BUZZARD	HORNBILL	OSTRICH	SPARROW
CARDINAL	HUMMINGBIRD	PARROT	STARLING
CASSOWARY	JACKDAW	PARTRIDGE	STORK
CHICKADEE	KESTREL	PEACOCK	SWALLOW
CONDOR	KINGFISHER	PELICAN	SWIFT
CORMORANT	KOOKABURRA	PENGUIN	THRUSH
CRANE	LAPWING	PHEASANT	TOUCAN
CUCKOO	LINNET	PIGEON	TURKEY
CURLEW	MAGPIE	PIPIT	VULTURE
EAGLE	MEADOWLARK	PLOVER	WOODPECKER

```
E E E D A K C I H C O R A V E N A R C E
G A O S T R I C H A D N A W A D K C A J
M A G P I E L O I R O B I N Y E R P S O
O B N L M E I O W D B G N I W P A L S Y
W L I N E Y V M P I L E R T S E K S O E
O A M A E G N I T N U B E L N K O D W K
O C A I R T G A S A E P T J U R W R A R
D K L R P E E S H L J K T N T A E A R U
P B F N O T P S W L A P I A H L L Z Y T
E I R N W D A L I O Y L B C A W R Z O R
C R K R O T S R O D R L Y I T O U U B O
K D S D E H S S M V A R E L C D C B H U
E G H S U R H T W I E R A E H A C S O T
R R O W A L L O W S G R A P N E D T N R
M O C K I N G B I R D A S P S M N A E L
G U D R I B E U L B I R N S F A R P S K
U S X N E H R O O M R D T K S O I D I O
M E E J O N E G R E T A D A M P D N L O
P E A C O C K P Y L R D E R D D G R L K
E R D O T E N N I L A H O N D F N Q I A
N U S R I S T T I N P C A O I A I U B B
G T L W P F S N J G S S S S K L F A N U
U L D R I B G N I M M U H D G C F I R R
I U F W P T O R R A P E K V L O U L O R
N V S N I G H T J A R H E R O N P C H A
```

CAPITAL CITIES

Here are sixty-four capital cities. They are also hidden in the grid below, but their names are written horizontally, vertically or diagonally, forward or back, always in a straight line without breaks. Can you find them all?

```
G N I J I E B B N U O G U O D A G A U O
A A V I M O N R O V I A R O V Z M R L E
T S E R A H C U B E R G A Z A S D R A D
T W A S R A W S S E S R A P T U S E N I
E T H N I C O S I A R L A E B M K B B V
L I L O N G W E L D B L R L O N O N A E
L N I K N I S L E H O D I S G S P A T T
A H W K U A S S A N A N C N O I J C O N
V E B N A H S U D M O O M E T O E T R O
A P E N A I R O B I W T B H A A R R T M
A M S J O H N S A E R S T T B I L I S I
C O P E N H A G E N L D T A Y U U P A S
C H U R R A N G O O N L A T W Q T O D C
U N T U K I P D S H T I I M U A E L D A
H P D S A X A C C R A H E V S R S I I R
D A B A M A L S I U A V Y V A S I L S A
A S U L P I A R O N D S A R N Z I E A C
J U D E A R P Y O N G Y A N G S A R B A
Y I A M L O U I Y L E H Y H A L D R A S
I N P K A T H M A N D U H R S O N U B P
R L E O P E D A R G L E B E D N U O A Y
K I S Q N R N O T G N I H S A W I A D D
L V T M B P R R U P M U L A L A U K A B
```

ACCRA	BUENOS AIRES	KUALA LUMPUR	PRETORIA
ADDIS ABABA	CAIRO	LA PAZ	PYONGYANG
ALGIERS	CANBERRA	LILONGWE	QUITO
AMSTERDAM	CARACAS	LISBON	RANGOON
ATHENS	COPENHAGEN	LONDON	RIYADH
BAKU	DUBLIN	MADRID	SKOPJE
BEIJING	DUSHANBE	MONROVIA	TBILISI
BEIRUT	HANOI	MONTEVIDEO	TRIPOLI
BELGRADE	HARARE	MOSCOW	ULAN BATOR
BERLIN	HAVANA	NAIROBI	VALLETTA
BOGOTA	HELSINKI	NASSAU	VIENNA
BRASILIA	ISLAMABAD	NICOSIA	VILNIUS
BRAZZAVILLE	JERUSALEM	OTTAWA	WARSAW
BRUSSELS	KAMPALA	OUAGADOUGOU	WASHINGTON
BUCHAREST	KATHMANDU	PARIS	YAOUNDE
BUDAPEST	KINSHASA	PHNOM PENH	ZAGREB

crosswords

(for answers *see* pages 393 to 397)

CROSSWORD 1

Across

7	Grain (6)
8	Stiff (6)
9	Rip (4)
10	American river (8)
11	Protectors (7)
13	Country (5)
15	Boat (5)
16	Adhesive label (7)
18	Any (8)
19	Nipple (4)
21	Infertile (6)
22	Development (6)

Down

1	This place (4)
2	Coolers (13)
3	Voted for (7)
4	Enlarge (5)
5	Message (13)
6	Precise (8)
12	Above (8)
14	Depot (7)
17	Happening (5)
20	Against (4)

CROSSWORD 2

Across

1	Leg wear (4)
3	Sample (8)
9	Odd (7)
10	Care for (5)
11	Shortening (12)
13	Draftsman (6)
15	Country (6)
17	Educationist (12)
20	Brotherhood (5)
21	Preparing (7)
22	Part of circle (8)
23	Applies (4)

Down

1	Spouses (8)
2	Clean vigorously (5)
4	Word attachment (6)
5	Building (12)
6	Reflectors (7)
7	Penury (4)
8	Freedom (12)
12	Corridors (8)
14	Country (7)
16	Ring (6)
18	Leaves (5)
19	Money in reserve (4)

CROSSWORD 3

Across

1	Twilight (4)
3	Continent (8)
9	Type (7)
10	Instrument (5)
11	Systems (12)
13	Rock faces (6)
15	Basement (6)
17	Verbal representations (12)
20	Body of water (5)
21	Light (7)
22	Intimates (8)
23	Just (4)

Down

1	Length (8)
2	Absolute (5)
4	Omitted (6)
5	Defending (12)
6	By the sea (7)
7	Mark (4)
8	Implication (12)
12	Detainee (8)
14	Sea hazard (7)
16	Flower (6)
18	Musical drama (5)
19	Animal collections (4)

CROSSWORD 4

Across

7	Substance (6)
8	In want of (6)
9	Physical damage (4)
10	Alumnus (8)
11	Animal skin (7)
13	Additional (5)
15	Thespian (5)
17	Most furious (7)
20	Obstinate (8)
21	Fictional villainous pirate (4)
22	Choosers (6)
23	0.125 expressed as fraction (6)

Down

1	March (6)
2	Particular (4)
3	Drawn slowly (7)
4	Someone acting as an informer (5)
5	Ensued (8)
6	Metal pot (6)
12	Distracted (8)
14	Early colonist (7)
16	Fabric (6)
18	Pathfinders (6)
19	Stoat (anag.) (5)
21	Vast (4)

CROSSWORD 5

Across

7   Higher temperature (6)
8   Score (6)
9   Body part (4)
10 Beaten (8)
11 Increased two-fold (7)
13 Newspaper industry (5)
15 Areas (5)
17 Moves boat (7)
20 Instructive reading (8)
21 Fathers (familiar) (4)
22 Mean (6)
23 Essential qualities (6)

Down

1   Fruit (6)
2   Point (4)
3   Seized (7)
4   Province (5)
5   Cited (8)
6   Those remaining (6)
12 Respires (8)
14 Communicating (7)
16 Removes unwanted
    substances (6)
18 Commodity (6)
19 Nutrients (5)
21 Touches lightly (4)

CROSSWORD 6

Across

1	Delves (4)
3	Merchandize (8)
9	Royalty (7)
10	Wed (5)
11	Enough (12)
13	Patted (6)
15	Apartment (6)
17	Lexicons (12)
20	Inn (5)
21	Clothes (7)
22	Anxious (8)
23	Communists (4)

Down

1	Alluviations (8)
2	Sorrow (5)
4	Former USSR (6)
5	Showed (12)
6	Orbited (7)
7	Tells (4)
8	By hazard (12)
12	Originates (8)
14	Decorator (7)
16	Stiff (6)
18	Egress (5)
19	Bear witness (4)

CROSSWORD 7

Across

1 Moldable (7)
5 Picture (5)
8 Acted (9)
9 Baked pastry (3)
10 Mounts (5)
12 Unwitting (7)
13 Promotional matter (13)
15 Mountainous republic in central Europe (7)
17 Hurry (5)
19 Deuce (3)
20 Remove (9)
22 Tables (5)
23 Nocturnal (7)

Down

1 Composition (5)
2 Mixed gasses (3)
3 Garment (7)
4 Message (13)
5 S. Asia republic (5)
6 Character sets (9)
7 Component (7)
11 Partitions (9)
13 Conformed (7)
14 Repeating (7)
16 Tall perennial grasses (5)
18 Each and all (5)
21 Behave (3)

CROSSWORD 8

Across

7	US state (6)
8	Engage (6)
9	Containers (4)
10	Anticipation (8)
11	Admonition (7)
13	Meanders (5)
15	Opponent (5)
17	Vocalists (7)
20	Without deviation (8)
21	Crosspiece (4)
22	Austere (6)
23	Bread portions (6)

Down

1	North American country (6)
2	Entangles (4)
3	Osculation (7)
4	Obtuse (5)
5	Accelerating (8)
6	Chucked (6)
12	Enumerated (8)
14	Form of transport (7)
16	Rackets (6)
18	Hired (6)
19	Additional (5)
21	Interpret (4)

CROSSWORD 9

Across

1 Fireworks (7)
5 Cervices (5)
8 Part of a circle (13)
9 Not me! (3)
10 Finest (9)
12 Sibling (6)
13 Missive (6)
15 Flat (Brit.) (9)
16 Medium for broadcasting (3)
18 Reference books (13)
20 Unclean (5)
21 Draws out (7)

Down

1 Stony (5)
2 Conditions (13)
3 Instrumentation (9)
4 Gentler (6)
5 And not (3)
6 Density (13)
7 Garment (7)
11 Handling (9)
12 Algae (7)
14 Dispatch (6)
17 Climbs (5)
19 Vociferation (3)

CROSSWORD 10

Across

7   Woody tropical grass (6)
8   Score plus ten (6)
9   Meddling (4)
10 Bunglers (8)
11 Diverting (7)
13 Connotation (5)
15 Hasten (5)
17 Four squared (7)
20 Discrete (8)
21 Curl (4)
22 Barely (6)
23 Formula (6)

Down

1   Absence of matter (6)
2   Conform (4)
3   Attacking with munitions (7)
4   Commonwealth (5)
5   Least heavy (8)
6   Garners (6)
12 Protections (8)
14 Chronicle (7)
16 Aristocrat (6)
18 Leave out (6)
19 Forefinger (5)
21 Deficiency (4)

CROSSWORD 11

Across

7 Woodland (6)
8 Suit (6)
9 Conceited (4)
10 Sufferers (8)
11 Travel (7)
13 Leans (5)
15 Chemise (5)
17 Garb (7)
20 Canopy (8)
21 Mammals (4)
22 Sternutation (6)
23 Spiralled (6)

Down

1 Tuber (6)
2 Edible seed (4)
3 Halted (7)
4 Exposure (5)
5 Sidewalk (8)
6 Declared (6)
12 Umpires (8)
14 Aromatic herb (7)
16 People (6)
18 Apple pie maker? (6)
19 Foreigner (5)
21 Lure (4)

CROSSWORD 12

Across

7 Cover (6)
8 Feet (6)
9 Circuit (4)
10 Functionary (8)
11 Entertainers (7)
13 Home of Mahatma
   Gandhi (5)
15 Anxiety (5)
16 Red (7)
18 Germs (8)
19 Small parasitic
   arachnid (4)
21 Clandestine (6)
22 Sufficient (6)

Down

1 Reverberate (4)
2 Iceboxes (13)
3 Inside (7)
4 Period at work (5)
5 Assiduity (13)
6 Proportional (8)
12 Apart (8)
14 Abraded (7)
17 Verity (5)
20 Coop (4)

CROSSWORD 13

Across

1 Fraction (7)
5 Confronted (5)
8 Perimeter (13)
9 Thee (3)
10 Youngsters (9)
12 Bug (6)
13 Sampled (6)
15 Affirmation (9)
16 Conjunction (3)
18 Books? (13)
20 Neglected? (5)
21 Broadens (7)

Down

1 Rot (5)
2 Conditions (13)
3 Facial hair (9)
4 Elevated (6)
5 Because (3)
6 Absorption (13)
7 Attired (7)
11 Habitation (9)
12 Alternatively (7)
14 Turn into (6)
17 Furniture (5)
19 Exclaim (3)

CROSSWORD 14

Across

1 Adhering to established standards and principles (7)
5 Jumps (5)
8 Intensifies (9)
9 Confound (3)
10 Square root of 64 (5)
12 Otalgia (7)
13 Logical proof (13)
15 Female relation (7)
17 Snow leopard (5)
19 Consume (3)
20 Flimsiest (9)
22 Fires (5)
23 Baby's room (7)

Down

1 Periodically repeated sequence of events (5)
2 Aspire (3)
3 Abbreviate (7)
4 Density (13)
5 Failure (5)
6 Fondness (9)
7 Four squared (7)
11 Acrobatic (9)
13 Academic awards (7)
14 Additional (7)
16 Plates (5)
18 Debut (5)
21 Hole in a needle (3)

CROSSWORD 15

Across

7 Frozen region (6)
8 Themes (6)
9 Fuzz (4)
10 Oblique (8)
11 Celebrate (7)
13 Questioned (5)
15 Regular transport (5)
17 Occasion for rest? (7)
20 Posts (8)
21 Additional (4)
23 Greenest (6)
24 Invitees (6)

Down

1 Domain (4)
2 Hunger (6)
3 Accomplish (7)
4 Contemplate (5)
5 Musical entertainments (6)
6 Dessert (8)
12 Uttered without voice (8)
14 Subject matter (7)
16 Preferably (6)
18 Motifs (6)
19 Vessels (5)
22 Locate (4)

CROSSWORD 16

1		2		3			4	5		6		7
						8						
9							10					
11					12							
	13	14					15					
16												17
18				19			20		21			
22					23							
24						25						

Across

1   Crude (6)
4   Electorate (6)
9   Adoration (7)
10 Appreciation (5)
11 Majestic (5)
12 Accept (7)
13 Nearing (11)
18 Tableland (7)
20 Fruit (5)
22 Appointments (5)
23 Fetch (7)
24 Seat (6)
25 Rhythms (6)

Down

1   Poltroon (6)
2   Regalia (5)
3   Student (7)
5   Frequently (5)
6   Oriental (7)
7   Confectioneries (6)
8   Outstanding (11)
14 Deep-rooted (7)
15 Fit (7)
16 Shovels (6)
17 Profundities (6)
19 Tripod (5)
21 Jewel (5)

CROSSWORD 17

Across

1	Mends (7)
5	Trusted (5)
8	Closest (7)
9	Lariat (5)
10	Panorama (5)
11	Wearing away (7)
12	Barbarian (6)
14	Nailed down (6)
17	Cock (7)
19	Coerce (5)
22	Clan (5)
23	Resolved (7)
24	Rush (5)
25	React (7)

Down

1	Relative status (5)
2	Serenity (5)
3	Cold floater! (7)
4	Sofa (6)
5	Greeting (5)
6	Aggressive (7)
7	Overwhelmed (7)
12	Graffito (7)
13	Instruments (7)
15	Brings about (7)
16	Monger (6)
18	Near objects? (5)
20	Wireless (5)
21	Concluded (5)

CROSSWORD 18

Across

1 Retainer (7)
5 Compact masses (5)
8 Emeritus (7)
9 Egress (5)
10 Hue (5)
11 Curdled milk (7)
12 Pouch (6)
14 More secretive (6)
17 Flat highland (7)
19 Heartbreak (5)
22 Organs (5)
23 Burrows (7)
24 Mobilize (5)
25 Contractile organs (7)

Down

1 Clean vigorously (5)
2 Magnitude relation (5)
3 Bring about (7)
4 Present ages (6)
5 Mendacious (5)
6 Depositories (7)
7 Protect (7)
12 Democratic (7)
13 Conduit (7)
15 Fables (7)
16 Tradition (6)
18 Try (5)
20 Nonpareil (5)
21 Hands (5)

CROSSWORD 19

Across

7 Fruit (6)
8 Nuclear (6)
9 Hither (4)
10 Cosmetic (8)
11 Obscure (7)
13 Honkytonks (5)
15 Nation (5)
16 Petition (7)
18 Downright (8)
19 Notion (4)
21 Times present (6)
22 Disappear (6)

Down

1 Factual (4)
2 External (13)
3 Guys (7)
4 Bivouacs (5)
5 Donations (13)
6 Rooms (8)
12 E.g., diary (8)
14 Get (7)
17 Cat (5)
20 Cardinal compass point (4)

CROSSWORD 20

Across

7 Less frigid (6)
8 Cleans with hot water (6)
9 Cab (4)
10 Plumage (8)
11 Facets (7)
13 Curiously (5)
15 Rap (5)
17 Male deliverer of mail (Brit) (7)
20 Water travel (8)
21 Groundless (4)
23 Large bodies of water (6)
24 Senior (6)

Down

1 Molten rock (4)
2 A group of countries under a single authority (6)
3 Earnings (7)
4 Habitual (5)
5 Way of doing (6)
6 Collapsible shelter (8)
12 Snack (8)
14 Languages (7)
16 Punctuation (6)
18 Result of dividing by three (6)
19 Beginning (5)
22 Bemused (4)

CROSSWORD 21

Across

7   Rather painful (13)
8   Curbs (8)
9   Relation (4)
10 Day (7)
12 Supernatural powers (5)
14 Aspects (5)
16 Small one-story house (7)
19 Menageries (4)
20 Dusk (8)
22 Unluckily (13)

Down

1   To (archaic) (4)
2   Time divisions (6)
3   Pertaining to a continent (7)
4   Triangular shape made of glass (5)
5   Fruit (6)
6   Embedding (8)
11 Mythical beasts (8)
13 Moves (7)
15 Sagacity (6)
17 Thrice X (6)
18 Say (5)
21 Vestibule (4)

CROSSWORD 22

Across

7 Lacking grace (6)
8 Word attachment (6)
9 Planet (4)
10 Wedlock (8)
11 Entirely (7)
13 Contributed (5)
15 Submit (5)
17 Rambling (7)
20 Single-celled organisms (8)
21 Tub (4)
22 Transparent opening (6)
23 Dancing halls (6)

Down

1 Edible tuber (6)
2 Sums (4)
3 Fauna (7)
4 Flicker (5)
5 Recalled (8)
6 Unmarried (6)
12 Height (8)
14 Warlocks (7)
16 Very sad (6)
18 Whimsy (6)
19 Gang (5)
21 Occupied (4)

CROSSWORD 23

Across

1	Slashes (4)
3	Taped (8)
9	Causing inconvenience (7)
10	Donated (5)
11	Therefore (12)
14	Weapon (3)
16	Sets of two (5)
17	Final resting place of apples? (3)
18	Accounts (12)
21	Separator (5)
22	Brusquer (7)
23	House servant (8)
24	Limbs (4)

Down

1	Carbonaceous material (8)
2	Owned (5)
4	Finish (3)
5	System (12)
6	Grow (7)
7	Completed (4)
8	Bugs (12)
12	Mating (5)
13	Assesses (8)
15	Most (7)
19	Further from middle (5)
20	Harsh or corrosive (4)
22	Winter transport (3)

CROSSWORD 24

Across

1 Vascular plant (4)
3 Something used to beautify (8)
9 Head protectors (7)
10 Interprets text (5)
11 Accordingly (12)
13 Demesne (6)
15 Feels (6)
17 Pertaining to scientific investigation (12)
20 Extremely sharp or intense (5)
21 Draw or pull out (7)
22 Benediction (8)
23 Quarrel (4)

Down

1 Conveyances (8)
2 A synthetic fabric (5)
4 Deliverance (6)
5 Orderly groupings (12)
6 Renders capable (7)
7 Flipping a coin (4)
8 However (12)
12 Diastole (anag.) (8)
14 The feel of a surface (7)
16 Bird (6)
18 Business deal (5)
19 A sweet innocent mild-mannered person (4)

CROSSWORD 25

Across

1	Sharp curve (4)
3	Dawn (8)
9	Demanding (7)
10	E.g., lawsuits (5)
11	Agitate (5)
12	Endured (6)
14	Tiny (6)
16	Happenings (6)
19	Utilize (6)
21	Absorbent cloth (5)
24	Cookers (5)
25	Welfare (7)
26	Bodily openings (8)
27	Exploited (4)

Down

1	Good-looking (8)
2	E.g., Carmen (5)
4	Spiritual beings (6)
5	Supports (5)
6	Oriental (7)
7	Osculate (4)
8	Surpassing in quality (6)
13	Detached (8)
15	Amounts (7)
17	Balloting (6)
18	Standing for (6)
20	Failure (5)
22	Swings at futilely (5)
23	Bony outgrowth (4)

CROSSWORD 26

Across

7 Deny food (6)
8 Condiment (6)
9 Precipitation (4)
10 Guidance (8)
11 Omnivorous nocturnal mammal (7)
13 Midsection (5)
15 Phones (5)
17 Brings together (7)
20 Capital of South Carolina (8)
21 Excavates (4)
22 Sebaceous (6)
23 Positions occupied by professors (6)

Down

1 Part of poem (6)
2 Gang (4)
3 Meeting (7)
4 Rate of travel (5)
5 Near (8)
6 Ball game (6)
12 Relating to arts (8)
14 A state of equilibrium (7)
16 On a ship (6)
18 Esteem (6)
19 Conforms (5)
21 Gully (US) (4)

CROSSWORD 27

Across
1 Closed (4)
3 Waver (8)
9 Copy (7)
10 Exams (5)
11 Modern (12)
14 Addition (3)
16 Location (5)
17 Gone by (3)
18 Accounts (12)
21 Denotes brief pause (5)
22 Tales (7)
23 Relating to the home (8)
24 Social insects living in organized colonies (4)

Down
1 Grip (8)
2 Pairing (5)
4 Hole in needle (3)
5 Carrefour (12)
6 European country (7)
7 Gentle (4)
8 Larvae (12)
12 Level open land (5)
13 Originates in (8)
15 The most (7)
19 Edible bulb (5)
20 Turns litmus red (4)
22 Implement for winter sport (3)

CROSSWORD 28

Across

1 A good deal (4)
3 Farm vehicles (8)
9 Apparels (7)
10 Famed (5)
11 Procreation (12)
13 Involving grief or death (6)
15 Repository (6)
17 Numerical (12)
20 Unit of weight (5)
21 Presently (7)
22 Freedom from normal restraints (8)
23 Heavy dull sound (4)

Down

1 Preside over (8)
2 Inexpensive (5)
4 Deliver (6)
5 Building (12)
6 Consequence (7)
7 Team (4)
8 Amazement (12)
12 Put into service (8)
14 Anti (7)
16 Diverted (6)
18 Hidden drawback (5)
19 Make filthy (4)

CROSSWORD 29

Across

1   Groups of, e.g., trees (6)
4   Smaller in amount (6)
9   Reaching destination (7)
10 Hobo (5)
11 Paragon (5)
12 Applauded (7)
13 Involving joint action (11)
18 Ocean (7)
20 Relation (5)
22 Precise (5)
23 Close-fitting pullover garments (7)
24 Conundrum (6)
25 Any mature animals (6)

Down

1   Not moving (6)
2   Concur (5)
3   Gradually acquire new characteristics (7)
5   More than is needed or required (5)
6   Cleansing agent (7)
7   Waterways (6)
8   A form of energy (11)
14 Grove (7)
15 Affected emotionally (7)
16 Look (6)
17 Meals eaten by service personnel (6)
19 Deadly (5)
21 A variable hue averaging a deep pink (5)

CROSSWORD 30

Across

1   Responses (7)
5   Chocolate drink (5)
8   To heat before eating (5)
9   Include (7)
10 In a relative manner (13)
11 Put up with (6)
12 Discontinued (6)
15 Delayers of decay (13)
18 Examine and note the similarities or differences (7)
19 Figure of speech (5)
20 A tentative attempt (5)
21 Meals (7)

Down

1   Garret (5)
2   Shut noisily (7)
3   Far more than usual or expected (13)
4   Relating to human society and its members (6)
5   A fee charged for work done (13)
6   Lifts and moves heavy objects (5)
7   Aroused to impatience or anger (7)
11 Localized pain (7)
13 Abdomen (7)
14 Expose (6)
16 Smokes (5)
17 Stalks (5)

answers

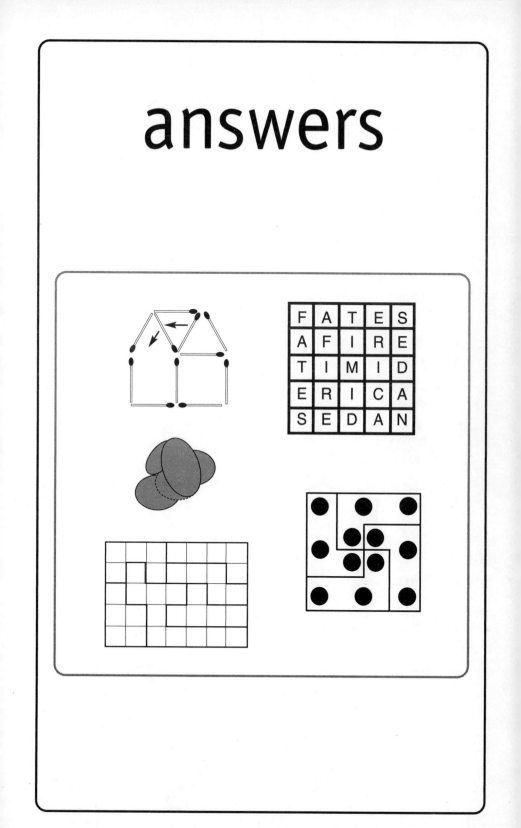

MATCHSTICK PUZZLES

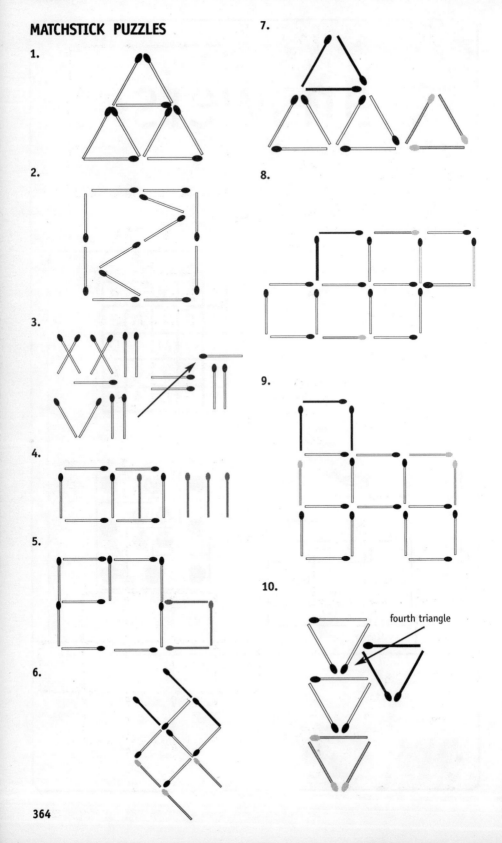

1.

2.

3.

4.

5.

6.

7.

8.

9.

10.

fourth triangle

11.

Answer 1   Answer 2

Answer 3   Any order of three is correct.

12.

13. square   The right match moves to make a square in the middle.

14.

15.

16.

17.

18.

19.

20.

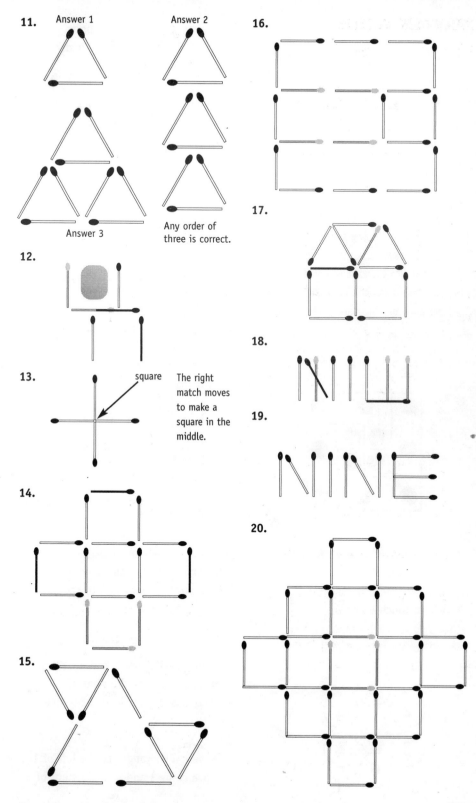

COIN GAMES

1. You can do it with 5 coins. Put one down and then place two more halfway and horizontally on the first coin. Now place the two remaining coins like a roof.

2. Move the bottom coin up two places.

3. Take a table knife and lay it at the side of the coin with the blunt edge facing the coin. Now strike the coin sharply with the knife and it will slip straight out. The inertia of the bottle keeps it from moving. This takes practice!

4. You push the cork into the bottle and shake the coin free.

5.

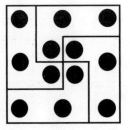

6. There are 2 coins at each corner.

7. These are the three moves:
Move 4 to touch 5 and 6.
Move 5 to touch 1 and 2.
Move 1 to touch 5 and 4.

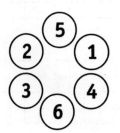

8. 1. Move 1 to below the bottom row and place it between and under 8 and 9.
2. Move 7 up two rows and place to the left of 2.
3. Move 10 up two rows and place it to the right of 3.

9.

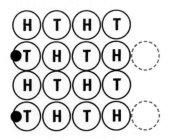

10. Put your first and second fingers on the marked coins and drag them round into the positions shown is the diagram below:

H T H T
T H T H ○
H T H T
T H T H ○

Keep your fingers on those same two coins and push six coins (those on the second and bottom rows) to the left. There, you've done it!

11.
1. Move coins 1 and 2 to the right of 6.
2. Move 6 and 1 to the right of 2
3. Move 3 and 4 to the right of five.

12.
1. Move coins 6 and 7 to the left of 1.
2. Move coins 3 and 4 to the right of 5.

3. Move 7 and 1 to the right of 2.
4. Move 4 and 8 to the right of 6.

13. Always count in the same direction, missing one coin each time before starting the next count.

14. Answer 1

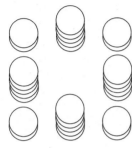

Two coins at each corner and piles of 5 coins between them.

Answer 2

Eight piles of 3 coins each.

Answer 3

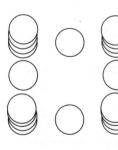

Four coins at each corner and single coins between them.

PENTOMINOES

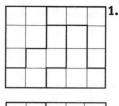

1.

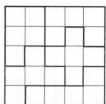

2.

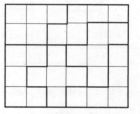

3.

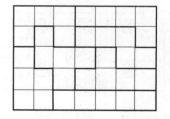

4.

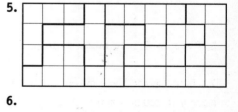

5.

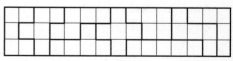

6.

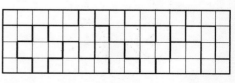

7.

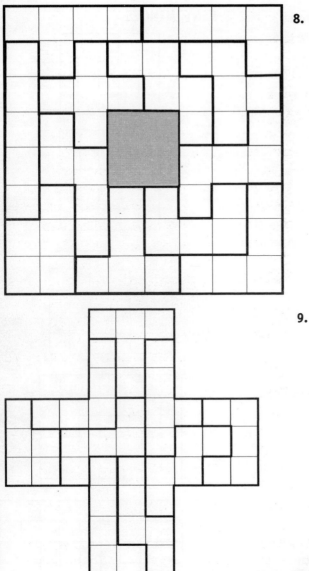

8.

9.

CHESS PROBLEMS

1. 1.Qd7+ Kh6 2.Qg7+ Kh5 3.Qh7+ Kg4 4.Qxg6+.

2. 1.Nb6+ (if 1...axb6, 2.Qa8 mate).

3. 1...f3+ (if 2.Kg1, there follows Qxf1+ 3.Kxf1 Rd1 mate).

4. 1...Rxh3 2.Rc5 (if 2.gxh3, 2...Nf3+) Qg3 3.Qxg3 Ne2+ 4.Kh1 Nxg3+ 5.Kg1 Ne2+ with a piece ahead. 3.fxg3 and 3.hxg3 each lead to a quick checkmate.

5. 1.Qxb4 axb4 2.Rxa8+ (if 2...Be8, 3.Bxd5 Qxd5 4.Rxe8 mate. If 2...Qe8, 3.Rxe8+ Bxe8; 4.Bxd5+ wins easily).

6. 1...Rxb2 2.Ra2 (if 2.Bxb2, Ne5 3.fxe5 g5 mate) 2...Rxa2 3.h3 Rh2 4.Rh1 Rxh1 5.Be3 Rxh3 mate.

7. 1. Rh1+ Kg8 2.Rh8+ Kxh8 3.Rh1+ Kg8 4.Rh8+ Kxh8 5.Qh1+ Kg8 6.Qh7 mate.

8. 1.Bxf6 Re2 2.Rc8+ Qxc8 3.Qxh6+ Kg8 4.Qxg7 mate.

9. 1.Qxd7+ Rxd7 2.Re8+ Rd8 3.R(either)xd8 mate.

10. 1...Qxg3 2.fxg3 Rd8+ 3.Kf1 Rxc8.

11. 1.Qd5+ Kh8 2.Nf7+ Kg8 3.Nh6+ Kh8 4.Qg8+ Rxg8 5.Nf7 mate.

12. 1...Qxe2 2.Rxe2 Rc1+ 3.Ne1 Rxe1+ (if 3...Rxe2? 4.Qb8+) 4.Rxe1 Rxe1 mate.

13. 1...Rxh2+ 2.Rxh2 Rxh2+ 3.Kxh2 Nf3+ 4.Rxf3 Qxd2+.

14. 1.Bg7+ Kf7 2.Qe6+ Nxe6 3.dxe6 mate.

15. 1.Bb5 Qxb5 2.Rxh7+ Kxh7 3.Qh5+ Bh6 4.Qxh6 mate.

16. 1.Be1 fxe1=Q 2.Rf8 mate.

17. 1.Ra1 bxa1=Q 2.Qb7 mate.

18. 1.Re8 Kxh1 2.Kf2 e1Q+ 3.Rxe1 mate.

19. 1.bxa8=N Kxg2 2.Nb6 Bxb6 3.a8=Q mate.

20. 1.Rh3 b3 2.Rh1 gxh1Q+ 3.Qxh1 mate.

21. 1.Qe7+ Nxe7 2.Nf6+ Kd8 3.Nxf7+ Kc7 4.Bf4+ d6 5.Bxd6 mate.

22. 1...Qxb2+ 2.Kxb2 R8a2+ 3.Kc1 Ba3 mate.

23. 1...Qh3+ 2.Kh1 Qf1+ 3.Bg1 Qxf3 mate.

24. 1.Rfg5 Kf8 (Kf7 2.Rxg7+) 2.Rxg7

Ke8 3.Rh8 mate.

25. 1.Bxh6 Ne8 (1...gx6 2.Qg3+ Ng4 3.Qxg4+ Qg5 4.Nxh6+) 2.Bxg7 Nxg7 3.Nxg7 Kxg7 4.Qg4+ Kh7 5.Rf5.

26. 1.Qxc6+ bxc6 2.Bxa6+ Qb7 3.Nxe7 mate (or 2...Kd7 3.Nf6 mate).

27. 1.Qg4 Qxg4 2.Bf6 mate (or 1...Qd6 2. Bf6+ Qxf6 3.Qxg8 mate).

28. 1.Qe4+ Kd7 2.Qg4+ Kc6 3.Qa4+ Kd5 4.Qe4 mate (or 1...Kb5 2.Rb1+ Ka5 3.Qb4+ Ka6 4.Qb5 mate).

29. 1.Nxc5+ dxc5 2.Qe7+ Kc6 3.Qxc7+ Kxd5 4.c4+ Ke4 5.Qxb7+.

30. 1.Rd3+ Kc8 2.Rc3+ Kb8 3.Qc7+ Ka8 4.Qa5+ Kb7 5.Qb4+ Ka6 6.Qa3+ Kb7 7.Qb2+ Ka8 8.Ra3 mate.

31. 1.Na3+ (not 1.Nc3+ or 1...Kxc2 2.Nxa2 stalemate) Kc1 2.Rb3 Qa1 3.Kd3 Qa2 4.Rb1+.

32. 1.Rxd4 cxd4 (if 1...Qxh5 2.Rxd8 mate) 2.Qxf5.

33. 1.Kf1 Kd2 2.Kf2 Kd1 3.Ke3 Ke1 4.Rc1 mate.

34. 1.Ra2 Kxa2 2.Nc3 mate (If 1...b3xa2 2.Na3 (or Nc3) mate.

35. 1.Qa1 Bxa1 2.Rb2 Bxb2 3.Bxb2 mate.

36. 1.Kf5 e6+ 2.Kf6 Kh8 3.Kf7 mate.

37. 1.Nf6 Kxh1 2.Ng4 Bh2 3.Nxf2 mate.

38. 1.Nh1 gxh1=Q+ 2.Qxh1 mate (any other move by Black also results in immediate mate).

39. 1.Bg2 a6, 2.Qxa6 mate (if 1...Rxg8+ 2.Qxg8 mate or 1...Bxg2 2.Qxg2 mate).

40. 1.Qc7 e3, 2.Qc2 mate (if 1...Ke3, 2.Qg3 mate.

41. 1.g4 e6 2.f3 Qh4 mate.

42. 1.Qxc6+ bxc6 2.Ba6 mate.

MEMORY GAMES

HANDBAG
Address book, Bandages, Bottle, CD player, Chewing gum, Chocolate bar, Comb, Compact, Diary, Eyeliner pencil, Keys, Lipstick, Magazine, Mascara, Mobile phone, Perfume, Purse, Sunglasses, Ticket, Toilet bag.

SCHOOLBAG
Apple, Calculator, Candy, Cap, Dividers, Eraser, Exercise book, Fruit juice, Magnifying glass, Pencil, Pencil case, Pencil sharpener, Report card, Ruler, Sandwich, Scissors, Schoolbook, Spinning top, Tickets, Yo-yo.

BACKPACK
Binoculars, Camera, Candy, Compass, First aid kit, Flask, Fleece, Gas point, Gloves, Map, Matches, Padlock, Pan, Penknife, Rope, Scarf, Sleeping bag, Socks, Torch, Whistle.

BEACH BAG
Beach ball, Book, Bucket & spade, Can of drink, CD player, Deck chair, Frisbee, Glasses, Goggles, Hat, Ice cream, Mobile phone, Net, Pillow, Purse, Sandals, Snorkel, Suntan lotion, Towel, Waders.

WHEELBARROW
Broom, Fork, Flower pot, Gloves, Gnome, Hat, Hoe, Hose, Markers, Plastic sacks, Rake, Secateurs, Seedling tray, Seeds, Shears, Spade, Trowel, Watering can, Weedkiller, Wellington boots.

BRIEFCASE
Apple, Bunch of flowers, Comb, Contract, Envelope, Folder, Hi-liter pens, Keys, Mobile phone, Newspaper, Palm pad, Paperclips, Pen, Pencil, Sandwich, Spectacles, Stamps, Tie, Umbrella, Wallet.

SHOPPING CART
Apples, Bananas, Bottle of soda water, Bread, Butter, Cake, Cans of drink, Cheese, Cherries, Corn, Eggs, Grapes, Milk, Peppers, Potatoes, Radish, Sausages, Spring onion, Tin of fish, Tomato.

GOLF BAG
Balls, Binoculars, Cup, Driver, Glove, Keys, Membership card, Mobile phone, Pencils, Putter, Rulebook, Scorecard, Shoes, Socks, Sunshades, Sweater, Tees, Umbrella, Visor, Windbreaker.

TOILET BAG
Compact, Cotton balls, Curling tongs, Dental floss, Deodorant, Duck, Hairbrush, Hairdrier, Handcream, Lipstick, Loofah, Nail polish, Nailclipper, Razor, Shampoo, Shaving foam, Soap, Tablets, Toothbrush, Toothpaste.

TOOLBOX
Drill, Flask, Glue, Hammer, Handcleaner, Hinge, Lunchbox, mallet, Nails, Pliers, Ruler, Scraper, Screwdriver, Stanley knife, Tape, Tape measure, Trowel, Vise, Wrench.

NUMBER PUZZLES

1. 10:00 a.m.
2. 784. Consecutive square numbers, reading top left, bottom right, top right, bottom left.
3. $8.
4. 5. 7 x 9 = 63; 5 x 5 = 25.
5. 15 mph.
6. 26. c = a + d; b = c + d; e = b + c.
7. 37c. Each letter in the first half of the alphabet is worth 7c; each letter in the second half of the alphabet is worth 3c.
8. 245. Add the last two numbers, then add 1 to obtain the next number.
9. The 98 employees received $22 each.
10. 23. Hearts = 7; Clubs = 9; Diamonds = 5; Spades = 2.
11. 224 miles.
12. 24 and 8.
13. Four minutes.
14. Nine. This works no matter what the number of baskets is.
15. $65.32.
16. Unfortunately this is a trick question! To make the average speed 60 mph, the car would have had to go from Boston to New York in no time at all – which is, of course, impossible.
17. $6.
18. One pen, nine pencils and 90 paperclips.
19. 30 and 44. The sequence comprises the non-prime numbers from 30 to 44.
20. 88.
21. 22. Alternately multiply by two and add two.
22. 6/14.
23. CCC
24. Dogs = 12; horses = 9; cats = 7; pigs = 5.
25. 45. Stars = 12; Crosses = 9; Flowers = 10.
26. Five.
27. Six ways. 20–5–0; 20–3–2; 15–10–0; 15–5–5; 12–10–3; 10–10–5.
28. 67.5 months.
29. 11 minutes 38 seconds.
30. Eight units long and five units wide.
31. Six and three.
32. 32. Peppers = 7, Suns = 13, Boxes = 4, Targets = 8.
33. 5. For each block of three numbers, the middle figure is the product of the other two.
34. 68 paces and 40 paces.
35. 6. Each pair of digits in the top row is a number representing the product of the two digits below it. 9 x 7 = 63; 7 x 8 = 56.
36. Ten.
37. $200.
38. 21 times.
39. 73.
40. Any number! This formula will always give you the number you first thought of, with 00 at the end.

VISUAL REASONING PUZZLES

1. B. It is the only figure which is not a Roman number rotated through 2700.
2. B.
3. C. When it is rotated it is a mirror image of the others.
4. 10
5. D. The figure rotates 90° clockwise each time.
6. E.
7. A. When it is rotated it is a mirror image of the others.
8. 10.
9. D. A and E form an opposite pair, as do B and C.
10. C.
11. B. When it is rotated, it is a mirror image of the others.
12. C.
13. B.
14. D.
15. A. When it is rotated it is a mirror image of the others.
16. 11.
17. A. The dots move alternately one position clockwise around the long figure.
18. A.
19. 27.
20. B.

LATERAL THINKING PUZZLES

1. The man was a lighthouse keeper and it was his responsibility to keep the light shining at all times. He had absent-mindedly turned off the light before going to bed and a ship had plowed into the rocks with terrible consequences.
2. "F" appears six times. "Of" appears twice and most people look for a "ph" sound.
3. By throwing the ball straight up in the air.
4. The friend was male and his name was Michael.
5. If, as we were told, there is no keyhole on the inside of the door, the lock must be of the Yale type. Fred simply turned the latch and walked out.
6. Eric is a teacher.
7. While the family was out, a pipe had burst and the floor was under two inches of water on which the balloons were floating.
8. The simplest way is to read the label on the end of the reel.
9. The night watchman was fired for sleeping on the job.
10. Horse racing.
11. He keeps ducks (or geese, or turkeys, or quail).
12. The cat. Fred and Ginger were goldfish, and the cat had knocked their bowl over.
13. The lady had suffered a heart attack and her heart had stopped. The man was a doctor. The punch to her chest had restarted her heart, after which he carried her to

his car and took her to the hospital where she made a full recovery.

14. The surgeon is the patient's mother.

15. Drop the egg from a height of four feet. It falls three feet without anything happening – 12 inches later, you have a mess on the floor.

16. The "housebreaker" was her husband and they had locked their keys inside the house.

17. None. The clock has four faces each with two hands, but Big Ben is the name of the bell inside the clock tower and not the clock itself.

18. The family had to sail across the sea before they could begin climbing. Unfortunately, their cabin went below the waterline once the ship was laden, and a faulty porthole had caused it to fill with seawater. The water pressure had held the door shut and the crew had been unable to save the family.

19. The man was a priest who presided over the marriage ceremonies of each of his sisters.

20. Arthur and Barry, along with their brother Charlie, are triplets.

LOGIC PUZZLES

1. 14 (eight females and six males).

2. From the information given, we know the girls' ages range from eight to eleven. The surname of Rebecca, the eleven-year-old (2), is not Black (1), Gray (5) or Green (6), so must be Brown. She was given the pony (3). The girl who received the CD player must therefore be the ten-year-old (5), whose surname is Green (6). This means that the daughter of the Grays must be the eight-year-old (5). She did not receive the pony or the CD player, or the doll (7), so must have been given the bike, and must therefore be Kelly (4). By elimination the surname of the nine-year-old must be Black. Her first name is Gemma (1). This means the eight-year-old is Kelly Gray and Tammy Green received the CD player.

3. 400 miles. The cyclists are going at 15 mph and 20 mph, so they close the gap between them at a combined speed of 35 mph. This means they meet after ten hours, having ridden 150 miles and 200 miles, respectively. The trick is to ignore the individual trips made by the fly and concentrate on the time it takes for the bikes to meet, which we have seen is ten hours. Therefore, the fly, flying at a speed of 40 mph, has covered 400 miles in total.

4. A. The series is of the second letter in the days of the week, from Monday. Saturday is next.

5. Step 1: Singer and guitarist walk across (2 minutes)
Step 2: Singer brings flashlight back (1 minute)
Step 3: Bass player and drummer walk across (10 minutes)
Step 4: Guitarist brings flashlight back (2 minutes)
Step 5: Singer and guitarist walk across (2 minutes)
(Steps two and four can be swapped.)

6. Yes. His birthday is on December 31 and it is now January 1. He turned 17 yesterday.

7. She was in a library. The $7 was a fine for returning the books late.

8. V. This series is the initial letter of signs of the Zodiac in chronological order. It begins with Aries, and is followed by Taurus, Gemini, Cancer, and Leo. The next one is Virgo.

9. They are aged 2, 5, 8, 11, 14, 17, 20, 23 and 26. The man's age is 48. The square of his age is 2,304 and the squares of the ages of his children (4, 25, 64, 121, 196, 289, 400, 529 and 676) add up to the same number.

10. Ed lives on the fourth floor. From the first to the sixth floors, the residents are Richard, Tim, Bob, Ed, Steve, Daniel.

11. The Welsh cycling fan is not Chloe (4), Adam (1), or Billy (3), so must be Donna, the lawyer (2). The Scottish accountant is male (5, Scotsman) and is not Billy (3), so must be Adam, the tennis fan (1). The Irish baker (6) is neither Donna nor Adam, nor Billy (3), so must be Chloe and as her sport is not cricket (6), she must be the soccer fan. By elimination Billy, the English cricket fan, is the nurse.

12. Three checks. Mr. Jones, Mr. Brown and Mr. Johnson should each give Mr. Smith a check for $10.

13. The barber is a woman.

14. He was at the South Pole and with his one pace he stepped across it. He was originally facing due south but as soon as he stepped over the Pole he was facing due north.

15. Second. From the front the positions are Rebecca, Jane, Sarah, Christine, Beth, Barbara.

16. N. This series is of the third letter in the month, starting from January. Next is June.

17. He was cleaning windows on the inside of the building.

18. 56. Mary had eight daughters, so each of Mary's daughters had seven sisters. All eight of them had seven daughters, so Mary had 56 daughters or granddaughters.

19. The husband of Gina, who lives in Delaware (3), is not Alan (1), Bob (2), or Chester (3), so must be David. Alice's husband of seven years (5) is not David, Alan (1), or Chester (3), so must be Bob. They live in Maine (2). Alan and Sarah are not celebrating their 15th (1), fifth (3), or seventh anniversaries (5), so they must be the couple who have been married for 12 years. (By elimination, David and Gina are celebrating their 15th

anniversary.) Alan and Sarah do not live in Vermont (4) and must live in New Hampshire. Therefore, Chester in Vermont is celebrating five years of marriage to Janet.

20. R. The series is of the penultimate letter of the planets in the solar system, starting with Mer̲cury and, moving away from the Sun, Ven̲us, Eart̲h, Ma̲rs, Jupit̲er. The next is Satur̲n.

WORD PUZZLES

1. Black.
2. Road.
3. Sun.
4. Fore
5. Well, Will, Sill, Silk, Sick.
6. Lose, Lone, Line, Fine, Find.
7. Meat, Moat, Most, Mist, Fist, Fish.
8. Fresh, Flesh, Flash, Clash, Clasp, Clamp, Cramp.
9. Overcoat.
10. Portugal.
11. Computer.
12. Election.
13. Pet.
14. Back.
15. Board.
16. Shot.
17. Hitchcock, Spielberg, Tarantino.
18. Linguini, Macaroni, Parmesan.
19. Copenhagen, Montevideo, Wellington.
20. Churchill, Mussolini, Roosevelt.
21. A bird in the hand is worth two in the bush.
22. *The Hitchhikers' Guide to the Galaxy*, Douglas Adams.
23. Winning isn't everything; it's the only thing.
24. Alas, poor Yorick, I knew him Horatio. A fellow of infinite jest.
25. Book (handbook, copybook, hymnbook, guidebook; bookmaker, bookworm, bookseller, bookmark).
26. Bill (waybill, twinbill, spoonbill, hornbill; billboard, billion, billfold, billposter).
27. Bath (footbath, bloodbath, birdbath, sunbath; bathtub, bathmat, bathroom, bathtime).
28. Hand (underhand, beforehand, backhand, shorthand; handsome, handmade, handling, handoff).
29. Disproportionate.
30. Incontrovertible.
31. Misunderstanding.
32. Parapsychologist.
33. Yes. The animals on the left can also be verbs; those on the right cannot.
34. Right. The first letters of the words on the left are men's names abbreviated; the last letters of those on the right are women's names abbreviated
35. Left. The words on the left use letters with only straight lines; all the ones on the right have some curves.
36. Left. The words on the left appear in their alphabetical order; the ones on the right in the reverse order.

37. Share, Homer, Ample, Relic, Erect.

S	H	A	R	E
H	O	M	E	R
A	M	P	L	E
R	E	L	I	C
E	R	E	C	T

38. Taper, Aware, Paras, Erase, Reset.

T	A	P	E	R
A	W	A	R	E
P	A	R	A	S
E	R	A	S	E
R	E	S	E	T

39. Fates, Afire, Timid, Erica, Sedan.

F	A	T	E	S
A	F	I	R	E
T	I	M	I	D
E	R	I	C	A
S	E	D	A	N

40. Local, Ozone, Conga, Anger, Learn.

L	O	C	A	L
O	Z	O	N	E
C	O	N	G	A
A	N	G	E	R
L	E	A	R	N

REBUS PUZZLES

1. Tall story.
2. Man overboard.
3. Three degrees below zero.
4. One for the road.
5. Square meal.
6. Hole in one.
7. Neon sign.
8. Bicycle.
9. Do you understand?
10. Standing ovation.
11. Broken promise.
12. Half price.
13. Feeling under the weather.
14. Half time.
15. Fishy business.
16. Birthday present.
17. Bridge over troubled water.
18. See eye to eye.
19. Power cut.
20. Weeping willow.
21. Cave man.
22. Head over heels in love.
23. To cut a long story short.
24. Seven seas.
25. Long time, no see.
26. Bingo.

JUMBLE WORDS

US PRESIDENTS

1. Ford and Nixon
2. Grant and Taft
3. Truman and Wilson.
4. Hoover and Reagan.

SCIENTISTS AND INVENTORS

5. Archimedes and Copernicus.
6. Einstein, Newton, and Celsius.
7. Galileo, Edison, and Pasteur.
8. Hawking and Herschel.

SINGERS

9. Christina Aguilera and Britney Spears.
10. Avril Lavigne and Pink.
11. Elvis and John Lennon.
12. Madonna and Shania Twain.
13. Kylie Minogue and Courtney Love.
14. Natalie Imbruglia.
15. Jessica Simpson and Norah Jones.
16. Frank Sinatra and Stevie Wonder.

MOVIE STARS

17. Julia Roberts and Angelina Jolie.
18. Ewan McGregor and Pierce Brosnan.
19. Keira Knightley and Johnny Depp.
20. Helena Bonham-Carter and Halle Berry.
21. Marlon Brando and Michael Caine.
22. Catherine Zeta Jones and Woody Allen.
23. John Wayne and Mickey Mouse.
24. Sean Connery and Donald Duck.

TRIVIA QUIZZES

FASTEST AND SLOWEST	HITS AND MISSES
1. b	1. d
2. d	2. c
3. c	3. c
4. a	4. a
5. b	5. b
6. b	6. c
7. d	7. a
8. b	8. d
9. d	9. b
10. d	10. d
11. c	11. a
12. d	12. d

HIGHS AND LOWS	KINGS AND QUEENS
1. a	1. d
2. d	2. b
3. b	3. c
4. d	4. a
5. c	5. b
6. d	6. d
7. a	7. a
8. c	8. c
9. b	9. a
10. c	10. d
11. d	11. c
12. c	12. d

ANSWERS

HUSBANDS AND WIVES
1. a
2. c
3. b
4. d
5. c
6. b
7. d
8. a
9. b
10. b
11. c
12. b

BROTHERS AND SISTERS
1. c
2. a
3. c
4. c
5. a
6. b
7. d
8. c
9. a
10. b
11. d
12. a

PARENTS AND CHILDREN
1. d
2. b
3. c
4. b
5. a
6. b
7. d
8. c
9. c
10. b
11. d
12. c

TRAINS AND PLANES
1. c
2. b
3. d
4. a
5. b
6. c
7. b
8. a
9. d
10. b
11. c
12. c

REDS AND BLUES
1. b
2. a
3. c
4. a
5. d
6. c
7. a
8. d
9. c
10. b
11. d
12. b

SWORD AND SORCERY
1. a
2. d
3. b
4. c
5. b
6. d
7. a
8. c
9. b
10. b
11. a
12. c

ACTRESSES AND BISHOPS
1. d
2. a
3. c
4. a
5. b
6. d
7. a
8. b
9. c
10. d
11. a
12. d

WET AND DRY
1. d
2. b
3. c
4. d
5. c
6. b
7. a
8. d
9. c
10. a
11. d
12. c

SWEET AND SOUR
1. c
2. a
3. b
4. d
5. c
6. d
7. b
8. a
9. d
10. c
11. a
12. d

SMITH AND JONES
1. a
2. d
3. b
4. c
5. a
6. c
7. d
8. a
9. b
10. c
11. a
12. c

LITTLE AND LARGE
1. b
2. a
3. b
4. d
5. c
6. a
7. c
8. d
9. b
10. a
11. d
12. c

UPS AND DOWNS
1. b
2. a
3. c
4. d
5. d
6. c
7. b
8. c
9. a
10. b
11. d
12. c

CATS AND DOGS
1. b
2. b
3. c
4. d
5. a
6. c
7. b
8. a
9. d
10. a
11. c
12. d

ROMEO AND JULIET
1. c
2. a
3. d
4. b
5. a
6. c
7. b
8. d
9. c
10. a
11. c
12. b

BEAUTY AND THE BEAST
1. d
2. c
3. a
4. b
5. c
6. d
7. a
8. c
9. a
10. a
11. c
12. b

YIN AND YANG
1. d
2. b
3. d
4. a
5. c
6. d
7. b
8. c
9. b
10. d
11. a
12. c

TRUE OR FALSE QUIZZES

IN THE SCIENCE LAB	ON THE SPORTS FIELD	AT THE MOVIES	IN THE ART GALLERY
1. TRUE.	1. FALSE	1. FALSE	1. TRUE
2. FALSE.	2. TRUE	2. TRUE	2. FALSE
3. FALSE.	3. TRUE	3. TRUE	3. TRUE
4. FALSE.	4. TRUE	4. FALSE	4. TRUE
5. FALSE.	5. FALSE	5. FALSE	5. FALSE
6. TRUE.	6. FALSE	6. TRUE	6. TRUE
7. TRUE.	7. TRUE	7. FALSE	7. FALSE
8. FALSE.	8. FALSE	8. TRUE	8. TRUE
9. TRUE.	9. TRUE	9. TRUE	9. TRUE
10. TRUE.	10. TRUE	10. TRUE	10. FALSE
11. TRUE.	11. FALSE	11. FALSE	11. FALSE
12. FALSE.	12. TRUE	12. TRUE	12. TRUE
13. TRUE.	13. TRUE	13. TRUE	13. FALSE
14. FALSE.	14. TRUE	14. TRUE	14. FALSE
15. FALSE.	15. FALSE	15. FALSE	15. FALSE
16. TRUE.	16. FALSE	16. FALSE	16. TRUE
17. TRUE.	17. FALSE	17. TRUE	17. TRUE
18. FALSE.	18. TRUE	18. FALSE	18. FALSE
19. TRUE.	19. TRUE	19. TRUE	19. FALSE
20. FALSE.	20. TRUE	20. FALSE	20. FALSE
21. FALSE.	21. FALSE	21. FALSE	21. FALSE
22. FALSE.	22. TRUE	22. TRUE	22. TRUE
23. FALSE.	23. TRUE	23. FALSE	23. FALSE
24. TRUE.	24. FALSE	24. FALSE	24. TRUE
25. FALSE.	25. TRUE	25. TRUE	25. TRUE
26. TRUE.	26. FALSE	26. TRUE	26. TRUE
27. TRUE.	27. TRUE	27. FALSE	27. FALSE
28. FALSE.	28. TRUE	28. FALSE	28. TRUE
29. TRUE.	29. FALSE	29. TRUE	29. FALSE
30. FALSE.	30. TRUE	30. FALSE	30. TRUE

IN OUTER SPACE	UNDERNEATH THE SEA	IN THE EYE OF THE STORM	IN THE RESTAURANT
1. TRUE			1. FALSE
2. TRUE	1. FALSE	1. FALSE	2. FALSE
3. FALSE	2. FALSE	2. FALSE	3. TRUE
4. FALSE	3. TRUE	3. TRUE	4. TRUE
5. FALSE	4. TRUE	4. FALSE	5. FALSE
6. TRUE	5. TRUE	5. TRUE	6. TRUE
7. TRUE	6. FALSE	6. TRUE	7. TRUE
8. FALSE	7. TRUE	7. FALSE	8. FALSE
9. FALSE	8. FALSE	8. TRUE	9. TRUE
10. FALSE	9. FALSE	9. FALSE	10. TRUE
11. TRUE	10. TRUE	10. TRUE	11. FALSE
12. FALSE	11. FALSE	11. TRUE	12. TRUE
13. FALSE	12. TRUE	12. FALSE	13. FALSE
14. TRUE	13. TRUE	13. TRUE	14. TRUE
15. FALSE	14. FALSE	14. FALSE	15. TRUE
16. TRUE	15. TRUE	15. TRUE	16. TRUE
17. TRUE	16. FALSE	16. FALSE	17. FALSE
18. FALSE	17. FALSE	17. FALSE	18. FALSE
19. FALSE	18. TRUE	18. FALSE	19. FALSE
20. TRUE	19. TRUE	19. TRUE	20. TRUE
21. FALSE	20. FALSE	20. FALSE	21. FALSE
22. TRUE	21. FALSE	21. TRUE	22. TRUE
23. FALSE	22. TRUE	22. TRUE	23. TRUE
24. FALSE	23. FALSE	23. FALSE	24. FALSE
25. TRUE	24. TRUE	24. TRUE	25. TRUE
26. FALSE	25. TRUE	25. FALSE	26. TRUE
27. TRUE	26. FALSE	26. TRUE	27. FALSE
28. TRUE	27. TRUE	27. FALSE	28. TRUE
29. TRUE	28. TRUE	28. TRUE	29. FALSE
30. FALSE	29. FALSE	29. FALSE	30. TRUE
	30. TRUE	30. FALSE	

ON THE TELEVISION	ON THE CATWALK
1. TRUE	1. TRUE
2. FALSE	2. TRUE
3. FALSE	3. FALSE
4. TRUE	4. FALSE
5. TRUE	5. TRUE
6. TRUE	6. FALSE
7. FALSE	7. TRUE
8. FALSE	8. FALSE
9. TRUE	9. FALSE
10. FALSE	10. TRUE
11. FALSE	11. TRUE
12. TRUE	12. FALSE
13. TRUE	13. TRUE
14. FALSE	14. TRUE
15. TRUE	15. FALSE
16. FALSE	16. FALSE
17. FALSE	17. TRUE
18. TRUE	18. FALSE
19. FALSE	19. TRUE
20. TRUE	20. TRUE
21. TRUE	21. TRUE
22. FALSE	22. TRUE
23. TRUE	23. FALSE
24. FALSE	24. TRUE
25. TRUE	25. FALSE
26. FALSE	26. FALSE
27. TRUE	27. TRUE
28. FALSE	28. FALSE
29. TRUE	29. FALSE
30. FALSE	30. TRUE

WORDSEARCHES

US PRESIDENTS

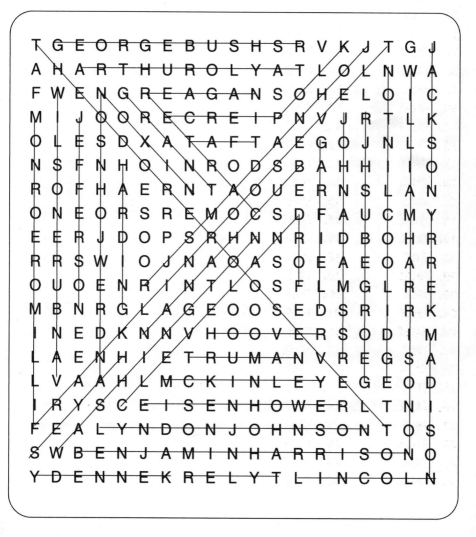

```
T G E O R G E B U S H S R V K J T G J
A H A R T H U R O L Y A T L O L N W A
F W E N G R E A G A N S O H E L O I C
M I J O O R E C R E I P N V J R T L K
O L E S D X A T A F T A E G O J N L S
N S F N H O I N R O D S B A H H I I O
R O F H A E R N T A O U E R N S L A N
O N E O R S R E M O C S D F A U C M Y
E E R J D O P S R H N N R I D B O H R
R R S W I O J N A O A S O E A E O A R
O U O E N R I N T L O S F L M G L R E
M B N R G L A G E O O S E D S R I R K
I N E D K N N V H O O V E R S O D I M
L A E N H I E T R U M A N V R E G S A
L V A A H L M C K I N L E Y E G E O D
I R Y S C E I S E N H O W E R L T N I
F E A L Y N D O N J O H N S O N T O S
S W B E N J A M I N H A R R I S O N O
Y D E N N E K R E L Y T L I N C O L N
```

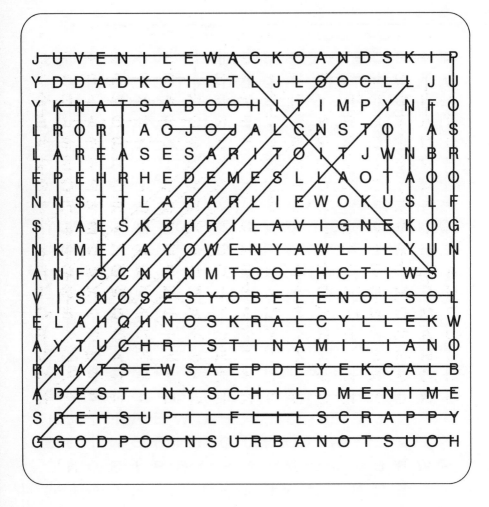

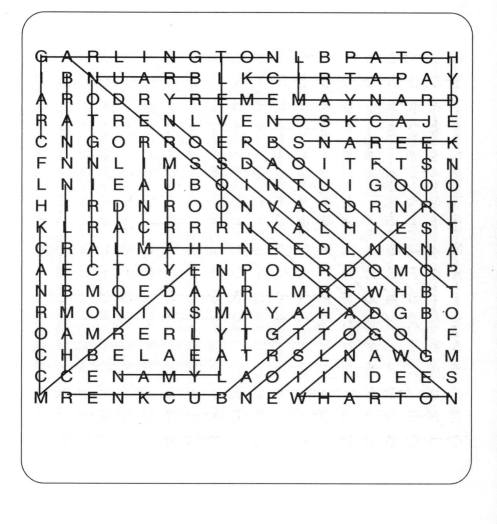

US GENERALS

```
G A R L I N G T O N L B P A T C H
  I B N U A R B L K C I R T A P A Y
A R O D R Y R E M E M A Y N A R D
R A T R E N L V E N O S K C A J E
C N G O R R O E R B S N A R E E K
F N N L I M S S D A O I T F T S N
L N I E A U B O I N T U I G O O O
H I R D N R O O N V A C D R N P T
K L R A C R R R N Y A L H I E S T
C R A L M A H I N E E D L N N A
A E C T O Y E N P O D R D O M O P
N B M O E D A A R L M R F W H B T
R M O N I N S M A Y A H A D G B O
O A M R E R L Y T G T T O G O F
C H B E L A E A T R S L N A W G M
C C E N A M Y L A O I I N D E E S
M R E N K C U B N E W H A R T O N
```

SUPERMODELS

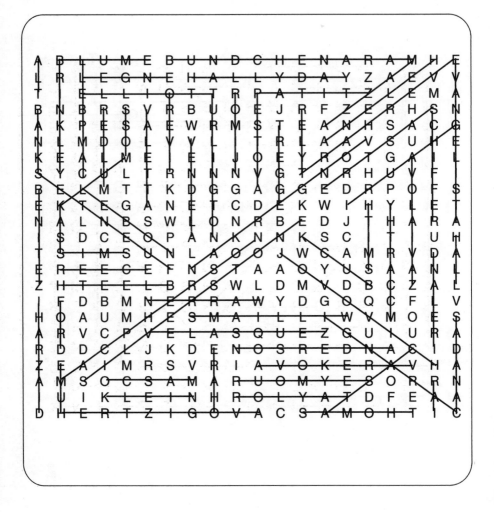

MYTHOLOGICAL CREATURES

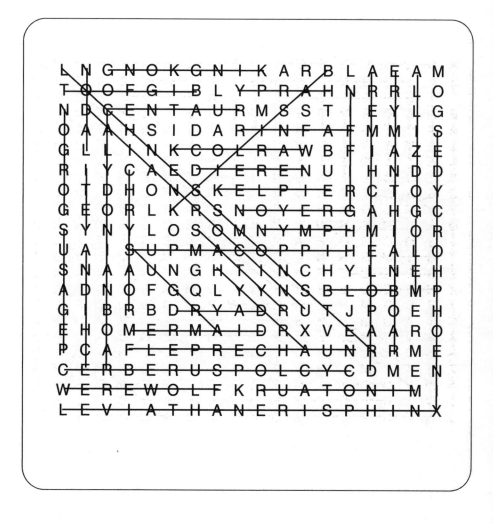

L N G N O K G N I K A R B L A E A M
T O O F G I B L Y P R A H N R R L O
N D C E N T A U R M S S T E Y L G
O A A H S I D A R I N F A F M M I S
G L L I N K C O L R A W B F I A Z E
R I Y C A E D I E R E N U H N D D
O T D H O N S K E L P I E R C T O Y
G E O R L K R S N O Y E R G A H G C
S Y N Y L O S O M N Y M P H M I O R
U A S U P M A C O P P I H E A L O
S N A U N G H T I N C H Y L N E H
A D N O F G Q L Y Y N S B L O B M P
G I B R B D R Y A D R U T J P O E H
E H O M E R M A I D R X V E A A R O
P C A F L E P R E C H A U N R R M E
C E R B E R U S P O L C Y C D M E N
W E R E W O L F K R U A T O N I M
L E V I A T H A N E R I S P H I N X

387

HOLLYWOOD IDOLS

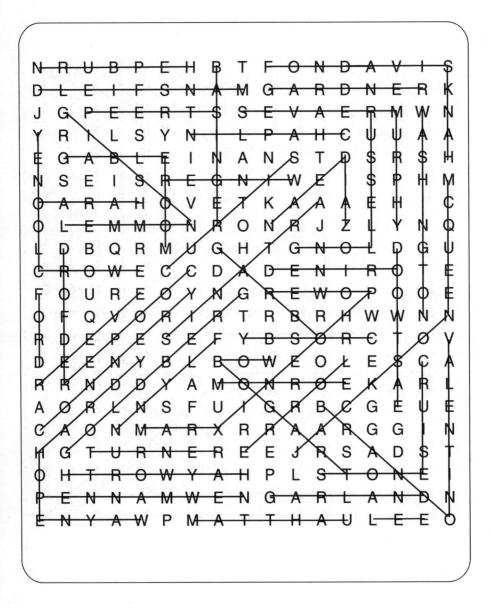

```
N R U B P E H B T F O N D A V I S
D L E I F S N A M G A R D N E R K
J G P E E R T S S E V A E R M W N
Y R I L S Y N L P A H C U U A A H
E G A B L E I N A N S T D S R S H
N S E I S R E G N I W E S P H M C
O A R A H O V E T K A A A E H C Q
O L E M M O N R O N R J Z L Y N Q
L D B Q R M U G H T G N O L D G U
C R O W E C C D A D E N I R O T E
F O U R E O Y N G R E W O P O O E
O F Q V O R I R T R B R H W W N N
R D E P E S E F Y B S O R C T O Y
D E E N Y B L B O W E O L E S C A
R R N D D Y A M O N R O E K A R L
A O R L N S F U I G R B C G E U E
C A O N M A R X R R A A R G G I N
H G T U R N E R E E J R S A D S T
O H T R O W Y A H P L S T O N E I
P E N N A M W E N G A R L A N D N
E N Y A W P M A T T H A U L E E O
```

ANIMALS

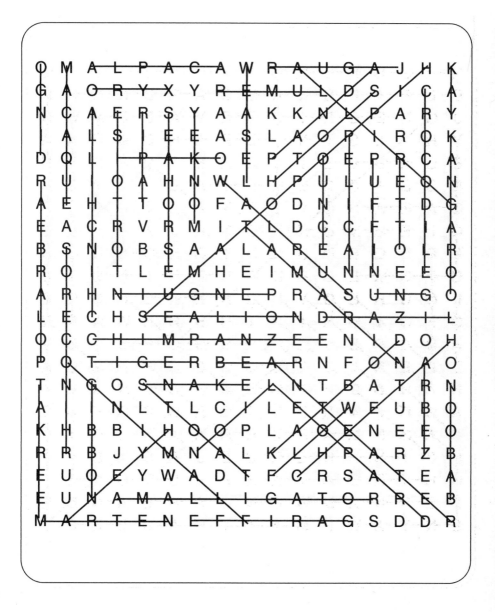

```
O M A L P A C A W R A U G A J H K
G A O R Y X Y R E M U L D S I C A
N C A E R S Y A A K K N L P A R Y
I A L S I E E A S L A O P I R O K
D Q L P A K O E P T O E P R C A
R U I O A H N W L H P U L U E O N
A E H T T O O F A O D N I F T D G
E A C R V R M I T L D C C F T I A
B S N O B S A A L A R E A I O L R
R O I T L E M H E I M U N N E E O
A R H N I U G N E P R A S U N G O
L E C H S E A L I O N D R A Z I L
O C C H I M P A N Z E E N I D O H
P O T I G E R B E A R N F O N A O
T N G O S N A K E L N T B A T R N
A N L T L C I L E T W E U B O
K H B B I H O O P L A C E N E E O
R R B J Y M N A L K L H P A R Z B
E U O E Y W A D T P C R S A T E A
E U N A M A L L I G A T O R R E B
M A R T E N E F F I R A G S D D R
```

NOVELISTS

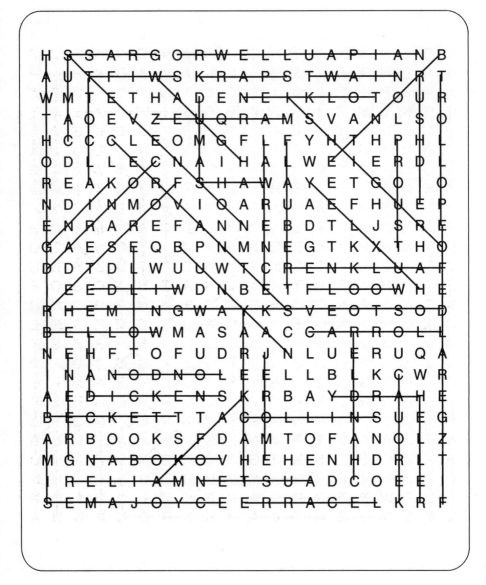

BIRDS

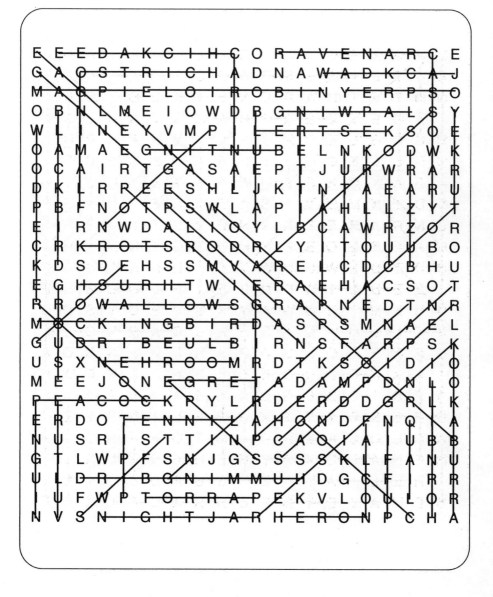

CAPITAL CITIES

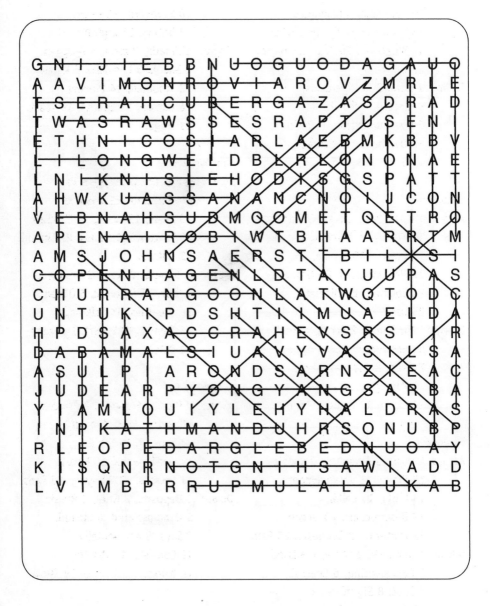

CROSSWORDS

Crossword 1

Across: 7 Cereal, 8 Wooden, 9 Tear,
10 Columbia, 11 Goggles,
13 India, 15 Ferry, 16 Sticker,
18 Whatever, 19 Teat, 21 Barren,
22 Growth.
Down: 1 Here, 2 Refrigerators,
3 Elected, 4 Swell,
5 Communication, 6 Definite,
12 Overhead, 14 Storage,
17 Event, 20 Anti.

Crossword 2

Across: 1 Hose, 3 Specimen, 9 Strange,
10 Nurse, 11 Abbreviation,
13 Drawer, 15 Russia,
17 Headmistress, 20 Union,
21 Cooking, 22 Diameter,
23 Uses.
Down: 1 Husbands, 2 Scrub, 4 Prefix,
5 Construction, 6 Mirrors,
7 Need, 8 Independence,
12 Passages, 14 America,
16 Circle, 18 Exits, 19 Fund.

Crossword 3

Across: 1 Dusk, 3 Americas, 9 Species,
10 Piano, 11 Arrangements,
13 Cliffs, 15 Cellar,
17 Descriptions, 20 Ocean,
21 Lantern, 22 Suggests, 23 Fair.
Down: 1 Distance, 2 Sheer, 4 Missed,
5 Representing, 6 Coastal,
7 Spot, 8 Significance,
12 Prisoner, 14 Iceberg,
16 Violet, 18 Opera, 19 Zoos.

Crossword 4

Across: 7 Matter, 8 Needed, 9 Harm,
10 Graduate, 11 Leather,
13 Other, 15 Actor, 17 Wildest,
20 Stubborn, 21 Hook,
22 Voters, 23 Eighth.
Down: 1 Parade, 2 Item, 3 Dragged,
4 Sneak, 5 Resulted, 6 Kettle,
12 Troubled, 14 Pioneer,
16 Cotton, 18 Scouts, 19 Toast,
21 Huge.

Crossword 5

Across: 7 Hotter, 8 Twenty, 9 Palm,
10 Battered, 11 Doubled,
13 Press, 15 Acres, 17 Paddles,
20 Textbook, 21 Pops, 22 Intend,
23 Nature.
Down: 1 Tomato, 2 Item, 3 Grabbed,
4 State, 5 Referred, 6 Others,
12 Breathes, 14 Talking,
16 Cleans, 18 Export, 19 Foods,
21 Pats.

Crossword 6

Across: 1 Digs, 3 Products, 9 Princes,
10 Marry, 11 Sufficiently,
13 Tapped, 15 Studio,
17 Dictionaries, 20 Hotel,
21 Dresses, 22 Worrying, 23 Reds.
Down: 1 Deposits, 2 Grief, 4 Russia,
5 Demonstrated, 6 Circled,
7 Says, 8 Accidentally,
12 Consists, 14 Painter,
16 Wooden, 18 Issue, 19 Show.

Crossword 7

Across: 1 Plastic, 5 Image, 8 Performed, 9 Pie, 10 Rides, 12 Unaware, 13 Advertisement, 15 Austria, 17 Haste, 19 Two, 20 Eliminate, 22 Desks, 23 Nightly.

Down: 1 Paper, 2 Air, 3 Trouser, 4 Communication, 5 India, 6 Alphabets, 7 Element, 11 Divisions, 13 Adapted, 14 Echoing, 16 Reeds, 18 Every, 21 Act.

Crossword 8

Across: 7 Hawaii, 8 Employ, 9 Bags, 10 Suspense, 11 Warning, 13 Winds, 15 Enemy, 17 Singers, 20 Directly, 21 Rung, 22 Severe, 23 Loaves.

Down: 1 Canada, 2 Mats, 3 Kissing, 4 Dense, 5 Speeding, 6 Tossed, 12 Numbered, 14 Bicycle, 16 Noises, 18 Rented, 19 Other, 21 Read.

Crossword 9

Across: 1 Rockets, 5 Necks, 8 Circumference, 9 You, 10 Prettiest, 12 Sister, 13 Letter, 15 Apartment, 16 Air, 18 Encyclopedias, 20 Dusty, 21 Extends.

Down: 1 Rocky, 2 Circumstances, 3 Equipment, 4 Softer, 5 Nor, 6 Concentration, 7 Sweater, 11 Treatment, 12 Seaweed, 14 Remove, 17 Rises, 19 Cry.

Crossword 10

Across: 7 Bamboo, 8 Thirty, 9 Busy, 10 Butchers, 11 Amusing, 13 Sense, 15 Speed, 17 Sixteen, 20 Distinct, 21 Lock, 22 Scarce, 23 Recipe.

Down: 1 Vacuum, 2 Obey, 3 Bombing, 4 State, 5 Lightest, 6 Stores, 12 Shelters, 14 History, 16 Prince, 18 Except, 19 Index, 21 Lack.

Crossword 11

Across: 7 Forest, 8 Hearts, 9 Vain, 10 Patients, 11 Journey, 13 Tends, 15 Shift, 17 Costume, 20 Umbrella, 21 Bats, 22 Sneeze, 23 Coiled.

Down: 1 Potato, 2 Bean, 3 Stopped, 4 Photo, 5 Pavement, 6 Stated, 12 Referees, 14 Tobacco, 16 Humans, 18 Mother, 19 Alien, 21 Bait.

Crossword 12

Across: 7 Screen, 8 Hooves, 9 Tour, 10 Official, 11 Singers, 13 India, 15 Worry, 16 Scarlet, 18 Bacteria, 19 Tick, 21 Secret, 22 Enough.

Down: 1 Echo, 2 Refrigerators, 3 Indoors, 4 Shift, 5 Concentration, 6 Relative, 12 Isolated, 14 Scraped, 17 Truth, 20 Cage.

Crossword 13

Across: 1 Decimal, 5 Faced,
8 Circumference, 9 You,
10 Teenagers, 12 Insect,
13 Tasted, 15 Statement,
16 And, 18 Encyclopedias,
20 Dusty, 21 Extends.

Down: 1 Decay, 2 Circumstances,
3 Moustache, 4 Lifted, 5 For,
6 Concentration, 7 Dressed,
11 Apartment, 12 Instead,
14 Become, 17 Desks, 19 Cry.

Crossword 14

Across: 1 Classic, 5 Leaps,
8 Compounds, 9 Fox, 10 Eight,
12 Earache, 13 Demonstration,
15 Grandma, 17 Ounce, 19 Eat,
20 Slightest, 22 Sacks,
23 Nursery.

Down: 1 Cycle, 2 Aim, 3 Shorten,
4 Concentration, 5 Loser,
6 Affection, 7 Sixteen,
11 Gymnastic, 13 Degrees,
14 Another, 16 Disks, 18 Entry,
21 Eye.

Crossword 15

Across: 7 Arctic, 8 Topics, 9 Hair,
10 Indirect, 11 Observe,
13 Asked, 15 Ferry, 17 Bedtime,
20 Stations, 21 Else, 23 Newest,
24 Guests.

Down: 1 Area, 2 Starve, 3 Achieve,
4 Study, 5 Operas, 6 Icecream,
12 Breathed, 14 Message,
16 Rather, 18 Themes, 19 Boats,
22 Site.

Crossword 16

Across: 1 Coarse, 4 Voters, 9 Worship,
10 Taste, 11 Royal, 12 Consent,
13 Approaching, 18 Plateau,
20 Apple, 22 Dates, 23 Attract,
24 Saddle, 25 Cycles.

Down: 1 Coward, 2 Array, 3 Scholar,
5 Often, 6 Eastern, 7 Sweets,
8 Spectacular, 14 Planted,
15 Healthy, 16 Spades,
17 Depths, 19 Easel, 21 Pearl.

Crossword 17

Across: 1 Repairs, 5 Hoped, 8 Nearest,
9 Lasso, 10 Scene, 11 Erosion,
12 Savage, 14 Pegged,
17 Rooster, 19 Force, 22 Tribe,
23 Decided, 24 Haste,
25 Respond.

Down: 1 Ranks, 2 Peace, 3 Iceberg,
4 Settee, 5 Hello, 6 Pushing,
7 Drowned, 12 Scratch,
13 Violins, 15 Effects, 16 Trader,
18 These, 20 Radio, 21 Ended.

Crossword 18

Across: 1 Servant, 5 Lumps, 8 Retired,
9 Issue, 10 Brown, 11 Yoghurt,
12 Pocket, 14 Closer, 17 Plateau,
19 Grief, 22 Lungs, 23 Tunnels,
24 Rally, 25 Muscles.

Down: 1 Scrub, 2 Ratio, 3 Arrange,
4 Todays, 5 Lying, 6 Museums,
7 Shelter, 12 Popular, 13
Channel, 15 Legends, 16 Custom,
18 Essay, 20 Ideal, 21 Fists.

Crossword 19

Across: 7 Orange, 8 Atomic, 9 Here,
10 Lipstick, 11 Unknown,
13 Dives, 15 State, 16 Request,
18 Absolute, 19 Idea, 21 Todays,
22 Vanish.

Down: 1 True, 2 International,
3 Fellows, 4 Camps,
5 Contributions, 6 Kitchens,
12 Notebook, 14 Receive,
17 Pussy, 20 East.

Crossword 20

Across: 7 Warmer, 8 Steams, 9 Taxi,
10 Feathers, 11 Aspects,
13 Oddly, 15 Knock, 17 Postman,
20 Swimming, 21 Idle,
23 Oceans, 24 Eldest.

Down: 1 Lava, 2 Empire, 3 Profits,
4 Usual, 5 Method, 6 Umbrella,
12 Sandwich, 14 Tongues,
16 Commas, 18 Thirds, 19 First,
22 Lost.

Crossword 21

Across: 7 Uncomfortable, 8 Contains,
9 Aunt, 10 Tuesday, 12 Magic,
14 Views, 16 Cottage, 19 Zoos,
20 Twilight, 22 Unfortunately.

Down: 1 Unto, 2 Months, 3 African,
4 Prism, 5 Banana, 6 Planting,
11 Unicorns, 13 Motions,
15 Wisdom, 17 Thirty, 18 State,
21 Hall.

Crossword 22

Across: 7 Wooden, 8 Prefix, 9 Mars,
10 Marriage, 11 Totally,
13 Added, 15 State, 17 Winding,
20 Bacteria, 21 Bath,
22 Window, 23 Discos.

Down: 1 Potato, 2 Adds, 3 Animals,
4 Spark, 5 Reminded, 6 Single,
12 Altitude, 14 Wizards,
16 Tragic, 18 Notion, 19 Crowd,
21 Busy.

Crossword 23

Across: 1 Cuts, 3 Recorded, 9 Awkward,
10 Given, 11 Consequently,
14 Arm, 16 Pairs, 17 Pie,
18 Explanations, 21 Comma,
22 Shorter, 23 Domestic,
24 Arms.

Down: 1 Charcoal, 2 Taken, 4 End,
5 Organisation, 6 Develop,
7 Done, 8 Caterpillars, 12 Union,
13 Measures, 15 Maximum,
19 Outer, 20 Acid, 22 Ski.

Crossword 24

Across: 1 Vine, 3 Ornament, 9 Helmets,
10 Reads, 11 Consequently,
13 Estate, 15 Senses,
17 Experimental, 20 Acute,
21 Extract, 22 Blessing, 23 Feud.

Down: 1 Vehicles, 2 Nylon, 4 Rescue,
5 Arrangements, 6 Enables,
7 Toss, 8 Nevertheless,
12 Isolated, 14 Texture,
16 Pigeon, 18 Trade, 19 Lamb.

Crossword 25

Across: 1 Hook, 3 Daybreak, 9 Needing,
          10 Cases, 11 Shake, 12 Lasted,
          14 Minute, 16 Events,
          19 Employ, 21 Towel, 24 Ovens,
          25 Benefit, 26 Nostrils, 27 Used.

Down: 1 Handsome, 2 Opera, 4 Angels,
         5 Backs, 6 Eastern, 7 Kiss,
         8 Finest, 13 Isolated,
         15 Numbers, 17 Voting,
         18 Symbol, 20 Loser, 22 Wafts,
         23 Horn.

Crossword 26

Across: 7 Starve, 8 Pepper, 9 Snow,
          10 Steering, 11 Raccoon,
          13 Waist, 15 Calls, 17 Gathers,
          20 Columbia, 21 Digs, 22 Greasy,
          23 Chairs.

Down: 1 Stanza, 2 Crew, 3 Session,
         4 Speed, 5 Approach, 6 Tennis,
         12 Cultural, 14 Balance,
         16 Aboard, 18 Regard, 19 Obeys,
         21 Draw.

Crossword 27

Across: 1 Shut, 3 Hesitate, 9 Imitate,
          10 Tests, 11 Contemporary,
          14 Sum, 16 Place, 17 Ago,
          18 Explanations, 21 Comma,
          22 Stories, 23 Domestic,
          24 Ants.

Down: 1 Suitcase, 2 Union, 4 Eye,
         5 Intersection, 6 Austria, 7 Easy,
         8 Caterpillars, 12 Plain,
         13 Consists, 15 Maximum,
         19 Onion, 20 Acid, 22 Ski.

Crossword 28

Across: 1 Much, 3 Tractors, 9 Dresses,
          10 Noted, 11 Reproduction,
          13 Tragic, 15 Museum,
          17 Mathematical, 20 Ounce,
          21 Shortly, 22 Latitude, 23 Thud.

Down: 1 Moderate, 2 Cheap, 4 Rescue,
         5 Construction, 6 Outcome,
         7 Side, 8 Astonishment,
         12 Employed, 14 Against,
         16 Amused, 18 Catch, 19 Soil.

Crossword 29

Across: 1 Stands, 4 Lesser, 9 Arrival,
          10 Tramp, 11 Ideal, 12 Clapped,
          13 Cooperation, 18 Pacific,
          20 Uncle, 22 Exact, 23 Tshirts,
          24 Riddle, 25 Adults.

Down: 1 Static, 2 Agree, 3 Develop,
         5 Extra, 6 Shampoo, 7 Rapids,
         8 Electricity, 14 Orchard,
         15 Touched, 16 Appear,
         17 Messes, 19 Fatal, 21 Coral.

Crossword 30

Across: 1 Answers, 5 Cocoa, 8 Toast,
          9 Contain, 10 Comparatively,
          11 Endure, 12 Ceased,
          15 Refrigerators, 18 Compare,
          19 Image, 20 Essay, 21 Lunches.

Down: 1 Attic, 2 Slammed,
         3 Extraordinary, 4 Social,
         5 Consideration, 6 Crane,
         7 Annoyed, 11 Earache,
         13 Stomach, 14 Reveal,
         16 Fumes, 17 Stems.

NOTES

ABOUT THE COMPILERS

Robert Allen is a psychologist and, before embarking on his writing career, was Director of Mensa Psychometrics. He has been creating puzzles and games for many years and his books have sold in huge quantities from Alaska to Australia and Germany to Japan. He lives in Cambridge, England, with his wife and two teenage children.

David Ballheimer has enjoyed solving word and number puzzles for more than 20 years and spent more than a decade editing and creating them for others. He has two sports books to his name and is contributing to another on his beloved Hendon Football Club. David appeared on the cult TV game show *Countdown* winning nine rounds. A book editor and weekend sports journalist, he lives in north-west London.

Jacqueline Harrod is an expert on Solitaire card games, having written *Pick of the Pack Patience Games* and contributed to *Card Games Made Easy*. She has also worked on two books about babies' names.

John Paines is an IT consultant, working chiefly in the life and pensions industry. He is an active and enthusiastic member of British Mensa and a trustee of the Mensa Foundation for Gifted Children. Since 1999 he has served on the Management Board of the British Chess Federation. He is single and lives in Bristol, England.